Contributions to International Relations

This book series offers an outlet for cutting-edge research on all areas of international relations. Contributions to International Relations (CIR) welcomes theoretically sound and empirically robust monographs, edited volumes and handbooks from various disciplines and approaches on topics such as IR-theory, international security studies, foreign policy, peace and conflict studies, international organization, global governance, international political economy, the history of international relations and related fields.

More information about this series at https://link.springer.com/bookseries/16658

Audrey Wells

The Importance of Forgiveness and the Futility of Revenge

Case Studies in Contemporary International Politics

Springer

Audrey Wells
Royal Holloway University of London
London, UK

ISSN 2731-5061 ISSN 2731-507X (electronic)
Contributions to International Relations
ISBN 978-3-030-87551-0 ISBN 978-3-030-87552-7 (eBook)
https://doi.org/10.1007/978-3-030-87552-7

This Springer imprint is published by the registered company Springer Nature Switzerland AG.
The registered company address is: Gewerbestrasse 11, 6330 Cham, Switzerland

Le Petit Journal

ADMINISTRATION
61, RUE LAFAYETTE, 61
Les manuscrits ne sont pas rendus
On s'abonne sans frais dans tous les bureaux de poste

15 CENT. — SUPPLÉMENT ILLUSTRÉ — 15 CENT.
29me Année — Numéro 1.490
DIMANCHE 13 JUILLET 1919

ABONNEMENTS

	SIX MOIS	UN AN
France et Colonies....	6 fr.	8 fr.
Etranger	8 fr.	13 fr.

A TON TOUR GERMANIA !

Le célèbre dessin de Janet-Lange, qui occupe le haut de cette page, montre les Allemands de 1871 imposant à la France le traité de Francfort. « Signe ou meurs ! », lui disent-ils. Aujourd'hui, c'est la France qui parle en maîtresse et qui dit à l'Allemagne : « Signe la paix de réparation, la paix de la justice et du droit. A ton tour, Germania ! »

Le Petit Journal July 13, 1919 (Gallica, Bibliotheque National de France, 84-S404)

TO
VAUGHAN, MARCELLE and IAN
WITH LOVE

Preface

Forgiveness is important in international politics because it can save thousands of lives. Its opposite, revenge, has played a significant part in many of the wars in the twentieth and twenty-first centuries. These conflicts are examined in this book, showing how forgiveness could have stopped the colossal ensuing bloodshed.

Despite its importance, forgiveness in international relations as a means of preventing the outbreak of war between states (as opposed to aiding reconciliation after a conflict) has been neglected as a subject of study. Indeed, it has also been ignored by politicians as a result of which there are few examples of forgiveness to study compared with those of revenge. This book reflects this but aims to change the situation by raising a public awareness of the importance of forgiveness in international affairs and the need to demand this of political leaders.

This book also provides a succinct, informative guide to the background of current affairs. Each chapter can be read independently of the rest and shows either forgiveness in action or the futility and loss of life caused by revenge, demonstrating where forgiveness could have made a dramatic difference.

In the first chapter, the concept of forgiveness is considered, specifically that of Jesus of Nazareth as discussed by the distinguished political theorist Hannah Arendt. Then revenge, the opposite of forgiveness, is discussed. Its negative effect in international relations is illustrated with a consideration of the Treaty of Versailles which was greatly influenced by France's desire for revenge. This aided the rise of Adolf Hitler leading to the Second World War.

The next six chapters deal with contemporary events where forgiveness is shown or denied towards a foreign enemy and the consequences. After the Second World War there might have been yet another cycle of revenge between France and Germany. However, the French Foreign Minister, Robert Schuman, was a devout Christian and understood the importance of forgiveness. He therefore constructively ended the age-old Franco-German revenge cycle by persuading both countries to cooperate in producing coal and steel. He invited Italy and the Benelux countries to join them in the European Coal and Steel Community which eventually became the European Union.

Unfortunately, in the twenty-first century such statesmanship has not been evident in other countries. The next five chapters deal with the responses of the USA and its allies to allegedly hostile Muslim states. Far from showing any forgiveness or empathy or reflecting on the cause of the hostility, the USA in particular has responded with destructive revenge to countries it regarded as harming its interests.

In the third chapter, the USA's war in Afghanistan is considered as being partly motivated by revenge. It has resulted in the longest war in its history ending only in 2021, after far more people have been killed than in the 9/11 attack. The fourth chapter discusses the invasion of Iraq which was also in part revenge for the 9/11 attack since President Bush erroneously thought Saddam Hussein was linked to al-Qaeda.

In the fifth chapter, the revenge cycle between the West and Libya, culminating in the overthrow of Gaddafi and a bloody civil war, is examined, while the sixth chapter looks at the age-long revenge cycle between the West and Iran.

The concept of a 'vengeful democracy' as characterised by wars abroad and capital punishment at home is then considered. The futility of revenge can be seen in the above chapters. Also obvious is the need for forgiveness in the form of restraining vengeful desires and attempting to dissolve hostility as Robert Schuman did after the Second World War.

Next in focus are the West's relations with their former Cold War enemies Russia and China. Here revenge is not the issue but the need not to be unforgiving, in the sense of being too harsh, is of paramount importance. The Ukraine conflict is studied in the context of Russophobia. I have argued that timely forgiveness and empathy could have prevented the massive loss of life. The need for forgiveness on all sides in Belarus is then discussed. Cooperation between the West and Russia could solve the problems presented in Belarus as well as Ukraine.

The following chapter is concerned with rising Sinophobia. It examines how the West has been unforgiving towards some of China's policies without trying to excuse or understand the reasons behind them, or find alternative ways of viewing them, or reflecting on their own chequered histories. The ways in which the successes of the Chinese Communists have been marred by political vengeance are then examined.

The focus of the book next moves to the importance of forgiveness towards an occupying power and how to remove it.

Gandhi's exemplary rejection of revenge is considered, his form of resistance being intrinsically bound up with forgiveness, holding that the enemy would be won over by a form of peaceful resistance where violence was not exchanged for violence.

The futile cycle of revenge that is distinctive in the long conflict between Israel and the Palestinians, together with the attempts of some of the latter to follow Gandhi's method, is then examined.

The Irish conflict is examined in detail as is Nelson Mandela's exemplary leadership of forgiveness that helped avoid bloodshed in South Africa.

The relevance of forgiveness to the Syrian civil war is next discussed: the causes of the conflict, the vengeance of Maher Assad (President Bashar Assad's brother),

ISIS, the Ministry for National Reconciliation, and the Grand Mufti's example of forgiveness are considered.

The attempts at reconciliation in countries after civil war are then examined: former Yugoslavian states, Rwanda, Sierra Leone, Colombia, and South Sudan are next considered. The idea of a leadership of forgiveness is then discussed.

Consideration is next given to the value of political apologies in encouraging forgiveness.

The book would not be complete without a consideration of the limits of forgiveness. Two contemporary cases of this are considered: Islamic jihadism in Africa and Myanmar under the generals.

Finally, the question of forgiveness of a country's debts to external creditors is examined.

In conclusion, I argue that this book provides overwhelming evidence that the world is best served not by revenge but by forgiveness which should be publicly encouraged.

London, UK Audrey Wells

Contents

Part V Further Aspect of Forgiveness in Politics

About the Author

Audrey Wells is an Honorary Research Associate at Royal Holloway College, University of London, where she taught twentieth-century history. Her doctorate was on Chinese political thought for which she studied at the London School of Economics and Ren Min University in Beijing. She has also taught at the London School of Economics and Goldsmiths College, University of London.

Also by Audrey Wells:

Britain and Soviet Communism (with F.S. Northedge)

The Political Thought of Sun Yat-sen

The Rule of Reverse Results

Chapter 1
Forgiveness and Revenge

In 1940, at a meeting at Caxton Hall in London, an Indian drew a gun and shot dead one of the speakers on the platform. Udham Singh had killed Sir Michael O' Dwyer in revenge for the massacre at Amritsar in 1919. Fortunately for Britain, Singh was not the leader of the Indian nationalist movement which was led by Mahatma Gandhi, who strongly deplored this act of vengeance [1]. Also, in 1940, another significant act of revenge took place for harm perpetrated in 1919, this time by the vindictive Versailles Treaty. Having invaded France, the Nazis forced the defeated French to sign an armistice in the very railway carriage where Germany had had to sign the armistice in 1918. Unfortunately for the whole world, the German Fuehrer, Adolf Hitler, was not a forgiving leader as was Gandhi.

Forgiveness, the opposite of revenge, is important in international relations because it can prevent the loss of life: sometimes on a colossal scale. 'Prevention' is the keyword here as this book is less about conflict resolution than conflict prevention. Forgiveness does not mean ignoring and forgetting a harmful action or, if the action is illegal, not punishing it by due process of law, but it does mean giving up all ideas of revenge, bitterness, and hatred towards the wrongdoer. Revenge, the desire to harm the offender, 'to get even' with them, often results in disproportionate injury done to them, as boiling rage and hatred sweep away reason in the mind of the victim, hell-bent on 'paying them back'. On a personal level, this occasionally might mean committing arson or a gun spree to kill a limited number of people, but in international relations, revenge can result in a far higher death toll, especially in a bloody cycle of retaliation in which millions die.

Forgiveness can manifest itself in many forms, such as an immediate refusal to lash out after being harmed, or in the case of an individual, a lengthy, personal internal process leading eventually to reconciliation, or a release from bitterness and hatred towards someone no longer alive, or a process of forgiveness and reconciliation between ethnic groups which have harmed each other. Whatever form forgiveness takes, it always means a disciplined refusal (which sometimes requires enormous willpower) to give way to the desire for revenge and harm the person or country that has harmed you. In international relations, it is important that this is

A. Wells, *The Importance of Forgiveness and the Futility of Revenge*, Contributions to International Relations, https://doi.org/10.1007/978-3-030-87552-7_1

done immediately and announced by the political leadership publicly to prevent any idea of vengeful reprisals. Then later, the leadership may try to empathise with the offending group or nation in an attempt to understand why the offence took place and respond to the root cause of the offence. This effort to see an offence from the offender's viewpoint and address it is an important part of forgiveness, reaching the higher ideal of empathy, the mark of maturity. Much of the overaction of revenge is caused by an almost infantile response that sees the world only in one's own terms. Of course, in international relations, the lengthy process which is often needed for interpersonal forgiveness is not relevant. What is needed is an immediate clamping down on any desire to respond militarily, unless the defence of the country is realistically threatened. If it is not, there should follow a period of calm reflection on the causes of the attack and the appropriate response.

1.1 Revenge

The distinguished psychologist Erich Fromm writes in 'The Anatomy of Human Destructiveness' of revenge thus:

'Vengeful destructiveness is a spontaneous reaction to intense and unjustified suffering inflicted upon a person or the members of a group with whom he is identified. It differs from normal defensive aggression in two ways: (1) It occurs *after* the damage has been done, and hence is not a defence against a *threatening* danger; (2) it is of much greater intensity, and is often cruel, lustful, and insatiable' [2].

Revenge indeed seems hard-wired into our brains, but unfortunately, forgiveness is not. The law of an 'eye for an eye' or 'lex talionis', the law of retaliation, can be found far back in ancient history, in the Babylonian Code of Hammurabi (the king of Babylon 1792-1750 BCE). There it was actually meant to ensure that the punishment was commensurate with the crime. The Jewish law of an 'eye for eye, tooth for tooth' [3] may have been derived from the Babylonian law. It certainly had the same meaning of restricting retribution.

Jesus Christ, however, in the Sermon on the Mount, asked for a more noble, heroic response to being harmed:

'Ye hath heard it hath been said, An eye for an eye, and a tooth for a tooth: But I say unto you, That ye resist not evil: but whosoever shall smite thee on thy right cheek, turn to him the other also.' [4]

This passage greatly influenced Mahatma Gandhi's thoughts which will be discussed later in this book. Unfortunately, many political leaders have not been guided by it but by a desire for revenge which can result in the mass deaths of people who have not had anything to do with the act being avenged but who have had the misfortune to belong to the same community or nation as the perpetrator of that act. Vengeance, which often engenders a cycle of retaliation, is a colossal negative and violent force that can often only be negated by forgiveness which is, therefore, a very important factor in international affairs, showing human beings at their most noble, disciplined and often empathetic.

1.2 Forgiveness and Christianity

The importance of forgiveness is emphasised in Christianity more than in any other religion. As the distinguished political theorist and writer Hannah Arendt (who was not a Christian) observed:

'The Discoverer of the role of forgiveness in the realm of human affairs was Jesus of Nazareth. The fact that he made this discovery in a religious context and articulated it in religious language is no reason to take it any less seriously in a strict secular sense. It has been in the nature of our tradition of political thought (and for reasons we cannot explore here) to be highly selective and to exclude from articulate conceptualization a great variety of authentic political experiences, among which we need not be surprised to find some of an even elementary nature....' [5]

It is not necessary to agree with Hannah Arendt that Jesus Christ actually 'discovered ' the role of forgiveness in human affairs to appreciate that no one before Him had given such emphasis to its importance. When, for example a disciple, Peter, asked, 'Lord, how often will my brother sin against me, and I forgive him? As many as seven times? 'Jesus replied,

'I do not say to you seven times, but seventy-seven times' [6]. Jesus practised what He preached. When He was dying on the Cross, He forgave those responsible for His death, uttering the immortal words: 'Father, forgive them, for they know not what they do' [7]. In this way, He set an example of forgiveness for all time. It remains one of the most noble and exalted responses to which human beings can aspire when harmed, revealing at such times perhaps the divine spark which may be in everyone. As Alexander Pope wrote:

To err is human
To forgive divine [8].

Hannah Arendt examined the matter closely: '...forgiveness is the exact opposite of vengeance, which acts in the form of re-acting against an original trespassing, whereby far from putting an end to the consequences of the first misdeed, everybody remains bound to the process, permitting the chain reaction contained in every action to take its unhindered course' [9].

Arendt argued that this 'chain reaction' can only be stopped by forgiveness which acts in an unexpected way. She wrote:

'Forgiving, in other words, is the only reaction which does not merely re-act but acts anew and unexpectedly, unconditioned by the act which provoked it and therefore freeing from its consequences both the one who forgives and the one who is forgiven. The freedom contained in Jesus' teachings of forgiveness is the freedom from vengeance, which incloses (sic) both doer and sufferer in the relentless automatism of the action process, which by itself need never come to an end' [10].

The Treaty of Versailles is a good example of this' relentless automatism' and will now be considered.

1.3 The Treaty of Revenge: Versailles 1919

The treaty, forced on Germany by the Allies, particularly France in 1919, was an act of vengefulness that would have the most cataclysmic consequences for the twentieth century, involving millions of deaths. France had long regarded Germany as its bitter enemy after its defeat in the Franco-Prussian war of 1871. With the Treaty, it wreaked its vengeance.

Indeed, on the 13th July 1919, the Parisian newspaper 'Le Petit Journal' published, on the front page of its illustrated supplement, a picture that showed how the French saw the peace treaty as their revenge. At the top of the page, the vanquished French were depicted signing the peace treaty with Germany in 1871. Below it was a second picture of a humbled Germany signing the Treaty of Versailles in 1919 while a shining victorious France looked on. The picture was captioned: 'A Ton Tour Germania'! (Your turn Germany!) (The picture is the frontispiece of this book) [11].

The Versailles Treaty blamed Germany 'solely' for the war (which was a debatable verdict) and included demands that Germany should pay £6,600 million in reparations while losing Alsace Lorraine to France, and other territories to Poland, Belgium, and Denmark as well as all her colonies. Germany's armed forces were severely limited and were forbidden from entering the Rhineland.

The Treaty naturally aroused the hatred of the Germans for France and a desire for revenge. This was witnessed by the writer Vera Brittain who in 1924 visited Germany. For example she records that she met a young German officer on a train:

'One day', he exclaimed exultantly, 'we will make war upon them and treat them as they have treated us! I am longing for that war' [12].

The Treaty of Versailles did not lead directly to the Second World War but was a major factor in the rise of Hitler, who came to power vowing to repudiate the treaty, end the payment of reparations and restore honour to Germany. There were other causes in Hitler's rise, probably the most important being the colossal increase in unemployment, but the Treaty of Versailles was an important factor. The economic crisis alone could well have helped some socialist or communist parties to power, but National Socialism also appealed to the nationalist pride of Germans angered over the peace treaty as well as unemployment.

In 1939 Hitler invaded Poland, which both Britain and France had pledged to defend. They, therefore, declared war on Germany. In 1940 Nazi Germany invaded and defeated France, which then had to sign the armistice in the Compiegne Forest in the same railway carriage where Germany had had to sign the armistice for 1918. Hitler sat in the very chair where General Foch had sat in 1918 for that signing, triumphantly showing how the Germans had been able to get their revenge on the French. This sort of revenge, like much of that in international relations, involved a restoration of national honour after a humiliation, as well as a desire to harm the enemy lethally.

Soon many other countries were swept up into the horror of the Second World War, which might well have been avoided if only France had acted with forgiveness and magnanimity towards Germany in 1919. The subsequent history of the latter could then have been very different. Hitler might never have come to power, nor would over 60 million people have been killed in the subsequent global war, neither would the Holocaust have taken place.

In 1915, in his Exhortation to the belligerent powers to seek a negotiated peace, Pope Benedict XV had warned of the cycle of vengeance '. . .Nations do not die; humiliated and oppressed, they bear the weight of the yoke imposed upon them, preparing themselves for their come-back and transmitting from one generation to the next a sad legacy of hatred and vendetta' [13].

After the Second World War, the 'sad legacy of hatred and vendetta' between France and Germany was ended by not a priest but a Christian politician, Robert Schuman, who, determined that the French should this time forgive the Germans, persuaded both countries to work together in the European Coal and Steel Community, thus creating a lasting peace between the two previously warring countries. He showed what one good person could achieve with power and the right will. His was an outstanding example of Arendt's idea of unexpected forgiveness. It is to this French statesman, Robert Schuman, that we shall turn in the next chapter.

However, as the chapters subsequent to that on Schuman show, his example was not followed by other Western political leaders for whom revenge was the default response. As a result, the twenty-first century opened with unnecessary bloody and futile conflicts, some of which lasted longer than did the First or Second World Wars.

References

1. Gandhi, M. *Harijan*, 15 March 1940. The assassination will be considered in the chapter on Gandhi and the Versailles Treaty later in this chapter.
2. Fromm,Erich'The Anatomy of Human Destructiveness' (Penguin Harmondsworth, Middx., England 1973)p.362-3
3. The Holy Bible,ESV (London 2012)Exodus 21.24
4. Ibid Matthew 5.38-39
5. Arendt, Hannah,' 'The Human Condition' (University of Chicago (1958) p.238
6. The Holy Bible, Matthew 18v21-22
7. Ibid, Luke 23v34
8. Pope, Alexander, 'An Essay on Criticism', in *Selected Poetry* (Oxford 1998), p. 14, line 525.
9. Arendt op.cit.p.241
10. Ibid
11. www.gallica.bnf.fr/Le Petit Journal, Supplement du Dimanche, 13-07-1919
12. Brittain,Vera,'Testament of Youth,'(London 1933)p.640
13. Pollard,John F.,'Benedict XV:The Unknown Pope and the Pursuit of Peace' (London 1999) p.117

Part I
Forgiveness Towards a Foreign Enemy and the Futility of Revenge

Chapter 2
Robert Schuman, Forgiveness and the Founding of the EU

After the Second World War, Robert Schuman, the French Foreign Minister, wanted the French people to forgive the Germans for their aggression and not to make the same mistakes as they had committed with the vindictive Versailles Treaty in 1919. He was determined to find a way of ending the decades long cycle of vengeance between the two countries, which had resulted in a colossal loss of life.

In 1951, as the French Foreign Minister, Schuman founded the European Coal and Steel Community with the specific aim of avoiding war between Germany and France again. The ECSC developed into the European Economic Community, which later became the European Union. Without Robert Schuman, the EU probably would never have been established: thus, he is known as 'the Father of the European Community'.

In 2012 the EU was awarded the Nobel Peace Prize for 'helping to transform most of Europe from a continent of wars to a continent of peace' [1]. Had he been alive then, Schuman would have deserved to receive that prize more than any other individual who had played a part in the creation of the European Union.

2.1 Early Life

Robert Schuman was ideally suited for the task of bringing France and Germany together as he had strong affinities with both countries. He was born a German citizen in June 1886 in Luxembourg. His father, originally a Frenchman born in Lorraine, had become a German when Lorraine was annexed in 1871. Robert Schuman's mother was a Luxembourger. He was educated in French-speaking schools but studied law in German universities. In 1912 he began practising as a lawyer in Metz, which was then German. However, after the First World war, it became French again, as did Schuman in 1919. In that year, he was elected as a deputy to the French parliament. As a result of his inter-cultural early life, Schuman was at home in the languages and cultures of both France and Germany.

A. Wells, *The Importance of Forgiveness and the Futility of Revenge*, Contributions to International Relations, https://doi.org/10.1007/978-3-030-87552-7_2

Furthermore, as a devout Christian who had considered entering the priesthood [2], Robert Schuman understood the importance of forgiveness in breaking the cycle of revenge between France and Germany. Indeed, during the Second World War, when on the run from the Gestapo, he had astonished those hiding him by talking about working with Germany to rebuild Europe after hostilities had ended [3]. After the war, he worked hard to bring this about. He also had a dream which he later expressed in his book 'Pour L'Europe' that a united Europe might be created in the geographical area once known as Christendom, based on the Christian principles which, according to him, gave rise to modern democracy:

'Democracy owes its existence to Christianity. It was born on the day when man was called to realise in his temporal life the dignity of the human being, in the freedom of each person, in respect for the rights of each and by the practice of fraternal love for all. Never before Christ had such ideas been formulated. Democracy. . .has recognised the primacy of the inner values which ennoble man. The universal law of love and charity has made each man our neighbour. . .it has by no means always been the believers who have made the most decisive progress for democracy. Christian ideas live on and are active in the subconscious of men who have ceased to practice a dogmatic religion but who continue to be inspired by its great principles' [4].

2.2 The Founding of the European Coal and Steel Community

Between 1947 and 1948 Robert Schuman became the Prime Minister of France, and afterwards the Foreign Minister. In this capacity, in 1950, he worked with the civil servant Jean Monnet on his plan to integrate the coal and steel industries of Germany and France so that, as steel would be jointly produced, the production of weapons for war by one of them would be impossible.

East Germany was then under the control of the Soviet Union but there were factors working in Schuman's favour. West Germany, led by Chancellor Adenauer, wanted to regain its sovereignty and trust from other nations, which was likely if it were part of such an arrangement. Moreover, there had already been Nazi-enforced collaboration during the Second World War between the Lorraine iron ore mines and the Saar coalfields, which were close to each other across the Franco-German borders.

Aware of the opposition to working with Germany, Schuman adroitly sprang the plan on the French Cabinet in May 1950 and demanded an instant response before any opposition could be organised. Some of the Cabinet members, such as the prime minister, Georges Bidault, were thinking in terms of a Franco-American alliance and needed persuading, but eventually, Schuman won them over, partly because the idea of France taking the initiative in European affairs appealed to the French Cabinet.

Few of its members could have envisaged the momentous consequences of their decision on that day.

Adenauer of West Germany was then approached and agreed to the Schuman Plan, which on 9 May 1950, Schuman revealed to the world. He declared that the coming together of the nations of Europe 'requires the elimination of the age-old opposition of France and Germany'. The plan proposed that Franco-German production of coal and steel be placed under a common High Authority, within a framework open to the participation of the other countries of Europe. It would be 'a first step in the federation of Europe' [5].

Italy, Belgium, the Netherlands and Luxembourg had also been invited to join the project, to which they agreed. However, Britain refused to participate as it wanted to preserve its independence. It believed it had a special relationship with the USA and that, together with the Commonwealth, was sufficient for its needs. Moreover, the Labour government intended to nationalise its coal and steel industries and thought involvement with Schuman's project might disrupt this.

Before the negotiations that would lead to the formation of the European Coal and Steel Community, Robert Schuman, Konrad Adenauer and Alcide de Gasperi the Catholic leaders of France, Germany, and Italy, met in a Benedictine monastery on the Rhine for fasting and prayer, aware that their great vision for Europe was a spiritual and moral one: the avoidance of war [6].

In 1951, by the Treaty of Paris, the European Coal and Steel Community was set up with the six members forming a common market in coal and steel. Supranational institutions were established to govern it, consisting of the High Authority, Council of Ministers, Parliament, and Court of Justice.

2.3 The European Economic Community

So successful was the ECSC that its six members decided to enlarge it into the European Economic Community in 1957.This was a common market of all their goods and services, with free movement of workers and capital. Its political institutions were to be a Commission to make proposals for the EEC as a whole, a Council of ministers from members states who could veto these proposals, a Parliament of Representatives from Members States' National Assemblies and an Independent Court of Justice.

Robert Schuman became the president of the European Parliamentary Assembly. In 1958 he declared:

'We are called to bethink ourselves of the Christian basics of Europe by forming a democratic model of governance which through reconciliation develops into a 'community of peoples' in freedom, equality, solidarity and peace and which is deeply rooted in Christian basic values' [7].

Although the EU has not developed into 'a democratic model' nor 'community of peoples' 'deeply rooted in Christian values' (such as being good neighbours and welcoming refugees), it has flourished economically until recently and buttressed the new democracies in Southern and Eastern Europe which have joined it. Above all, there has been peace between Germany and France.

Britain, which could have made a major contribution to the development of the EU, did not join the Common Market until 1971, thus missing a historic opportunity to be at its inception and influencing its formation. Having declined to join the European Coal and Steel Community in 1951 and the negotiations for the European Economic Community in 1957, Britain then changed its mind in the early1960s. A committee set up under the former President of the Board of Trade, Sir Frank Lee, found that the economic growth rate of the EEC was two and a half times that of Britain. Therefore in 1962, Britain's Conservative government under Harold Macmillan applied to join the EEC. However, its application was rejected by President De Gaulle of France, who feared Britain's economic and political clout would be used to stop France from exploiting the EEC agriculturally with the Common Agricultural Policy he was introducing. For this reason, De Gaulle also blocked Britain's application in 1967. However, he need not have worried. When Britain did enter the EEC in 1971, it did not use its muscle to reform the organisation either economically or politically. It became more bureaucratic and allowed France to exploit it. The EEC enlarged gradually to twenty- eight members after the collapse of the Soviet bloc, and decision-making became more complex. By 2020 the EU had many problems regarding the economy, free movement of workers, refugees and migration, terrorism, secession movements within countries, the euro, further integration, and seemingly increasing German dominance, as well as other issues. Unfortunately, instead of trying to reform the EU, Britain, after a referendum in 2016, decided to leave it. By this time, much of Robert Schuman's idealism had been lost.

In 1963, the year of his death, Robert Schuman wrote that the 'New Europe':

'cannot and must not remain an economic and technical enterprise; it needs a soul, the conscience of its historical affinities and of its responsibilities in the present and in the future, and a political will at the service of the same human ideal' [8].

In 2003 Romana Prodi, the President of the European Commission, launched three high-powered working groups to examine the EU's core values, chaired by the Polish philosophy professor Krystof Michalski, in a bid to demonstrate that the Union has a 'soul' and is not solely a technical construction. The groups were to rethink the principles that guided European society and were to reflect in particular on the challenges posed by immigration, by a dialogue with the Muslim world and whether Europe's social model needs rejuvenating [9].

However, despite the efforts of Prodi and others, the EU does often seem 'soulless', its early inspirational idealism destroyed by materialistic concerns. Nevertheless, it has been an effective model of how an age-old cycle of revenge can be replaced by cooperation for the good of all involved. Many countries such as Israel and her Arab neighbours could benefit if another Robert Schuman, in the form of an Arab or Jewish politician, fluent in Hebrew and Arabic and aware of how to integrate their economies, could lead the people into forgiveness and peace.

Today the problem in Europe is tension not between Germany and France but between Russia and the West. But this, too, could probably be overcome in Europe by following Robert Schuman's example of forgiveness, empathy with both sides and using economic cooperation to create peace. This will be discussed in another chapter.

References

1. www.europarl.europa.eu/eu-wins-2012-nobel- peace-prize
2. Mowat, R. C.'Creating the European Community', (London1973) p.44
3. Ibid p.44
4. Schuman,Robert, 'Pour L'Europe' (Paris)1963p.56-70
5. http://europa.eu/about-eu/basic-information/symbols/Europe-day/schuman-declaration
6. **John Paul II addressing European Christian Democratic politicians in 2003, "Omission of Christianity from EU text 'unjust'** from 'The Irish Examiner' November 08,2003
7. Fountain,Jeff,'A Christian Europe:the Forgotten Legacy of Robert Schuman,'(Amsterdam 2014) p.5
8. Schuman,Robert, op.cit. p.58
9. Spinant, Dana, *European Voice* 2nd May 2003

Chapter 3
9/11: The USA'S Revenge on Afghanistan

After the Second World War, Robert Schuman, by overcoming the age-old cycle of revenge between Germany and France, showed what forgiveness could achieve.

However, half a century later, vengeance in the form of military response, not forgiveness and reflection on the cause of the hostility, was still the default response for a country attacked by another. This was shown in 2001 by the USA's response to the 9/11 onslaught.

On 11 September 2001, just after 8.45 am, an American airliner bound for California crashed into the north tower of the World Trade Centre in New York, killing all onboard and hundreds in the tower. Less than twenty minutes later, a second plane rammed into the south tower, which soon collapsed, along with the north tower, killing over two thousand people. A third plane then crashed onto the Pentagon. A fourth targeted Washington but was brought down by some brave passengers before it could harm the seat of government. All in all, 2996 people were killed, and over 6000 were injured. Nothing constructive was achieved.

3.1 Al-Qaeda's Revenge

This attack by al-Qaeda was revenge for the USA's harming the Palestinian people by its support for Israel and also for the presence of American troops in Saudi Arabia, the land of Mecca and Medina.

On 7 October 2001 al-Qaeda's leader, Osama bin Laden, explained his thinking: 'I swear to God that America will not live in peace until peace reigns in Palestine, and before all the army of infidels depart the land of Mohammed. Peace be upon him.' [1]

The next year he declared that:

'The blood pouring out of Palestine must be avenged.' [2]

Bin Laden had been much influenced by Dr. Abdullah Azzam, a Palestinian refugee and scholar who had wanted to avenge the wrong done to his people. He had

A. Wells, *The Importance of Forgiveness and the Futility of Revenge*, Contributions to International Relations, https://doi.org/10.1007/978-3-030-87552-7_3

worked with bin Laden to recruit Muslims worldwide to fight with the mujahidin in Afghanistan. In a 'fatwa' Azzam had declared that both the Afghan and the Palestinian struggle were 'jihads' in which Muslims had a moral duty to kill non-believers in those lands [3].

3.2 Forgiveness and Revenge in Islam

Revenge is not condemned in Islam, but forgiveness is held as a higher virtue, although it is not distinctively emphasised as it is in Christianity. Three words are used in the Koran to mean 'forgive', each one having a different shade of meaning.'Afa', translated as 'forgive' means to forget or to obliterate from one's mind.'Safaha', is also translated as forgive, and means to turn away from, ignore, or treat the matter as not affecting one.' Gaffar' means to cover up something as an act of grace.

In the Koran, believers are told:

'. . .if you overlook their offences and forgive and pardon them, then know that God is forgiving and merciful.' [4]

If nevertheless revenge is decided upon, it must be only commensurate with the injury received and never be more than that. Moreover, the Koran teaches that it would be best still to exercise self-restraint:

'If you punish, let your punishment be commensurate with the wrong that has been done to you. But it shall be best for you to endure your wrongs with patience.

Be patient, then: God will grant you patience. Do not grieve for the unbelievers, nor distress yourself at their intrigues. God is with those who keep from evil and do good works.' [5]

However, despite these clear Koranic teachings, a minority of Muslims have carried out catastrophic acts of bloody revenge on innocent people. The attack on the World Trade Centre in 2001 was one of these.

As there is now no caliphate to give leadership on the Koran's teachings, extremists feel free to interpret them as justifying bloody revenge. In 2019 the leader of ISIS, al-Baghdadi, declared that the suicide bombings of packed churches in Sri Lanka on Easter Sunday were revenge for ISIS's loss of its territory in Syria. He called for more such attacks [6].

3.3 MI5 Discerns Vengeance Unlike President Bush

To their credit, the British members of MI5, who had flown to Washington in the wake of the 9/11 attack, did see it as an act of revenge for the USA's foreign policy. As the then head of M15, Eliza Manningham-Buller, explained in her Reith Lectures:

'It would, though, be wrong to suggest that all terrorists belonging to al-Qaeda, or its affiliates, or merely inspired by it, share an identical motivation. But a single narrative compelling to some, seems to prevail, namely that it is the duty of good Muslims to wage jihad against the West, to avenge their Palestinian co-religionists, and more recently those in Iraq and Afghanistan, as well as elsewhere.

If you watch the chilling video wills made by the British 7/7 bombers, or those convicted in London for the ambitious plot of 2006 to destroy a series of transatlantic aircraft, to mark the fifth anniversary of 9/11, it is clear that their perception of revenge is the main motive.' [7]

However, President George Bush neither saw the attack as revenge for the USA's foreign policy nor considered a change in America's policy in the Middle East as being the best method of preventing further attacks. Instead, Bush announced :

'America was targeted for attack because we're the brightest beacon for freedom and opportunity in the world. And no one will keep that light from shining.' [8]

In contrast, Manningham-Buller stated that a change in America's policy was vital to prevent another such onslaught. In the British Embassy in Washington:

'we mulled on the various options open to the US Government and, more widely to other Western governments. I recall that one of those present argued that the peace process between Israel and the Palestinians needed to be revived, an explicit recognition that the West needed to re-address the open sore in the Middle East that could well have contributed to these events. Those present agreed. It was important, even at this early stage, following a monstrous crime, to consider all possible ways of reducing the likelihood of further attacks'. [9]

3.4 If Bush Had Shown Forgiveness...

However, as well as not asking whether its foreign policy was to blame for the attack, the USA did not consider forgiving the attackers as a possible option, despite the frequent references to God in the USA's political rhetoric and despite the fact that most Americans claim to be of the Christian faith which emphasises the importance of forgiveness. Had America announced that it forgave those who had bombed it and that it would not be retaliating in the same vein, it would have shown that it was operating on a higher ethical plane than are most other countries. Above all, this action could have saved thousands of innocent lives, including those of children, and prevented the USA from becoming involved in a conflict that has been the longest in its history. The funds wasted on destroying Afghan civilians and their homes could have been used to improve their living standards, thereby winning their support. The USA could still have issued international arrest warrants for the perpetrators of the 9/11 attack, who would be then be subjected to the due process of law, as forgiveness does not deny justice but revenge. The USA might then have reflected on the root cause of the attack, considered the view of British intelligence on this and used its influence with Israel to secure justice for the Palestinians as well as for the Jews there.

It is not clear how far the British apprised the American government as to the views of MI5.What is clear is that, as usual, Britain did not act as a candid friend to the USA but instead supported its military action against Afghanistan. Had the British Prime Minister, Tony Blair, as a fellow Christian, persuaded President Bush to forgive the 9/11 attackers, issue arrest warrants for them, but not embark on a war against the innocent people of Afghanistan, he would have prevented a massive shedding of blood not only in Afghanistan but also later in Iraq which Bush held erroneously as being also linked to the al-Qaeda attack on America. A true friend of the USA would have tried to calm the American President and government when their national anger was at boiling point, American pride deeply hurt. What was needed was a period of quiet reflection and consideration of the possible causes of the attack with regard to an appropriate response.

However, on the night of 11 September Blair broadcast his view: 'This mass terrorism is the new evil in our world. The people who perpetrate it have no regard whatever for the sanctity or the value of human life. . .This is not a battle between the United States of America and terrorism, but between the free and democratic world and terrorism. . .' [10]

He declared that Britain would stand 'shoulder to shoulder' with the USA to defeat this 'evil' [11].

It was thus clear that Britain would support the use of force by the USA. Forgiveness, in the sense of military restraint, together with a consideration of alternative responses, was not on the cards. Had it been so, thousands of lives would have been saved. But the USA had been hurt and humiliated and wanted revenge.

The people who had a platform and a moral obligation to lobby for a forgiving response to the 9/11 attack were, of course, the heads of the Christian churches. Influential Christian church leaders, well-informed about current affairs, might have persuaded President Bush to think more constructively and with forgiveness. However, no such persons emerged in the USA. The distinguished American sociologist and pastor Tony Campolo, who had been an adviser to President Clinton, did comment on the desire for retaliation and the 'bellicosity' in the USA [12] but with little effect.

In Rome, the Vatican kept quiet on the issue of what should be the USA's response. In Britain, the Archbishop of Canterbury, George Carey, led a national remembrance service at St Paul's Cathedral for the victims of the 9/11 attack. However, instead of speaking in his sermon of the need to forgive and consider the reasons why the tragedy had occurred, he spoke, as had George Bush and Tony Blair, in binary terms of the USA being good and the attackers 'evil' and 'barbaric'. Some scholars have argued this encouraged those who wanted military action [13]. This was unfortunate as Archbishop Carey had a good record of building bridges with Muslims in Britain.

However, there was one lone prophetic voice in the wilderness. This was from the Archbishop of Wales, Dr. Rowan Williams, who later became the Archbishop of Canterbury and who did courageously warn against mere revenge for the 9/11 attack. He had himself experienced its horror, having been at that time in Washington at a church meeting near the World Trade Centre. He said, immediately after the attack, that while the perpetrators needed to be punished:

'the challenge before the USA and its allies today, I believe, is to ask what is to be done beyond punishment to make any such punishments more than revenge.' [14]

He suggested this must be recognisable as more than retaliation and therefore accompanied by some new initiatives such as ' a further round of debt cancellation, a concerted initiative to break the deadlock in the Holy Land and to bind the security of the Israelis and Palestinians together; a review of the sanctions on Iraq...' [15].

Regarding the dehumanising effect of anger that facilitates killing people, he warned:

'Anger always blurs the real human features of those we're angry with. If it didn't, no-one would ever be persuaded to violent action' [16].

However, he was not speaking at some grand national event but giving the Presidential Address to the Governing Body of the Church in Wales, University of Wales, Lampeter on 20 September 2001. His speech was not therefore given the media coverage it deserved, and his words went unheard.

It is possible that had Dr. Williams been the Archbishop of Canterbury, then he might have had more clout and access to the governments in Britain and the USA. One person could have made a great difference to events here. Also effective could have been the churches' encouraging their congregations to demonstrate in the name of forgiveness. Indeed, there should have been a loud thundering for it from the pulpits. Unfortunately, the desire for churches in the USA to steer clear of politics might have inhibited such response there. Furthermore, academics who believed revenge was not the most constructive way forward could have spoken out. The philosopher Jacques Derrida whose theory of 'pure forgiveness 'or 'forgiving the unforgivable' was arguably relevant to the situation, kept silent about the 9/11 attack. Even though he gave an interview on his work just after the attack, he did not mention the latter. For this, he has been rightly criticised [17].

Indeed, the silence of many who were well placed -whether in the church, academia, or politics -to query whether military action was the most constructive response to 9/11 was shameful.

3.5 The USA'S Revenge

The USA chose revenge, not forgiveness, as its response to the 9/11 attack. The consequences of this policy demonstrated the truth of Hannah Arendt's concept of the chain reaction set in train by vengeance. Washington decided on a massive bombing campaign, launching in October 2001 Operation Enduring Freedom (OEF) with the support of the British Armed Forces and the Afghan Northern Alliance. The official objective of OEF was to find bin Laden and other al-Qaeda leaders and bring them to trial, to destroy al-Qaeda and oust the Taliban from power to stop it harbouring al-Qaeda. However, that there was also the desire by the USA to wreak its own revenge on the Taliban and al-Qaeda is shown by its excessive bombing of

Afghanistan. This was clearly not the most ethical or efficient way to find Osama bin Laden. Indeed, by alienating the local populations in Afghanistan and northwest Pakistan with its attacks, the USA made intelligence gathering on bin Laden's whereabouts far more difficult for itself.

Of course, President Bush would never admit that such a base motive as revenge had motivated the American bombing campaign. On 25 September 2001, he told employees at the FBI:

'Ours is a nation that does not seek revenge, but we do seek justice' [18]

However, some distinguished spiritual leaders saw the matter differently. In December 2001, Pope John Paul11 issued a strong statement, without referring to the USA, on the importance of limiting military action, even when the action is justified [19]. Meanwhile, Dr Rowan Williams wrote a small book, 'Writing in the Dust' (published in January 2002) in which he denounced the war in Afghanistan as morally 'tainted' [20]. He said that the bombing campaign in Afghanistan had lost credibility and was morally equivalent to the terrorism it sought to defeat:

'From the point of view of a villager in Afghanistan whose family have died in a bombing raid, a villager who has probably never heard of the World Trade Centre, the distinctions between what the US troops are doing and what was done on 11 September will be academic.' [21]

Operation Enduring Freedom, which was not authorised by the UN, was part of President Bush's vaguely named 'war on terror'. Of such a war Eliza Manningham–Buller made the following insightful comments, which were shared by her colleagues in the British Intelligence Services:

'Despite talk of military action, there was one thing we all agreed on: terrorism is resolved through politics and economics not through arms and intelligence, however important a role these play'. [22]

Of the 9/11 attack on the USA she observed: 'I call it a crime, not an act of war...' [23].

3.6 The Islamic Republic of Afghanistan

However, the USA was not interested in resolving terrorism through politics and economics. After a colossal bombing campaign, the OEF forced the Taliban out of Kabul in a matter of weeks. The Islamic Republic of Afghanistan was set up with an interim government under Hamid Karzai. In December 2001, the International Security Assistance Force (ISAF) was established by the UN Security Council at the end of December 2001 to secure Kabul. NATO assumed control in 2003 of the ISAF, which consisted mainly though not entirely of NATO troops.

With regard to Afghanistan's governance, in 2002, Western-backed Hamid Karzai was chosen as the President of Afghanistan's Transitional Administration by the grand assembly of tribal chiefs. In 2004 his government was democratically elected to power by the Afghan people. The women were given more rights and education, but these had not been the aims of the USA's OEF in 2001 and could have been achieved by more peaceful means using the money that would otherwise have been spent on weapons.

It is true that the coalition forces did oust the Taliban from power and kill some of the leaders of al-Qaeda. But it was not until after ten years of war, in May 2011, that the USA actually found and assassinated Osama bin Laden in his hideaway in Pakistan. Moreover, the USA did not destroy al-Qaeda, which simply operated from other countries, while its spin-off, ISIS, then terrorised the Middle East.

3.7 The Price of the War

Al-Qaeda's 9/11 vengeful attack on the USA was futile, achieving nothing. However, the USA's vengeful retaliation, leading to nearly 20 years of war, was also largely futile, certainly not worth the very high price paid. By 2014, when most of the international forces left Afghanistan, the war had already cost the USA over 2300 soldiers' lives, the UK 453 [24]. Additional lives had been lost by other coalition forces, not to speak of the enormous death toll of innocent civilians as well as soldiers and insurgents on the Afghan side and those in Pakistan caused by the drone attacks. The USA's response to the 9/11 assault thus killed almost as many of its own citizens and those of its allies as the nearly 3000 lost in the original attack. The financial costs were colossal. Precise figures are difficult to obtain, but the Congressional Research Service estimated that the USA had spent about $444 billion on the war by 2011 [25]. In 2012 it was reported that the UK had spent an estimated £4 billion a year on the war and probably the total would be about £20 billion at the end of the conflict [26]. The coalition forces have, of course, spent additional sums. By 2017 the war in Afghanistan was estimated to have cost $850 billion [27] with prospects of caring for the veterans of the war years after its end increasing the totals [28].

3.8 The Situation Deteriorates

Sadly, less than three years after NATO announced an end to combat operations in Afghanistan, the situation deteriorated. In 2017 attacks on Kabul were worse than ever. According to the UN 10,400 civilians had been killed in that year alone [29].

Even al-Qaeda was now back in Afghanistan, though not on the same scale as before [30]. ISIS had at least 1000 militants there [31]. The Kabul government controlled only 64% of the population, the Taliban controlled 12%, and the remaining 24% lived in 'contested' territory [32].

In August 2017, the USA announced that it was sending more troops (an estimated 3900) to Afghanistan. These would join the 12,000 NATO troops already there, more than half them being American [33]. President Trump was aiming to stop the Taliban from overthrowing the Afghan government, not to defeat them. He was hoping for a political reconciliation with the insurgents that would enable him to bring the American troops back home. To this end in July 2018, he sent envoys to Afghanistan to open direct talks with the Afghan Taliban [34]. At the end of the year, he announced that he planned to bring half the 14,000 US soldiers back [35].

Peace negotiations were later opened between the USA and the Taliban, resulting in senior officials from both sides signing a peace in Doha, Qatar, in February 2020, ending nearly 20 years of war, the longest in the USA's history. The Taliban agreed to cut all ties with al-Qaeda and to negotiate with the Afghan government. The USA would withdraw their troops gradually only if this political reconciliation took place. However, for this, there needed to be mutual forgiveness. It seems there has been none. Nevertheless, President Trump's government agreed with the Taliban to withdraw its troops by 1 May 2021. In April of that year, the new American administration under President Joe Biden announced the date had been postponed to 11 September 2021.

By May 2021, there had still been no ceasefire, and the Taliban had not been defeated. Indeed it portrayed itself as the victor, as the NATO troops were leaving. Despite President Biden's announcement of a postponement of the USA's troops withdrawal, by July, they had all left, other than those needed for security. In August the Taliban took control of Afghanistan amid mass panic and chaos. Thousands of Afghans who had worked for NATO forces tried to flee for fear of the Taliban's revenge. Its leaders, however, said that the Afghans would be forgiven [36]. At the time of writing (August 2021) that remains to be seen.

The final price of the war has been estimated at 2,442 US deaths and 20,660 injured; 457 UK deaths and 2,209 injured; the Afghan army lost 69,000 men and 47,245 Afghan civilians were killed The war cost the USA approximately 2 trillion dollars and the UK just over 27 billion pounds [37]. In addition the other NATO allies also, of course, suffered fatalities and financial losses,while the costs of caring for injured servicemen will be on going.

If 20 years earlier, after the 9/11 attack, an enlightened American government and people had decided to forgive al-Qaeda (only issuing arrest warrants for the crime's perpetrators) and re-consider its foreign policy as a cause of the hostility, thousands of people in the USA, Afghanistan, and elsewhere, would now still be alive. Billions of dollars that could have been better spent, and the USA would have stood tall among nations as an exemplar of the moral heights to which a people can aspire.

References

1. Halliday,Fred, 'Two Hours that Shook the World' (London 2002) p234
2. Observer 24th Nov 2002
3. Azzam,Abdullah, 'Defence of the Muslim Lands', www.religioscope.com

4. The Koran with a Parallel Arabic Text,trans by N.J.Dawood (Penguin ed,Harmondsworth, Middx England 1994)64.14 p556
5. Ibid 16.126,p.280
6. The Times April 30th 2019
7. Manningham-Buller,Eliza,Reith Lectures 6th September 2011 http://www.bbc.co.uk/reithlectures Lecture 1 Terror
8. http://archives.cnn.com/2001/US/09/11/bush.speech.text
9. Manningham-Buller op.cit.
10. Tony Blair, A Journey, (London 2010) p.356-7
11. He declared that Britain would stand 'shoulder to shoulder' with the USA to defeat this 'evil'.
12. Megoran,Nick 'God On Our Side? The Church of England and the Geopolitics of Mourning 9//11' Geopolitics (Routledge 2006),11:p.566
13. Ibid p.570
14. Williams, Rowan,Presidential Address to the Governing Body of the Church in Wales,University of Wales,Lampeter,20thSeptember 2001,https://www.churchinwales.org.uk
15. Ibid
16. Ibid
17. Strawser,Michael, *'Forgiving Derrida:From Terrorism to Self-Forgiveness'*,in 'Forgiveness: Probing the Boundaries,'eds Bloch-Schulman,Stephen and White,David,(Oxford 2009)
18. 'FBI needs Tools to Track Down Terrorists', Remarks of the President to Employees at the FBI, Office of Press Secretary, September 25 2001
19. Henneberger,Melinda,New York Times, December 12,2001
20. Williams,Rowan,'Writing in the Dust Reflections on 11th September and its aftermath' (London 2002) p.34
21. Ibid p.35
22. Manningham-Buller op.cit.
23. Ibid
24. www.icasualties.org/OEF
25. Bellasco,Amy 'The Cost of Iraq, Afghanistan, and other Global War on Terror Operations since 9/11',Congressional Research Service, March 29, 2011. www.crs.gov
26. The Daily Telegraph 19th May 2012 (www.telegraph.co.uk)
27. Evans,Michael,The Times,28th August 2017
28. Ibid
29. Rossi,Alex, Sky News,'War in Afghanistan:Threat of attacks 'worse than ever'19th February 2018
30. Evans,op.cit.
31. Ibid
32. Ibid
33. Ibid
34. The Daily Telegraph 16th July 2018 (www.telegraph.co.uk)
35. www.nytimes.com/2018/12/20/us/politics/afghanistan-troop-withdrawal
36. The Guardian 17th August 2021
37. The Sunday Times 22nd August 2021

Chapter 4
Iraq 2003: Deluded Revenge

It was not only Afghanistan that suffered from the USA's vengeful bombing for the 9/11 attack, but also Iraq, despite the fact that Saddam Hussein's regime had absolutely nothing to do with the attack, nor with al-Qaeda, to which Saddam was strongly opposed. Deluded as to Saddam's involvement, on 18 March 2003, President Bush authorised the invasion of Iraq as being consistent with the policy of the USA to take action against those who 'aided the terrorist attacks that occurred on September 11, 2001' [1].

The USA did have further motives for invading Iraq, including removing a brutal dictator who possibly possessed weapons of mass destruction and who also happened to possess the fourth-largest oil reserves in the world, but the rush to attack Saddam in the deluded belief he had harboured members of al-Qaeda was expressly one of the reasons.

4.1 The USA's Blind Revenge

Bush's decision to avenge the 9/11 attack bloodily by bombing not only Afghanistan but also Iraq resulted in the lethal chain reaction that Hannah Arendt had decades earlier warned would result from revenge:

'. . .forgiveness is the exact opposite of vengeance, which acts in the form of re-acting against an original trespassing, whereby far from putting an end to the consequences of the first misdeed, everybody remains bound to the process, permitting the chain reaction contained in every action to take its unhindered course' [2].

The invasion of Iraq destroyed hundreds of thousands of lives, homes, and livelihoods, causing tragic mayhem from which fled floods of refugees. In addition, as I will show later, the invasion led to the terrifying rise of ISIS/Isil or Daesh (the Islamic State of Iraq and Levant). None of this would have occurred Bush decided to forgive the 9/11 attack in the sense of forbearing to retaliate militarily while

A. Wells, *The Importance of Forgiveness and the Futility of Revenge*, Contributions to International Relations, https://doi.org/10.1007/978-3-030-87552-7_4

considering the causes of the attack and constructive responses to it. As Arendt argued:

'Forgiving, in other words, is the only reaction which does not merely re-act but acts anew and unexpectedly, unconditioned by the act which provoked it and therefore freeing from its consequences both the one who forgives and the one who is forgiven' [3].

Without this, she argued, the chain reaction of the revenge process need never end.

However, President Bush had other ideas.

On 22 January 2002, in his State of the Union address, he announced that Iraq was part of the 'axis of evil' which, along with North Korea and Iran threatened the USA's interests [4].

Between 2002 and early 2003, Bush urged the UN to ensure that Saddam Hussein did not restart a nuclear weapons programme nor possess weapons of mass destruction which he was forbidden to do by UN sanctions after the first Gulf war in 1991. Whether Bush's administration manipulated CIA reports to argue that Saddam did have WMD's is still a controversial issue.

In November 2002, under UN Security Council Resolution 1441, Hans Blix and Mohammed El Baradei led a team of UN weapons inspectors to restart the investigation of the state of Saddam's armaments. By March 2003, Blix had found no stockpiles of weapons of mass destruction and stated that although there was not always immediate Iraqi cooperation, the key remaining disarmament tasks would be resolved in a matter of months. Nevertheless, the USA tried and failed to get the UN Security Council to pass a resolution to authorise the use of force against Saddam.

Without UN authorisation, the USA would probably never have invaded Iraq had not the UK agreed to support the invasion. However, despite a huge protest by the British people in March 2003, their government led by Tony Blair did join the USA's military action against Iraq. Australia and Poland sent much smaller contingents than those of the USA and UK. Thus was launched the second Gulf War,' Operation Iraqi Freedom', on 19 March 2003 against Iraq to destroy the weapons of mass destruction which Saddam was alleged to have possessed and to remove him from power.

By 1 May the war was over. Saddam Hussein was deposed, but there were no weapons of mass destruction to be found. This might have been made clear by the weapons inspectors had they been given more time in Iraq.

Tragically the USA was so blinded by its desire to take revenge on Iraq for its alleged connection with the 9/11 attack that it could not wait for the weapons inspectors' investigations, nor did it have time to ascertain the truth about the situation. There were, in fact, no members of al-Qaeda in Iraq ironically until the American invasion. Saddam's rule was secular in Iraq and had no connection with the 9/11 attack.

4.2 The UK and Iraq

The British Prime Minister Tony Blair did not invade Iraq out of revenge but supported the USA's vengeful action. As usual, Britain did not act as the candid friend to the USA: it did not point out the errors of America's analysis of the situation. Blair might have been able to enlighten Bush that Saddam Hussein had nothing to do with the 9/11 attack, which was still reverberating in the American mind. Blair could have at least urged the USA to wait for the verdict of the weapons inspectors.

In a debate in the House of Commons leading up to the war on 26 February 2003, Alex Salmond (then a Scottish Nationalist MP and later his party's leader) pointed out that the coming war was partly an irrational retaliation for the 9/11attack and that Tony Blair was in a position to 'put the brakes on such a policy'. He argued that:

'it is the job of a candid friend to tell his friend the truth in times of crisis. That is particularly so in this case given that the friend, America, is gripped in the trauma of the aftermath of 11September,18 months ago. The fact that the Prime Minister has failed to do that is his central culpability,because he was in a position to put the brakes on that sort of policy, and he still is in such a position' [5].

He then humbly and courageously warned:

'Let us consider morality. The Prime Minister is a religious man and I respect that. It does him great credit. I have nothing like his record of church going or observance. However, I too, have faith and conviction. I believe that if an immoral and unjust war takes place, with thousands of casualties and the spilling of innocent blood, the person responsible for arguing for it, will answer one day to a much higher authority than the House of Commons' [6].

Across party lines MP's opposed the war but in insufficient numbers. Within the Labour Party, Robin Cook, the former Foreign Secretary, resigned as Leader of the House, the Health Minister Lord Hunt and the Home Office Minister John Denham also quit the government, while about a quarter of the Labour MP's voted against attacking Iraq. Meanwhile, one of the largest protests ever seen in Britain demonstrated against the impending war.

However, the leader of the Conservative opposition, Iain Duncan Smith, far from opposing the war, was one of the first politicians to call for military action against Iraq, which he erroneously believed was involved with the 9/11 attack on the USA. Indeed, as early as November 2001, soon after he became the Conservative Party leader, he tried and failed to win over Prime Minister Tony Blair to his view. He went to New York to hold talks on the matter with senior US administration officials, including Vice-President Dick Cheney, the National Security Advisor Condoleezza Rice and Paul Wolfowitz, the Deputy Defence Secretary and a leading advocate of military strikes against Iraq [7]. Had the Conservatives been led by someone such as Kenneth Clarke, who argued eloquently against the war in 2003 [8] or Malcolm Rifkind, who unfortunately had to oppose the war from outside parliament, the history of the West and Iraq might have been very different. Much depended on individual leadership in these circumstances.

4.3 The Churches' Opposition

The Pope and church leaders in the USA, other than of the Southern Baptist Convention, condemned the prospective war in Iraq, but it was to no avail. Probably face to face meetings between church leaders and Prime Minister Tony Blair and US President George Bush would have been more effective. In September 2002, the Archbishop of Canterbury, Dr. George Carey, declared there were 'no grounds whatsoever' for war against Iraq at that time [9]. In February 2003, Dr. Rowan Williams, the new Archbishop of Canterbury, spoke out against its possibility, issuing a joint a statement with Cardinal Cormac Murphy-O'Connor: 'The events of recent days show that doubts still persist about the moral legitimacy as well as the unpredictable humanitarian consequences of a war with Iraq' [10]. The year before Dr. Williams and other Anglican and Catholic bishops had signed a Pax Christi petition with 3000 other people protesting against the illegality and immorality of an American-led assault on Iraq.

The petition declared:

'It is deplorable that the world's most powerful nations continue to regard war and the threat of war as an acceptable instrument of foreign policy, in violation of the ethos of both the United Nations and Christian moral teaching...

The way to peace does not lie through war but through the transformation of structures of injustice and of the politics of exclusion, and that is the cause to which the west should be devoting its technological, diplomatic and economic resources.' [11]

The petition was handed into PM Tony Blair's office, where, however, it seems to have had little impact. It seems there was not enough protest or persuasion that could stop the war. Perhaps church leaders could have urged their congregations to write to their MP's to protest and stop the expected massive loss of life incurred by the proposed invasion of Iraq. They might well have done if they could have seen the consequences of the invasion.

In September 2012, in an interview to launch his memoirs, the former UN Secretary General Kofi Annan said that Tony Blair could have stopped the war in 2003 had he refused to support the USA without a second UN Resolution over Iraq [12].

4.4 The Dossier

Blair may have sincerely believed Saddam Hussein had weapons of mass destruction, was a cruel dictator and should be removed, but this does not explain his haste in going to war. Whatever his motives may have been, they were certainly clouded by the methods used to persuade Parliament of the need for war against Iraq. In particular, Blair's Director of Communications, Alastair Campbell, and a Ministry of Defence official, Paul Hamill, prepared a dossier that exaggerated the intelligence findings. In it, much was made of a claim that Iraq had weapons of mass destruction that could be activated within 45 mins. Based on dubious intelligence from a single source passed to an Iraqi exile group in London, it seems that the real claim was not about WMD but about battlefield weapons that could be fired at British troops in Cyprus. The dossier used unprocessed intelligence parts of which were flagged up and even used material plagiarised from an American-Iraqi student's thesis [13].

At the Iraq Inquiry in May 2011, Major General Michael Laurie, Director General of Intelligence Collection, stated that the purpose of the dossier was to make a case for war rather than setting out the available intelligence.

Tony Blair should have queried the findings in the dossier and had the sources independently investigated in view of his great responsibility as a Prime Minister about to take his country into a war with all the bloodshed and suffering that would result. Ideally, he should have made President Bush realise that he was motivated by a desire for revenge for 9/11with which Saddam Hussein had no connection. Instead, Blair charged into Iraq alongside the USA, although there was no exit strategy worked out before the invasion, which shows how much it was driven by visceral emotion and not rigorous thought.

4.5 The Cost of the Iraq War to the USA

Nearly 4500 American servicemen lost their lives in the war [14], with many more wounded. Obviously, the USA's coalition partners also suffered losses. Hundreds of thousands of Iraqis were also killed, and their country severely damaged. The war had cost the USA $806 billion by 2011 [15].

4.6 The Cost of the War to the UK

Besides the huge loss of Iraqi life and that of Coalition partners mentioned earlier, the war also resulted in the loss of 179 British servicemen [16], many more wounded, and cost Britain £8.2 billion [17]. Moreover, by supporting the USA's vengeful policies, the UK incurred revenge attacks from extremist Muslims. The actual invasion of Iraq by the USA and Britain was probably the most important reason for Britain's being subjected to the suicidal bombing in London on 7 July 2005 that caused 52 deaths.

Besides the loss of life on all sides, the US's invasion led to the rise of ISIS whose reign of terror spread worldwide.

4.7 The USA Inadvertently Enables Al-Qaeda to Enter Iraq

Ironically Saddam had, in fact, been keeping al-Qaeda out of Iraq. In 2003, just before the invasion, a Jordanian militant, Abu Musab al-Zarqawi had linked up with a Kurdish Islamist militant group in the north of Iraq, Ansar al-Islam. This group Saddam had viewed as a threat to Iraq and had had his intelligence service watching it. Zarqawi had previously run an Islamic training camp in Afghanistan. Saddam's removal meant that now the organisation was able to establish itself in the country.

With some of Ansar al-Islam and other Islamic supporters, Zarqawi formed a group 'Jama'at al-Tawid wal-Jihad' ('JTJ)'with the aim of forcing the US-led coalition to leave Iraq where he wanted to establish a pure Islamic state [18]. In 2004 he and his group declared allegiance to al-Qaeda [19]. He contributed greatly to the bloody chaos in Iraq as his tactics were suicide bombings and videoed beheadings. In 2006 he was killed, but his al-Qaeda jihadists, who were Sunni, continued their violence. (In Iraq, roughly 65% of the population are Shia, 20% Sunni, and the rest are either Kurds (also Sunni) or of other faiths).

Meanwhile, the ill-advised American Administrator of the Coalition Provisional Authority, Paul Bremer, had foolishly disbanded the Iraqi army, police, and intelligence officers in an attempt to rid Iraq of the influence of the Baathist party. As a result, there was not only a breakdown in law and order but thousands of disaffected soldiers and police looking for employment. It was these men that later filled the ranks of ISIS.

By 2006, the USA realised that it needed the moderate Sunni tribal leaders (or 'sheikhs') to help deal with the Sunni extremists in al-Qaeda. Therefore, America paid the sheikhs to unite against al-Qaeda and reduce the violence. At first, this movement, called 'the Sunni Awakening', was successful. However, the Shia Iraqi Prime Minister, Nouri al-Maliki, refused to allow the Sunnis to integrate fully with the Iraqi Security Services or to accommodate them in his administration. The Sunnis were therefore resentful. When the last American troops had left Iraq in 2011 'the Awakening' had become less effective.

4.8 The Rise of ISIS

A new dark chapter in the history of al-Qaeda was opening as some of its members in Iraq went to Syria to fight with the rebels, including the al-Nusra Islamists, against Assad's government. In 2013 al-Qaeda in Iraq announced it was allied to al-Nusra. This new group called itself 'Islamic State of Iraq and al-Sham', which is abbreviated to ISIS. ('Al-Sham' is Arabic for Levant, and the organisation also called itself ISIL or the Islamic State of Iraq and Levant). Practising Salifiya jihadism, it aimed to create the whole area into one caliphate or one Sunni Islamist state.

4.9 Al-Baghdadi

The caliph was to be the ISIS leader, Abu Bakr al-Baghdadi. It seems that in 2010 he was appointed to the position by a group of former Iraqi intelligence agents, led by Haji Bakr, who had been one of Saddam Hussein's military intelligence chiefs and, according to documents found after he had been killed in Syria, had masterminded ISIS's rise to power [20]. He and the other intelligence officers were Sunnis who had been sacked by Paul Bremer. Indeed, the ranks of ISIS were swelled by disaffected Sunni army officers who had likewise lost their jobs and by those Sunnis who believed that the Iraqi government was discriminating against them on behalf of the Shia [21].

By 2014, ISIS controlled vast swathes of territory in Syria and Iraq, amounting to the size of the UK. Some of ISIS's methods were so brutal that even al-Qaeda split from it. Nevertheless, young radicalised Muslims in other countries were attracted to the ideas of ISIS and secretly travelled out to join it.

ISIS took to kidnapping foreign hostages and beheading them, showing executions on the social media to try to press governments for ransoms or, in 2014, to stop airstrikes against it from the West. The establishment in Iraq of al-Qaeda, its development into ISIS and the USA's further military involvement against it would never have happened had Bush decided in 2001 to forgive al-Qaeda for the 9/11 attack, reflect on its possible causes and address them while issuing international arrest warrants for the perpetrators of the crime.

To believe that al-Qaeda was in Iraq and, in 2003, to invade that country was utter folly, causing the colossal death toll and deadly chaos there. ISIS would not have arisen to terrorise that country nor gone into Syria, where it caused more bloody horror with its nightmarish efforts to establish itself. It helped drive thousands of Syrians to flee as refugees into Europe, where right-wing parties rose in response. The long-term effects of the USA's thirst for vengeance after being attacked by al-Qaeda in 2001 are still being grimly played out.

Eighteen years after its invasion of Iraq, the USA has finally announced that by the end of 2021, it will withdraw its troops from Iraq (while some will remain to provide training and intelligence). However, that country has not yet recovered from the invasion of 2003, nor has ISIS been completely defeated in Iraq, Syria, or elsewhere in the Middle East from where it is supporting terrorism in Africa.

References

1. Letter from President to the Speaker of the House of Representatives, March 18, 2003 http://georgewbush-whitehouse.archives.gov/news/releases/2003/03/print/20030319-1
2. Arendt, Hannah,' 'The Human Condition' (University of Chicago (1958) p.241
3. Ibid
4. http://georgewbush-whitehouse.archives.gov/news/re/eases/2002/
5. Salmond,Alex,Hansard,26th Feb 2003,Column 323

6. Ibid
7. *The Independent* 30 November 2001
8. Clarke,Kenneth,Hansard,26th February 2003 Column 293
9. *The Daily Telegraph,* 30th September 2002
10. Norton-Taylor,Richard, 'Church leaders petition No 10', www.theguardian.com/politics/2002/aug/07/uk.religion
11. Norton-Taylor,Richard, 'Church leaders petition No 10', www.theguardian.com/politics/2002/aug/07/uk.religion
12. *The Guardian* 29th September 2012
13. *The Independent* 22nd June 2003
14. Casualties in Iraq. Antiwar.com
15. Bellasco,Amy:The Cost of Iraq, Afghanistan, and other Global War on Terror Operations since 9/11.Congressional Research Service, March 29, 2011. www.crs.gov
16. BBC World News,21st Jul 2010 http://www.bbc.co.uk/news/uk-10637526
17. *Daily Mail* 21st June 2010
18. 'Al-Qaeda leaders have proclaimed Iraq a major front in their global terrorist campaign'. Office of the Director of National Intelligence, USA,July 9,2005
19. Zarqawi pledges allegiance to Osama *Dawn* October 18 2004
20. *The Times* April 21st 2015
21. Caerusassociates.com/news 23 September 2014/Who the US Should Really Hit in ISIS –see also: www.vox.com/2014/6/20/5824480/why-the-iraqi-army-cant-defeat-isis.

Chapter 5
Libya and the West: A Cycle of Revenge

A lethal cycle of revenge between Libya and the West may well have resulted in the Lockerbie bombing and the overthrow of Muammar Gaddafi, which has led to bloody chaos in that country. If in the earlier stages of the retaliatory cycle there could have developed a more forgiving attitude by either side, accompanied with a referral of disputes to an international arbiter, the later colossal loss of life could have been avoided.

5.1 Gaddafi's Rule Resented

The West never forgave Gaddafi when in 1969, he nationalised the oil industry and expelled the West's military and commercial presence in Libya without compensation, having, at the age of only 27, with his fellow officers, overthrown the corrupt King Idris in a bloodless coup. Gaddafi used hard-line tactics with foreign oil companies to quadruple Libya's oil revenues during his first five years in power. With the money, he established an Islamic welfare state. This was a dictatorship that transformed Libyan society rapidly and crushed the opposition of the wealthy. Despite the lack of democracy, Gaddafi may well have done more for the impoverished in his country than many Western leaders have done for theirs. In the words of the distinguished African historian, Ali A. Mazrui, writing in 1984:

'The transformation of Libya's social services since the revolution is astonishing. Medicine is free and tuberculosis cases have dropped by more than 80 per cent since 1971. Education is free and compulsory. Between 1969 and 1976 the number of schoolchildren doubled and that of university students quadrupled. Vast construction programmes have rehoused shanty-dwellers in practically free accommodation. There is full employment and comprehensive social security' (1).

Indeed, by the time of his overthrow by the Western powers in 2011, Gaddafi had provided so well for the Libyan people in terms of free education to university level, free healthcare and cheap housing (using Libya's oil wealth for these services) that

A. Wells, *The Importance of Forgiveness and the Futility of Revenge*, Contributions to International Relations, https://doi.org/10.1007/978-3-030-87552-7_5

the UN Human Development Report of 2010 ranked Libya far higher than any other North African state in terms of health, education, and income: Libya was placed 53rd, Tunisia 81st, Algeria 84th, Egypt 101st, and Morocco 114th. Libya was also placed higher than oil-rich Saudi Arabia, which was put at 56th (2).

The Western media, however, gave Gaddafi no credit for the good he had done for the Libyan people but portrayed him as a 'mad dog', sometimes extremely unfairly. For example journalists once reported that he had declared that Shakespeare was an Arab. They had not realised that this was an old Arab joke-a pun on 'sheikh' (3).

5.2 Cycle of Revenge

The Western powers remained resentful of their loss of cheap oil, but it was probably Gaddafi's foreign policy that was the main reason why the NATO powers wanted to overthrow him in 2011. He had alienated the West by supporting terrorists whom he regarded as freedom fighters. Thus, he helped the IRA with finance and weapons as well as pro-Palestinian groups, including that of Syria-based Abu Nidal whose terrorism stemmed from Israel's occupation of his family's prosperous estates in Palestine.

Furthermore, a deadly cycle of revenge developed between Gaddafi and the USA when, in March 1986, a naval clash broke out between the USA and Libya in the Mediterranean, in the Gulf of Sidra, over whether the waters were Libya's or international. The matter should have been referred to international arbitration. Instead, during the naval clash, the USA killed 35 Libyan seamen.

Libya's response was probably the bomb which was planted, on 5 April 1986, in a discotheque, 'La Belle', in Berlin, which was frequented by American servicemen. Three people were killed by this explosion, a Turkish woman and two US Army sergeants and about 230 people were injured, including 79 American soldiers. President Reagan blamed Libya for the attack and ordered retaliatory strikes on that country.

5.3 USA's Revenge

Therefore, on 15 April 1986, American warplanes launched a series of bombing raids from British bases against Tripoli and Benghazi, killing over 100 Libyans. Many more were injured. This bloody revenge of the USA, which was particularly inappropriate in a country that often publicly refers to the Christian faith of its people, achieved nothing positive and may have sealed the fate of those who were later killed in Lockerbie.

Had the USA forgiven Gaddafi in the sense of not taking revenge and embarked only on legal proceedings, the tragedy of Lockerbie might not have occurred, for it was probably Libya's revenge for the USA's attacks in 1986.Indeed, the British Prime Minister, Margaret Thatcher, warned President Ronald Reagan that this might happen when he asked her for permission to use RAF bases for the attacks on Libya in 1986:

'My worry is that this risks getting us into a cycle of revenge and counter revenge in which many more innocent lives will be lost' (4).

But she did give her permission, the USA bombed Libya, and two years later, the Lockerbie bombing took place.

Of course, it might be argued that Gaddafi could have forgiven the USA for killing the Libyan seamen, refused to take revenge and take the whole dispute to international arbitration. However, Islam, the faith of Gaddafi and of most Libyans, does not emphasise the importance of forgiveness as much as does Christianity. Indeed until 2004, Libya celebrated unashamedly the 'Day of Vengeance' when the country rejoiced over the expulsion from Libya in 1970 of Italian settlers and also Jews. Therefore, Gaddafi could not have been expected to show forgiveness in the circumstances as could President Reagan.

Had the USA not taken revenge on Libya in 1986, there probably would have been no Lockerbie bombing. Then, later the West would not have turned so strongly against Gaddafi and supported violent regime change by a conflict which, in 2021, is still smouldering and has caused a heavy death toll.

5.4 Lockerbie

In December 1988, a bomb on board Pan Am Flight 103 blew up over Lockerbie, Scotland. All 270 people on board were killed, including 189 Americans. Libya was held responsible for this by the USA, although there is still some debate as to who was really was to blame. Some commentators have argued that an Iranian-sponsored terrorist group based in Syria, the Popular Front for the Liberation of Palestine-General Command, was behind the atrocity, which was Iran's revenge for the accidental shooting down of Iran Air Flight 655 by USS *Vincennes* in July 1988, killing all 290 people on board (5).

Gaddafi always denied he had ordered the Lockerbie bombing. It is, however, possible that his security services acted without his authorisation. Indeed, such services do not always keep their governments informed of their activities. (The British Prime Minister, Harold Wilson, for example found in 1976 that he was being investigated by his own intelligence service, MI5, as well as the CIA).

Despite the lack of incriminating evidence, in 1992 UN sanctions were placed against Libya for refusing to hand over two Libyans who were accused of being behind the Lockerbie bomb. These sanctions put pressure on Libya's economy. In addition, Gaddafi was facing the developing problem of Islamic fundamentalism in his country. He realised that he needed friends in the West and decided to be more cooperative with them. He had always argued the two suspects would never get a fair trial in Scotland, but in 1999 he agreed to hand them over to be tried by Scottish judges at a neutral venue in the Netherlands. Gaddafi made it clear that he himself had not ordered the bombing, but that he would accept responsibility for his officials. His son Saif said he was buying peace rather than accepting guilt (6). In 2001 one of the officials, Abdel Baset Al Megrahi was found guilty of the bombing and sentenced to 27 years imprisonment.

In December 2003, Libya announced that it had abandoned its weapons of mass destruction programme. The next year at a meeting in Libya with the British Prime Minister Tony Blair he agreed to renounce terrorism in return for having international oil companies help him extract Libya's massive oil reserves. In addition, Gaddafi provided help to find the killers of WPC Yvonne Fletcher (who was killed by a bullet meant for an opponent of Gaddafi's regime outside the Libyan embassy in 1984).

In 2008, after a court case in the USA, Libya agreed to pay $1.5 billion into a fund to compensate the victims of the Lockerbie bombing, the 1986 Berlin bombing as well as, surprisingly, the Libyan victims of the US bombing in 1986. In addition, Libya also agreed to pay compensation to the victims of the French plane bombing UTA Flight 772, which exploded over the Sahara in 1989. (The plane was bound for Paris and 54 Frenchmen were killed as well as victims from many other countries. A French court had blamed Libya for the bomb. It was thought that was possibly Libya's revenge over France's support for Chad over a border dispute.)

Gaddafi's policy of normalising Libya's relations with the West appeared to be making progress. He seemed to be coming in from the cold and be more acceptable to Western governments. However, he was then caught up in events that lethally reawakened the West's old hostility and probably their unfulfilled desires for revenge for Gaddafi's bombings in the 1980s.

5.5 Protest

In February 2011, a protest movement in Benghazi developed. It was inspired by the Arab Spring, which was a series of pro-democracy Arab uprisings. The people in Benghazi (who were not of the same tribe as Gaddafi) also felt discriminated against in matters of housing and employment. In addition, they were commemorating a demonstration five years earlier against the Italian embassy when 14 civilians had died. An Italian MP's perceived anti-Islamic comments regarding some Danish cartoons of the Prophet had then sparked outrage.

The Libyan police were heavy handed, and violence on both sides grew. When the police opened fire, the mob retaliated by torching police stations. Soon more Libyans in Benghazi rose up against Gaddafi's regime. Surprisingly they unfurled flags of the former corrupt King Idris: some may have been former royalist supporters who had lost their wealth under Gaddafi's socialist reforms.

Although there was a lack of democracy in Libya, there was much that could have been praised and appreciated there, since Gaddafi had used the country's oil revenues well to provide the people with free education to university level, free healthcare and cheap housing. He should have been given some credit for this, especially as he was held responsible for all that went on in that country, but Western governments did not give it to him, neither did the rebels in his country.

Then on 22 February Gaddafi made a fatal mistake. In a speech broadcast to the Libyan people about the rebels, he declared:

'Get out of your homes, to the streets, secure the streets, take the rats, the greasy rats out of the streets. We are coming tonight . . .Prepare yourselves from tonight. We will find you in your closets' (7)

This was the extreme language of an eccentric leader who had spoken like this before so that many Libyans had tended to ignore his speeches (8). Gaddafi no doubt did think that the al-Qaeda members were 'rats' (as he claimed they were) stirring up rebellion against him since, according to Wikileaks, he had been passing the names of hundreds of Islamic extremists in that region to the CIA (9). Whatever his intentions, his speech was broadcast outside Libya and caused justifiable alarm that a massacre might take place.

On 26 February 2011, the UN Security Council passed Resolution 1970, demanding an end to the violence in Libya, deciding to refer the matter to the International Criminal Court while imposing an arms embargo on the country as well as a travel ban and an assets freeze on the family of Gaddafi and certain government officials.

5.6 National Transitional Council and France

On 27 February the rebels in Benghazi formed the National Transitional Council with the aim of overthrowing Gaddafi, claiming that it was the only body legitimately representing the Libyan people.

France was the first country to recognise the TNC. This was seemingly the result of the initiative of just one man: the flamboyant French public intellectual Bernard–Henri Levy. On 23 February he was in Cairo and watched the TV coverage of Gaddafi's threatening speech. Alarmed, he then crossed to eastern Libya, spoke to the rebels, phoned President Nicolas Sarkozy, and suggested that he ought to speak to them. Levy then organised their being flown to France to meet its president. After talking with them, Sarkozy decided to recognise their National Transitional Council and summon up international support for it. Whether this was for humanitarian reasons or because appearing as an international statesman would increase his chances of success in the coming French presidential election is difficult to ascertain. Whatever the probably mixed motives, other nations followed France in recognising the NTC.

B-H Levy went further, arguing for military intervention in Libya. Sarkozy agreed and persuaded the British Prime Minister, David Cameron, to support a 'no-fly zone' in Libya under the UN auspices. President Barack Obama of the USA was similarly approached but he was more cautious. However, he was finally persuaded to agree to the 'no-fly zone' by Hillary Clinton, the USA Secretary of State, Susan Rice, the USA's ambassador to the UN, and Samantha Power, the White

House adviser. The Arab League also agreed to support the 'no-fly zone', which meant that intervention in Libya could not been seen as a purely Western action.

5.7 No-Fly Zone

Therefore, on the night of 17 March 2011, the Security Council approved UN Resolution 1973 with five members abstaining and ten in favour. It set up a 'no–fly zone' over Libya, imposing a ban on all flights in the country's airspace. It further demanded an immediate ceasefire in Libya, an end to attacks on civilians and the tightening of sanctions against Gaddafi's regime and its supporters. The Security Council authorised member states, acting nationally or through regional organisations or arrangements, to take' all necessary measures to protect civilians' under threat of attack in the country, including Benghazi, while excluding a foreign occupation force of any form on any part of Libyan territory. Member states were requested immediately to inform the Secretary-General of such intended actions.

It was the phrase 'all necessary measures to protect civilians' that was later extended by the USA, UK, and France to mean regime change. Russia and China would no doubt have used their veto had they known what was to happen. As it was, they agreed to abstain.

On 19 March a multi-state coalition began a military intervention in Libya to implement the UN Resolution 1973 and established a naval blockade. The effort was initially led by France and Britain, with command shared by the USA. Had only a no-fly zone been established and regime change ruled out, the Libyan state would not have later collapsed into the bloody chaos that it did.

5.8 Revenge and Regime Change

However, the USA, UK, and France were driven by an apparent thirst for revenge: for ousting Gaddafi, although they had no plan for his replacement. This shows they were motivated more by destructive desires than by constructive thought. Without waiting to see if Gaddafi accepted the no-fly zone, the US launched missiles against Libya's air defences, Britain and France undertook sorties across Libya, and the latter carried out airstrikes against Libya's tanks. On 31 March, NATO took charge of the Libya mission, but instead of acting impartially to protect lives, NATO militarily supported the rebels.

5.9 Demonisation of Gaddafi

The Western mass media went into overdrive to demonise Gaddafi. He was now regarded as the international pariah he had once been before normalising his country with the West. There was no appreciation of any good that he had done, such as his being responsible for Libya's unrivalled position with regard to healthcare and education in North Africa. The anti-Gaddafi onslaught by NATO and the media probably resulted from the fact that the West had never forgiven Gaddafi for ejecting their oil companies from Libya, for his perceived support of terrorism, including the IRA, and his bombing attacks, especially the Lockerbie bombing and that of the French UTA Flight 772. However, even if Gaddafi was at least partly responsible for the tragedies, these were the culmination of a series of mutual revenge attacks for which the West must take part of the blame. If the USA had not bombed Libya in 1986, for example the Lockerbie bombing might never have occurred.

In Britain, the respected peace negotiator, Lord John Alderdice, warned:

'It should not be that we are backing the rebels against Colonel Gaddafi but that we are backing international law for the protection of all of the citizens of Libya, of whichever side, and much beyond...' (10)

He was supported by others in the House of Lords, including the distinguished lawyer, Baroness Helena Kennedy:

'We are now falling into the same trap as we did in Iraq, where we are over-reading resolutions 1970 and 1973 in order to justify what was not within the ambit of those who voted in favour of them. Resolution 1970 made it clear that there was a total embargo on providing arms to either side. Resolution 1973 did not vary that position. It said that 'all necessary means' should be used to prevent a massacre, but that is not the same as providing arms to the rebels. Neither is it about regime change' (11).

5.10 Gaddafi's Overthrow

However, such pleas were in vain as the airstrikes continued. In October 2011, NATO's military support enabled the rebels to overthrow Gaddafi's regime. They could not have done this without such backing; all in all, NATO flew over 26,000 sorties. One of them bombed Gaddafi's convoy as he was leaving his hometown of Sirte. Gaddafi was captured by the rebels, humiliated and shot. However, beforehand, one Western politician admirably did try to save him. Former Prime Minister Tony Blair telephoned him, with the permission of the NATO powers, and urged him to flee, but Gaddafi would not (12).

5.11 The Futility of the Attack

Regime change in Libya had been achieved without the UN's authorisation, nor with any plans for a new government. As with the invasions of Afghanistan and Iraq, there was no exit strategy. This again indicates how the attacks were driven more by visceral feelings, not by rigorous thought.

5.12 Death Toll

The objective of NATO in Libya was to protect the lives of civilians. However, in September 2011, the interim Health Minister in Libya announced that at least 30,000 people had been killed in the civil war, and over 50,000 had been wounded, while 4000 were still missing. He expected the final figure for the dead to be higher (13). Libya's population had been just over 6 million.

5.13 Spread of Islamic Extremism

Besides the high death toll, much of Libya's infrastructure was destroyed, while thousands of migrant workers were displaced. Moreover, Islamic extremism, which Gaddafi was trying to combat in Libya, increased. In September 2012, Islamists in Benghazi killed the American Ambassador, Christopher Stevens, and three other diplomats from the USA. NATO's intervention may well have helped the spread of Islamism in Libya and beyond. This is the last thing that the West wanted for that oil-rich region so near to the West. Thousands of Tuareg fighters (nomadic Berbers), whom Libya had been recruiting since the 1990s, returned home to Mali with their weapons. This resulted in an Islamic takeover of the north of that country. The West's intervention destabilised the area, which became awash with weapons. The effect on the sub-Sahara of the fall of Gaddafi has been extremely harmful (14).

5.14 The Syrian Conflict

Furthermore, as an even greater disaster unfolded in Syria, the UN Security Council has been unable to intervene because Russia and China, feeling betrayed by the West over Libya, believe that a UN Resolution on Syria would be used by NATO forces to overthrow the Syrian government which Russia and China do not want to happen. Hundreds of thousands of lives have been lost in the Syrian war.

5.15 Refugees

At the time of writing (in 2021), the bloody chaos into which Libya collapsed in 2011 continues part of it involving senseless revenge killings (15). Meanwhile, thousands of refugees and migrants have streamed from Africa through the weakened Libyan borders trying to reach Europe, where they impose strains on the economies of the host nations if they sadly have not already drowned in their rotting boats in the Mediterranean. Their presence has encouraged the rise of right-wing parties in Europe.

All of this might have been avoided if earlier the West had responded with forgiveness, not military retaliation to Gaddafi, made an effort to understand his viewpoint and to try to normalise relations with him, rather than mounting violent attacks of revenge on him and his people. The importance of individuals cannot be overestimated in this. Had Mrs. Thatcher acted on her own advice that she gave President Reagan and refused to help him wreak his vengeance on Gaddafi in 1986, she might have saved not only lives then but also stopped the cycle of revenge before it reached the Lockerbie stage. If this had not happened, then it is unlikely that the USA, UK, and France would have enthusiastically supported the rebels in overthrowing Gaddafi's regime and precipitating the country into a decade of civil war.

References

1. Mazrui,A.A. and Tidy,M. 'Nationalism and New States in Africa' (Oxford1989) p.267
2. UN Human Development Report www.hdr.undp.org
3. The Times 4 August 1989,2a
4. Horne,Marc,'Thatcher warned US of reprisals…'*The Times*,March 22 2019
5. Foot,Paul:www.guardian.co.uk/uk/2004/mar/31/Lockerbie.libya. See also Schindler,John R.,'The Truth Behind This Bomb…'*The Observer* 21st December 2018 and Horne,Marc www.thetimes.co.uk-lockerbie-files-bombing-originally-thought-to-be-by-Iranian terrorists 30th November 2018
6. Hilsum,Lindsey, 'Libya in a Time of Revolution'(London 2012)p.119
7. http:mydd.com/users/inoljt/posts/gaddafis-fateful-speech. Politikalblog:http://thepolitikalblog.wordpress.com/2011/12/9/gaddafis-fateful-speech
8. Ibid
9. The Times March22 2011
10. Alderdice,Lord, Hansard 1 April 2011 Column 1472 www.publications.parliament.uk/pa/ld201011/ldhansrd/text/110401-0001.htm
11. Kennedy,Baroness,Ibid
12. www.independent.co.uk. 9th December 2015
13. Huffington Post 8th September 2011 (www.huffingtonpost.com/2011/09/08/libya-war-died_n_953456.html)
14. Melly, Paul, 'Gaddafi's Guns Trigger Collapse', The World Today, Volume 68, Number 11
15. McLoughlin,Paul,'ICC condemns bombing, revenge killings in Libya's Benghazi' https://english.alaraby.co.uk 27th.January 2018

Chapter 6
USA and IRAN

'There will be severe revenge', declared Iran's Supreme Leader, Ayatollah Ali Khamenei, on learning that the USA had assassinated one of Iran's most important and popular generals, Qasem Solemeini, commander of the Iranian Revolutionary Guard's Quds force [1]. He was killed by an American drone strike while being driven from Baghdad airport on 3rd January 2020, together with four members of his entourage, including Abu Mahdi al-Muhandis, the deputy head of the Popular Mobilisation Forces and commander of the Kataib Hezbollah forces. The Ayatollah's declaration demonstrated the difference between Islamic and Christian views of revenge. To Muslims, it is not something to be deprecated, but to Christians it certainly is. Western leaders, even though not Christian, would not dream of speaking openly of wanting revenge lest they be condemned for such a base motive due to the influence of Christianity's emphasis on the importance of forgiveness. Nevertheless, President Trump, while not explicitly expressing a desire for revenge, did so implicitly when he vowed to hit 52 sites 'very hard' if Iran retaliated [2].

This number referred to the 52 American diplomats and citizens that Iran had taken hostage in 1979, holding them for 444 days. Trump was indeed threatening revenge: both for past and present Iranian offences against Americans. To matters worse, he even said that some of the sites would be cultural, thereby striking at the heart of the Iranians heritage, which would have been illegal under international law if it had taken place.

The world waited with bated breath. Solemeini had been responsible for the deaths of many perceived enemies of Iran, within and without the country, and had been designated a terrorist by the UN, but President Trump's decision to kill him with a drone strike seemed ill-advised and without consideration of the consequences. If he thought it might improve his media image and divert attention away from his imminent impeachment, it did not. (This process, indeed, may well have played on his mind, making him more unstable and inclined to lethal risks.).To make matters worse, Trump had not consulted any of his allies before the assassination, which ironically united the Iranians in calling for revenge against the USA. In

A. Wells, *The Importance of Forgiveness and the Futility of Revenge*, Contributions to International Relations, https://doi.org/10.1007/978-3-030-87552-7_6

previous months there had been protests by the Iranians against their government over the state of the economy. President Trump's retaliation had backfired on him.

Iran did in fact retaliate, firing a barrage of ballistic missiles at the American military bases in Baghdad, but probably intentionally did not kill anyone. Nevertheless, the Iranians feared revenge from America. On 8 January a local base of Iran's Revolutionary Guard Corps spotted a Ukrainian plane leaving Tehran airport. In the tense atmosphere, believing it was an American cruise missile, the Revolutionary Guard shot it down, killing all 176 passengers aboard. After an initial denial, President Rouhani admitted Iran's 'unforgivable' mistake [3].

The tragic shooting down of the Ukrainian airliner shows the risks involved in a cycle of revenge: huge, lethal mistakes made in the heat of the moment and absence of any strategy. Indeed the Iranian Foreign Minister wrote on Twitter that it was the USA which created the tense atmosphere in which Iran's Revolutionary Guard Corps accidentally launched a missile at Ukrainian Airlines flight 752 [4].

In Canada, which lost 57 of its citizens in the crash, Justin Trudeau, its Prime Minister, also said that the USA was partly to blame for escalating the tension, declaring that if the USA had not killed General Soleimani the 57 Canadians killed in the crash would still be alive [5].

6.1 Background to the Revenge Cycle Between the USA and Iran

Relations between Iran and the USA have been hostile ever since the Iranian Islamic revolution in 1979. It is possible that the USA and the UK were to blame for this. In 1953 they removed from power the very able and popular Iranian Prime Minister, Mohammed Mossadeq, to stop him from nationalising Iran's oil fields, and restored the Shah to his throne. Without this interference, Iran's subsequent history would probably have been very different.

The Shah owed his position and power to the USA, which encouraged him to westernise. This alienated many sections of society: the clergy, the villagers who had to leave their homes in the countryside and work in towns where they paid high rents and the bazaar merchants who resented the new banking system. In addition, the middle classes wanted a voice in the running of the country and resented the corruption and oppression [6]. By 1978, as inflation rose, there was increasing unrest with demonstrations against the Shah and strikes were taking place. Martial law was imposed, and protesting civilians were shot. By December 1978, the Shah realised he had lost the support of the army as well as of the people who were calling for the exiled Ayatollah Khomeini to return and replace him. In January 1979, the Shah left Iran and the next month Ayatollah Khomeini returned from exile to become the Supreme Leader of Iran, establishing a theocracy.

In November 1979, a group of Iranian students took over the American embassy and seized 52 members of the staff there, holding them hostage until January 1981.

Their action was revenge for the USA's support of the Shah. Ayatollah Khomeini referred to the USA as 'the Great Satan'.

The Iranians then began exporting their Islamic revolution, funding the anti-Israel Hezbollah organisation in 1982. Between 1980 and 1988, Iran was at war with Iraq which was backed by the USA. Relations between Iran and the West deteriorated further.

One of the many concerns of the USA after the Islamic Revolution was that America had provided the Shah's regime, in 1957, with nuclear technology and resources for peaceful purposes. The USA was concerned that this know-how might enable Iran to develop a nuclear bomb. Eventually, in 2015 the USA and Iran agreed to the multilateral nuclear deal known as the Joint Comprehensive Plan of Action. This was signed in 2015 by Iran, all the five permanent members of the UN Security Council, together with Germany and the EU. Its object was to prevent Iran from developing a nuclear weapon. If Iran complied with the plan, the economic and financial sanctions against it would be dropped. However, in May 2018, although the International Atomic Energy Agency confirmed that Iran was complying with the Plan, President Trump, influenced by questionable evidence produced by the Israeli government [7], withdrew the USA from the deal, stating that Iran was not complying with it. He then reimposed crippling sanctions. A series of 'tit-for-tat' skirmishes followed.

In May 2019, Trump designated Iran's Revolutionary Guard Corps a terrorist organisation. In June in the Gulf of Oman, explosions hit six oil tankers for which the USA blamed Iran. In the same month, Iranian forces shot down a US military drone over the Straits of Hormuz. The USA said it was over international waters, but Iran said it was over its territory. Denying this was so, President Trump decided to strike three Iranian targets in retaliation. But then, surprisingly, he showed he could resist the desire for revenge. Possibly because of a telephone call from Tucker Carlson, the influential Fox News host and strong advocate against a military response, or because he had watched his programme, Trump asked the military how many deaths would result from the operation. Informed that there would be about 150 people killed, at the 11th hour, he called off the operation, declaring that the resulting Iranian deaths would be disproportionate in relation to the shooting down of an unmanned American drone [8]. Trump of course incurred the wrath of the hawks in the White House, especially John Bolton, the Security Adviser. Trump's was a brave late decision, saving many lives and possibly preventing an outright conflict between Iran and the USA. It was courageous because Trump would have known he would be ridiculed for indecision. This incident shows what one person's advice against military action could achieve.

Meanwhile, Iran's economy fell into a recession because of the sanctions, resulting in riots against the government, which announced it was rolling back its commitments under the nuclear deal. The cycle of revenge between Iran and the USA was then resumed and ratcheted up to a higher level of military action.

On 27 Dec 2019, an American airbase in Kirkuk province in Iraq was attacked by more than 30 rockets killing an American civilian contractor and injuring four US service members and two Iraqi security forces personnel. The US blamed the

Iranian-backed Kata'ib Hezbollah militia, a sub group of Iraq's Popular Mobilisation Forces, for the attack. America took revenge on 29 December with airstrikes on five weapon storage facilities and command and control locations in Iraq and Syria, killing 25 militia members and wounding 55 more. In retaliation on 31 December 2019, the Kataib Hezbollah militiamen and their Popular Mobilisation Forces (PMF) supporters and sympathisers attacked the US Embassy in the Green Zone. This may have made Trump decide to assassinate General Solemeini [9], although he claimed it was to prevent the general from carrying out imminent attacks on American bases in Iraq. This reason was soon being questioned even in the USA [10].

After the assassination of Solemeini, the Iranian people, at least temporarily, were united with the government in grief for him. Instead of protesting about the economic situation, as they had been doing, they demanded revenge on the USA. In Iraq there were calls for the USA to withdraw its troops from the country. Moreover, Iran announced it was not being restricted by the nuclear deal and was enriching uranium again. These were not the results that the USA had wanted to achieve, and they demonstrate the futility of its retaliatory responses.

Nothing constructive or positive has been achieved by the 40-year-old cycle of revenge between the USA and Iran. Instead, it has resulted in unnecessary bloodshed and loss of life as well as wasting funds that could have been better spent to relieve poverty. Moreover, it has made the world a more dangerous, not safer place.

Had the USA forgiven Iran for its recent violent attacks and lifted the economic sanctions against Iran, it could probably have made that country more cooperative. Ultimately America wants regime change in Iran. It is more likely to achieve it bloodlessly, without encouraging free trade and the opening up of the country to commerce and visitors.

The issue of Israel must be addressed since the pro-Israel lobby in the USA, especially AIPAC, the American Israel Public Affairs Committee, greatly influences American foreign policy. The USA should realise its support for Israel is part of the problem in the Middle East. It was Israel that told Trump that Iran was allegedly not keeping to the nuclear deal. Israel fears Hezbollah, but this organisation was only founded (in 1982) to support the Palestinians against Israel's oppression. If Israel allows the Palestinians their own state Hezbollah's main raison d'etre would disappear. Moreover, while the USA imposes sanctions against Iran to stop it from getting a nuclear bomb, it actually protects Israel from any criticism that it has an undeclared nuclear weapon. The USA should address these issues in atmosphere of forgiveness and enlightenment with the help of other countries' mediation. Unfortunately, this does not seem likely to happen.

Obviously, if Iran, for its part, could show forgiveness and understanding towards the USA, foregoing any form of military response to attacks but demanding international mediation, that would be an outstanding contribution to peace in the Middle East and a good advertisement for the Iranian's Muslim faith. However, as forgiveness is not the most important of Islamic values and Iranian leaders encourage the expressions of hatred for the USA, this is not likely to happen either.

Fortunately, in 2020 Donald Trump lost the American presidential election to Joe Biden. A new and more hopeful chapter in the USA's relations with Iran might have begun.

References

1. www.bbc.co news middle east 3rd January 2020
2. *The Guardian* 5th January 2020
3. *The Guardian* 11th January 2020
4. www.nytimes.com>2020/01/11.world.middleeast>plane-crash
5. www.ft.com 14/01/20
6. Halliday, Fred and Alavi, Hamza', State and Ideology in the Middle East' (London 1988)
7. www.bbc.co.uk 1st May 2018
8. Baker, Peter et al., 'Urged to launch an Attack, Trump listened to the Skeptics. . .' *The New York Times,* June 20th 2019; Wintour, Patrick and Borger, Julian,' Trump says he stopped airstrike on Iran because 150 would have died', *The Guardian*, 21 June 2019
9. *The New York Times*, January 4th 2020
10. www.washingtonpost.com>opinions>2020/01/07>Trumps

Chapter 7
Is America a Vengeful Democracy?

In the last four chapters, I have endeavoured to show that the USA, although an avowedly Christian country, 'united under God' as it is often claimed, has been vengeful, not forgiving, reflective, or empathic in its foreign policy. Indeed, as will be shown, it has been classified as a 'vengeful democracy' not only because of its war record but also because it has another characteristic for that classification: the death penalty, which may be regarded as a form of revenge.

It is often assumed that democracies are more reasonable and less belligerent in their foreign policies than are autocracies. It is certainly true that no democracy goes to war with another democracy. Moreover, a democratically elected government has to take public opinion into consideration far more than does an autocratic leader.

7.1 Vengeful Democracies

Obviously, states go to war for many different reasons, such as the defence of national interests, to secure economic benefits, for ideological reasons, or to protect minorities. However, it is clear that some democracies are more belligerent than others. Recent research has shown that in fact democracies vary according to their core values. Some are in fact more vengeful than others and therefore are more likely to support military action against another power [1]. It has been asserted by Professor Rachel Stein, of George Washington University, that one of the characteristics of a vengeful democracy (where revenge is widely endorsed) is the retention of capital punishment [2].

Stein has compared two large democracies, the USA and India, with West European democracies [3]. Both the former two countries retain the death penalty and have fought a disproportionately large number of wars since 1945 compared with those engaged in by Western European countries, which have not retained the death penalty. The USA was vengeful in its wars in Afghanistan, Iraq, and Libya.

A. Wells, *The Importance of Forgiveness and the Futility of Revenge*, Contributions to International Relations, https://doi.org/10.1007/978-3-030-87552-7_7

For its part, India fought four wars after independence in 1947 against Pakistan and also fought against China and Portugal.

Stein's concept of revenge in her article is the: 'belief that wrong doers *deserve* to be repaid for their crimes. In this view, taking an 'eye for an eye' is a moral good in and of itself, regardless of its impact on future outcomes' [4]. In other words, it is not a matter of punishment to induce better behaviour. To go to war in a democracy, Stein argues, a leader must convince the public that the use of military force is repayment for some act of wrongdoing on the part of the adversary [5] (which is what such leaders usually try do). This argument of repayment of harm for harm is also used to justify the use of capital punishment, although there is no empirical evidence of its being an effective deterrent.

7.2 The Death Penalty: Revenge as 'Justice'

In support of Stein's argument, it can be said that capital punishment has indeed long been regarded by its critics as a form of revenge but it is often clothed as a form of 'justice'. Even Christians in the USA often demand it as 'justice' for a family member who has been killed and seem to gain visceral satisfaction from watching the killer being executed through glass windows in a room adjacent to the execution chamber. They usually show no forgiveness or attempt to understand the criminal who often has from a brutalising background and is 'more sinned against than sinning'.

The relatives of murdered victims often demand that execution be not postponed as they do not want 'justice' delayed for their dead relative. For example in California in March 2019, Governor Gavin Newsom imposed an executive moratorium on the use of the death penalty in his state, thus sparing the lives of 737 inmates. The mother of a murdered man, expecting to witness the execution of his killer, said of Newsom: 'He stole justice from us like a thief in the night'. She said 'I don't want my grandchild growing up and spending 35 or 40 years before he sees his father's killer's execution carried out' [6].

Often governors of states in the USA have the power to grant clemency but fear they will lose the support of the vengeful voters if they seem to be going soft on the death penalty. Thus the governor of Ohio refused to commute the death sentence of a 69-year-old man, Alva Campbell, who was already dying of cancer, walking with a zimmer frame and wearing a colostomy bag. In the execution chamber, in November 2017, because of Campbell's state of health, the executioner could not find a vein to inject the lethal drugs. After half an hour, the execution was aborted. A new execution date for June 2019 was set for him, but in March 2018, he died from his illnesses. Ron O'Brien, the Franklin County prosecutor, said on Twitter that due to Cambell's post-conviction litigation, 'he successfully ran the clock out on justice due to the state and the victim's family' [7].

In 2015 Pope Francis spoke out against the death penalty saying: 'It does not render justice to the victims, but instead fosters vengeance' [8]. If revenge at the heart of the American judicial system is allowed to pass for justice without a national outcry against it or at least a thundering condemnation from the churches, it is small wonder that revenge attacks have been part of the USA's foreign policy. It is Professor Stein's argument that the death penalty and a vengeful foreign policy are linked as revenge seems to be a core value in the USA.

There are of course exceptions to Stein's argument such as the UK, which has abolished the death penalty but has militarily supported many of the USA's vengeful wars, although this was not because it wanted revenge for itself and often it was amid much public protest.

However, there does seem to be some validity in Stein's thesis. Therefore, those who wish to change the vengeful, belligerence ethos of their country to one of forgiveness should surely protest against the use of the death penalty as well as against military ventures, endorsing forgiveness and deprecating acts of revenge whenever they occur. Such a task has been made much easier by the Pope's condemnation of the death penalty as 'inadmissible' in all cases in August 2018 [9]. He has shown a leadership of forgiveness here which needs to be copied by political leaders if the massive loss of life often incurred by vengeance is to be avoided. Britain could make a valuable contribution here by protesting strongly to the USA about the use of its death penalty since its worldwide abolition is one of the aims of the UK's foreign policy.

References

1. Stein, Rachel M, 'War and Revenge: Explaining Conflict Initiation by Democracies', American Political Science Review Vol 109, No 3, August 2015, p.558–559
2. Ibid 562,567
3. Ibid 567
4. Ibid 557
5. Ibid 559
6. Chakrabarti, Meghna and Hardzinski, Brian, 'How Murder Victims' Families Are Responding To Death Penalty Halt' (WBUR Boston University Radio Station), On Point, March 20 2019
7. Connor, Tracy, March 4 2018 NBCNews.com
8. *The Guardian* 20th March 2015.
9. www.bbc.co.uk/news/world-europe-45042130 2nd August 2018

Part II
The West's Unforgiving Responses to Russia and China

Chapter 8
Russophobia: The Ukraine Conflict, the Skripal Affair

Just as the age-long relationship of hatred and suspicion between France and Germany was ended by Robert Schuman's bringing the two states together in a productive, economic community, so it should be possible for another great statesman or woman to conclude the centuries-old enmity between Russia and the West. Both sides could work together in an economic relationship in a spirit of mutual empathy and forgiveness for past wrongs. Had this happened earlier the violent unrest that broke out in Ukraine in 2014 could have been avoided. The West moreover could have co-operated with Russia to end the Syrian civil war expeditiously. The form of forgiveness towards Russia by the West that was needed did not involve restraining a desire for revenge, since that was not a major issue in this conflict. Rather what was required was a refusal to take punitive action against a state that genuinely believed itself to be threatened and adjusting the perceived threatening behaviour. As Hannah Arendt pointed out, punishment is an alternative to forgiveness although not its opposite [1].

Furthermore, the forgiveness that was needed to improve Russo-Western relations was that in which governments forgave Russia its trespasses, knowing their own states had also trespassed all around the world. However, there was no such enlightened response by the West, only often a Russophobic one.

I have examined in detail the history and causes of Russophobia in an earlier work [2]. Here I shall summarise it and then consider in more detail the current tensions between the West and Russia which show the importance of forgiveness and empathy.

The conflict in Ukraine should be seen in the context of the West's perennial hostility towards Russia, feelings which stemmed from the early nineteenth century with the erroneous belief that Russia had designs on the West and indeed on the world. Russia, in turn, was suspicious of the West's ambitions in Eastern Europe.

A. Wells, *The Importance of Forgiveness and the Futility of Revenge*, Contributions to International Relations, https://doi.org/10.1007/978-3-030-87552-7_8

8.1 Russophobia

As early as 1817 the *Morning Chronicle* declared:

'A very general persuasion has long been entertained by the Russians that they are destined to be the rulers of the world and this idea has been more than once stated by publications in the Russian language' [3].

Whatever were Russia's hopes, it was of course Britain that had both wanted and achieved global imperial domination. Russia was often seen as a threat to this. By the time of the Crimean War (1854–1855) alarm at Russia's ambitions was intensified. Lord Palmerston warned that Russia' bestriding the Continent from north to south . . .could become dangerous to the liberties of Europe' [4].

Throughout the nineteenth century, press and politicians expressed intense hostility towards Russia's alleged designs of aggrandisement, its intentions to seize the Black Sea, to control Turkey, the Mediterranean, and to extend itself to Persia and India. It was a perpetual threat to Britain's own possessions.

As the historian JH Gleason wrote in his authoritative 'The Genesis of Russophobia in Britain': 'Within the United Kingdom there developed early in the 19th century an antipathy towards Russia which soon became the most pronounced and enduring element in the national outlook on the world abroad' [5].

In the twentieth century the Bolshevik revolution increased the West's paranoia of Russia. Fear of the spread of communism, together with a desire to regain vested interests led to some Western countries invading Russia in 1918, but to no avail. After the Second World War in which the USSR's courageously strong resistance to Nazism played a decisive part in its defeat, there was a constant irrational fear of Russian expansion in Europe which became two armed camps threatening each other. During the Cold War, the West showed little understanding of the Soviet Union's need to surround itself with a ring of buffer states. Having been invaded by Nazi Germany, which cost 20 million Russian lives, and earlier by Western countries, the USSR was determined that this should never happen again. It was certainly in no fit state to want another war by taking over Western Europe, neither did it want this. Nevertheless, the West believed that Russia was a threat and set up the North Atlantic Treaty Organisation. Russia, feeling also threatened, responded with the Warsaw Pact. As mutual suspicion intensified in this Cold War there developed an unnecessary arms race which wasted trillions of dollars that could have been used for humanitarian purposes. Each side failed to attempt to understand the other's point of view. The West remained unforgiving and uncomprehending of Russia's attempt to protect itself.

Meanwhile, as Russia sought to safeguard itself from Western attack by controlling Eastern Europe, the USA showed equal anxiety over its own backyard: Latin America. America feared communist infiltration there and intervened in the internal affairs of many Latin American states. Both Russia and the USA fought each other in limited wars in Korea and Vietnam while also seeking to curb each other's influence elsewhere.

In 1985, Mikhail Gorbachev came to power as General Secretary of the Communist Party in Russia. He was a genial, unusually liberal-minded Russian leader who knew the USSR needed to reform. Thus, he introduced his new policies of 'glasnost (openness)' and 'perestroika' (restructuring). People could discuss and criticise the political system and also not be fearful of admitting mistakes. To this extent he was a 'transformational leader of forgiveness' [6], introducing a new culture where criticism is valued, the leader is not vindictive, and mistakes are treated with understanding. Gorbachev was aware of the harm done when in 1986 there was a delay in revealing that the Chernobyl nuclear reactor had exploded. In the past such situations would be covered up for good in the USSR [7].

By 1989, the USSR's increased expenditure on arms and grain and decreased revenue from oil brought it to the point of collapse. Mikhail Gorbachev understood his country's need to end the Cold War and held talks with the American President George Bush to achieve this officially in December 1989. A month earlier the fall of the Berlin Wall marked the demise of communism in Eastern European countries which soon asserted their independence from Russia. A lesser Russian leader might well have been tempted to use force against them. It is a tribute to his 'forgiving' personality that Gorbachev did not. In December 1991, the Soviet Union came to an end. Gorbachev had been its last president 1990–1991.

8.2 Conflict in Ukraine 2014

Although the Cold War ended with the USSR's demise, Russophobia resurfaced during the West's confrontation with Russia over Ukraine in 2014. After the conflict the Western countries decided to punish Russia without attempting to understand its actions or remember their own chequered histories. Forgiveness and empathy would have avoided much bloodshed.

The events in Ukraine will now be considered as they illustrate how unforgiving and unempathetic the West has been and still is of Russia.

8.3 The Budapest Memorandum 1994

In 1994, the leaders of Ukraine, Russia, Britain, and the USA had agreed in the Budapest Memorandum that as Ukraine consented to give up its nuclear weapons (which comprised about a third of the former USSR's) and join the Non-Proliferation of Nuclear Weapons Treaty, the other three states would respect the sovereign independence and existing borders of Ukraine. They would also refrain from the threat or use of force against the territorial integrity of Ukraine and never use their weapons against Ukraine save in self-defence or in accord with the UN Charter. Moreover, they would refrain from using economic coercion in Ukraine to secure advantages for themselves.

8.4 NATO Bucharest April 2008

Russia nevertheless feared that NATO would encircle it. In April 2008, this concern seemed justified when at a NATO summit meeting in Bucharest, President George Bush lobbied for Georgia and Ukraine to join NATO. One of the reasons for this could have been the Baku–Tbilisi–Ceyhan pipeline which passes through Georgia, supplying Europe and bypassing Russia and Iran, thus making the West more independent of Middle East oil. But Bush's action worried France and Germany which warned that the USA's proposal would give 'unnecessary offence to Russia' [8].

Despite this, the heads of states and governments at Bucharest issued a Declaration that included Clause 23:

'NATO welcomes Ukraine's and Georgia's Euro-Atlantic aspirations for membership in NATO. We agreed today that these countries will become members of NATO. . .MAP (Membership Action Plan) is the next step for Ukraine and Georgia on their direct way to membership. . .' [9].

8.5 Georgia August 2008

This, as Germany and France had predicted, did indeed alarm Russia. In August 2008, when mainly Russian-speaking rebels in Georgian-ruled South Ossetia rose against their government, President Vladimir Putin promptly sent them military support as he did later their fellow-rebels in Abkhavia, finally occupying those regions. A ceasefire was later negotiated by President Sarkozy of France.

The West should have been warned by Russia's actions in Georgia that the latter would not tolerate the threat of NATO encirclement. But no such lesson was learned.

8.6 Russia's Alarm over Ukraine

In 2013, Russia became particularly alarmed by the USA's attempts to win Ukraine over to its sphere of influence. Indeed, as a first step, it seemed that Ukraine was moving closer to the EU with which it was about to sign an associate agreement. However, in November of that year, Putin persuaded the President of Ukraine, Viktor Yanukovich, not to sign it, offering him a 15 billion dollar loan and cheaper gas from Moscow.

8.7 The Uprising in Western Ukraine

The people in Western Ukraine were furious, wrongly thinking that the associate agreement with the EU would give greater benefits. They rose in protest in February 2014, demonstrating in Maidan Square, in Kiev, and elsewhere. As a result, the elected president Yanukovich fled.

8.8 The USA's Involvement

During the uprising, the US's Assistant Secretary of State for European and Eurasian Affairs, Victoria Nuland, was seen in Maidan Square, talking to the protestors. In February 2014, a recording of a phone call between Nuland and the US ambassador to Ukraine, Geoffrey Pyatt, was published on YouTube. The phone call, made on 28th January, was probably recorded by the Russians. In the recording, Nuland referred dismissively to the EU, talked of the opposition politicians in Ukraine, discussing those whom the USA wanted to get in power and the strategy for this, thereby showing the extent of American involvement [10]. Not all American politicians approved of this activity. The American Congressman Ron Paul condemned his country's use of $5 billion since 1991 to meddle in Ukrainian affairs, stating that the USA had helped to overthrow an elected president which was not a democratic procedure [11].

8.9 Far-Right Attempts to Ban Russian Language

The Kiev parliament sacked Yanukovich and appointed an interim president Oleksandr Turchynov who in turn appointed an interim government. However, the far-right Svoboda party in the Kiev parliament then attempted to ban the use of Russian as an official language. This greatly alarmed those for whom Russian was their only tongue. Although Turchynov refused to sign the bill banning the Russian language, the alarmed Russian speakers in eastern Ukraine asked to join Russia.

8.10 Putin Seizes Crimea

Seizing the opportunity, after a hasty referendum, in March 2014 Putin annexed the Crimea which had only been transferred to the administrative region of Ukraine in 1954, and not meant by the USSR to be in a foreign country. Moreover, Crimea was at the historic heart of Russia. Furthermore, strategically it was important because of its ports on the Black Sea. Russia had been paying Ukraine millions of dollars each year to use them. There were Tartars in Crimea who did not want to join Russia but it seems that most of the Russian-speaking population there did.

8.11 Need for Forgiveness and Understanding

Instead of understanding any of these reasons for Putin's actions, appreciating that Crimea is a special case because of its unusual history and holding an internationally monitored referendum to ascertain the wishes of the Crimean people, the USA and the EU took the moral high ground and decided to punish Russia by imposing sanctions on certain Russian individuals and businesses. Some other governments and organisations did the same. What was needed here was forgiveness in the sense of an absolute pardon for the action of taking Crimea in recognition of its unusual history making it a special case. The West should not have punished Russia but held an internationally monitored referendum in Crimea to determine whether the majority of its inhabitants wanted to remain part of Russia. If they do, they should be allowed to stay as such.

8.12 The War in Donbass

Meanwhile unmarked troops, probably Russian special forces, entered Ukraine to support the armed resistance of rebels in the Donbass region, where much of the population was Russian speaking. This eastern region of Ukraine then disintegrated into an armed conflict where Russia was clearly supporting the rebels who wanted to break away from Ukraine. However, it was unlikely that Russia wanted to absorb this region and it seemed to have bitten off more than it could chew. The prospect of more autonomy for eastern Ukraine seemed a possible solution. In May 2014, a presidential election was held in Ukraine and was won by Petro Poroshenko. His bloc also won the general election in October of that year, but in the Donetsk region there were no elections, instead there was a bloody civil war. By December 2014, over 4300 people had died in the rebellion there. A peace agreement made in September at Minsk, Belarus, had no effect as the rebels ignored it. The West increased its sanctions on Russia as the conflict in Ukraine spread.

At the same time Western politicians and media demonised Putin and, as in the Cold War, attributed to Russia sinister intentions of westwards aggressive expansion. They did not realise that the Russian speakers in Ukraine genuinely feared the far-right parties there. It was these, not Putin, that had made them ask for Russian protection.

Moreover, the West did not understand that Russia feared NATO encirclement which was why Putin did not want Ukraine to go to the West's sphere of influence. Whatever might have been the reality regarding NATO's intention it was essential that the West understood how Russia saw it: as an attempt to encircle it. The West should have understood that Russia was paranoid about this and therefore the West's worst response would be a hostile one of imposing sanctions. The West might also have remembered its own chequered history and how it had invaded other countries. In particular the USA had regarded Latin America as its own backyard. In 1954, it had overthrown the democratically elected government of Guatemala which had led to a civil war. In 1971, the USA did the same in Chile.

8.13 The 'Russian Threat'

During the Ukraine crisis, Western media and politicians started again speaking of the Russian threat, as if a needle in a record-player had slipped into a well-worn groove. The former US Secretary of State, Hillary Clinton, compared Putin's action with those of Adolf Hitler in the 1930s [12]. She later depicted Putin as a mortal threat to sovereign European countries and U.S. interest and called for a sustained commitment to keep Russia contained [13]. The British Prime Minister, David Cameron, also referred to the Nazi threat of the 1930s:

'We have to be clear about what we are dealing with. It is a large state bullying a smaller state in Europe. We have seen the consequences of that in the past and we should learn the lessons of history and make sure we don't let it happen again' [14].

Many Western politicians as well as the mass media seemed to portray Putin as single-handedly stirring up the eastern Ukrainians into rebellion into order to expand his power. They ignored the fact that many Russian speakers in Ukraine wanted to be Russian citizens, that Putin was not a dictator in the Soviet sense and was working in accordance with the wishes of the Russian government and citizens, and that Putin and his government did not really want Eastern Ukraine (although they wanted Crimea) and were probably looking for a compromise.

The West stated that its sanctions on Russia would not be lifted until Russia implemented the Minsk peace agreement by which Russia was to withdraw from Ukraine its men and materials. As the rouble slumped so did the price of oil, hitting Russia on two fronts. However, Westerners who wanted to trade with Russia were also hit by the sanctions, while Russia turned to China as a trading partner for its gas, as well as to Turkey. In December 2014, Putin cancelled a proposed £25 billion gas pipeline to southern Europe (which the EU had refused to approve) and announced it would be replaced with a new route via Turkey that would bind Ankara closer to Moscow. Putin also promised a 6% cut in the price that Turkish customers would pay for Russian gas [15].

In February 2015, Chancellor Angela Merkel of Germany and President Francois Hollande of France held 17-h all-night talks with President Putin and President Poroshenko of Ukraine in Minsk. The next day they announced an agreement which was signed by the so-called Contact Group: representatives of the east Ukrainian separatists and OSCE (the Organisation for Security and Cooperation in Europe) as well as Moscow and Kiev. The Minsk 2 agreement stipulated that there would be a ceasefire by midnight, 15th February, the withdrawal of heavy weapons, and greater autonomy for east Ukraine. It was to be monitored by the OSCE.

However, the tragic conflict in Ukraine continued, and is still doing so in the Donbass region at the time of writing (2021), having already caused the deaths of over 13,000 people. This war was the result of both the USA and Russia trespassing in the affairs of Ukraine, creating a dire situation which was the opposite of the benefits that both sides had wanted. Neither side was prepared to emphasise with the other. The West took an unjustified moral high ground in condemning and punishing Russia's actions instead of showing empathy and forgiveness.

Ukraine has emerged as one of Europe's poorest countries and most corrupt [16]. The situation in Ukraine is worse than before the Maidan uprising. In despair its citizens have elected a comedian as their president: Volodymyr Zelensky. It was a vote more against Poroshenko than for him. This situation could have been avoided through enlightened cooperation between the West and Russia.

8.14 The Salisbury Poisonings

Western powers have continued to vilify President Putin. In particular he has been accused of attempting lethally to poison a former Russian double agent Sergei Skripal and his daughter Julia, in Salisbury in the UK in March 2018. There is no hard evidence for this allegation. It is most unlikely that Putin would have wanted to kill a former spy who had already had a presidential pardon—yet alone his daughter. This in no way would benefit Putin and would reflect very badly on him—a blackening effect which many Western commentators are trying now to achieve. Besides he has more important things with which to be concerned.

Some Russians were no doubt involved in the attempted murder in Salisbury but that does not justify stating that 'Russia' was involved and by implication President Putin. The speed with which he was condemned by politicians and the media, ignoring the fact that he had the right to be regarded as innocent until proved guilty (as stipulated in Article 11 of the International Declaration of Human Rights) and the hasty expulsion of 23 Russian diplomats from the UK, showed the alarming resurgence of Russophobia.

The most likely explanation for the poison attack is that it was an act of revenge by a former GRU (foreign military intelligence) colleague, either betrayed by Skripal or acting on behalf of someone else who was. Such a person could have gained access to the state manufactured nerve agent, novichok, either through bribery or during the chaos when the Soviet Union broke up. This person could well have bribed or ordered the two Russian men who were caught on CCTV in Salisbury to commit the crime. These two Russians may not have been told they were going to commit murder but to give Sergei Skripal some well-deserved pain (This would account for their carelessly throwing away the perfume bottle which held the poison and which later led tragically to the death of a woman who sprayed herself with it). The fact that the two men were working for the GRU does not mean that Putin was involved. Quite apart from the fact that the head of the GRU reports not to Putin but to the Russian Minister of Defence, acts of insubordination are not unknown in intelligence services.

The poisoning of the former Russian spy Alexander Litvinenko in 2006 has also been linked to Putin but again there is no hard evidence for this. Indeed, poison has often been used by Russians to kill their enemies. Even churches in former USSR territory do not seem exempt from this tradition. In 2017, a Georgian Orthodox priest, Giorgi Mamaladze, was caught with sodium cyanide in his luggage allegedly intending to kill a high ranking church leader [17].

Poisoning might indeed be an idea that comes more easily to people who live in some countries than in others—and the state does not have to be involved. However, another poisonous tradition can be detected in the Skripal affair—that of Russophobia which has been such a destructive force in international relations for the last two centuries. Its antidote is empathy and forgiveness for trespassing in search of security.

Putin and the Kremlin have also been accused of interfering with the USA presidential election in 2016 and in European elections. The evidence for this is debatable but if Russia was involved it would be because it wants to get governments into power which could lift the sanctions against it. It regards the imposition of the sanctions as an unfair hostile act.

It is surely in the best interests of both sides that the West and Russia forgive each other for their involvement in Ukraine and, each remembering their own chequered history, attempt to forge strong links of friendship between each other. This would be the most constructive way forward. One way of doing this is to give each other credit for their achievements. Unfortunately, during the 75th D-Day celebrations in 2019, the Allies ignored the enormous and vital part Russia played in destroying Nazism. Acknowledging this and inviting the Russians for a prominent part in the celebrations would have been a golden opportunity to relax unnecessary tensions.

After the Second World War Robert Schuman saw that in order to end the perennial enmity between France and Germany, the former should forgive the latter for its military aggression and join it as a founder member of the European Coal and Steel Community which later grew into the EU. Just as economic concerns can create war so they can create peace. Russia has a wealth of natural resources such as oil, gas, gold, and diamonds which the West could help it to exploit in a new economic relationship, while at the same time giving support to Russia's democratic institutions. Each side could profit from trading freely with each other. Moreover, such a relationship would greatly decrease the need for arms expenditure on defence for both sides, when neither fears an attack by the other. Furthermore, peace in Syria as well as in Ukraine would be easier to achieve if warmer relations were established between the West and Russia.

In a letter to 'The Times' in 2018, the Rev. Canon Malcolm Rogers, Chaplain of St Andrews, Moscow, and the Archbishop of Canterbury's representative to the Patriarch of Moscow and all Russia, summed up the problem with the West's relations with Russia:

'There is a completely unjustified level of fear of Russia and Russians, particularly in the UK. . .

Sadly, the Russia that I read about in the Western media or that I hear spoken about by our politicians bears little reality to the Russia in which I live, or the Russia experienced by those who have come.

The danger is that if we represent each other simply as monsters, then we will only look for monster-like behaviour, and we will find it' [18].

References

1. Arendt, Hannah, 'The Human Condition' (University of Chicago 1958) p.241
2. Northedge, F.S. and Wells, Audrey, 'Britain and Soviet Communism' (Macmillan 1982)
3. Ibid p.138
4. Ibid p.139
5. Gleason J.H., 'The Genesis of Russophobia in Great Britain', (Cambridge, Mass 1950) p.1
6. Kets de Vries, Manfred, 'The Art of Forgiveness: Differentiating Transformational Leaders' (April 18, 2013) INSEAD Working Paper No.2013/52/EFE
7. For an interesting account of the Gorbachev era, see Ch.21, McMauley, Martin, 'The Rise and Fall of the Soviet Union' (Harlow, England 2008)
8. www.nytimes.com/2008/04/03/world/europe/03nato.html
9. Clause 23 in www.nato.int/cps/en/natolive/official_texts_8443.htm
10. BBC News Online 7 Feb 2014
11. Ron Paul Institute for Peace and Prosperity 23 March 2014
12. News.sky.com/ 6th March 2014
13. www.washingtonpost.com/blogs/right-turn/wp/2014/10/14/hillary-clinton
14. www.telegraph.co.uk 14th November 2014
15. The Times 2 December 2014 p35
16. www.atlantic.council.org/ what is wrong with the Ukrainian economy/26 April 2019
17. www.bbc.com/nws/world-europe-38966787-14thFeb-2017
18. The Times 5th July 2018 p.26

Chapter 9
Belarus: Forgiveness; Russophobia Impedes Mediation

At the time of writing, the crisis over the presidential election in Belarus has suddenly arisen. The outcome is uncertain, and this chapter will be short.

The unrest in Belarus that began in August 2020 over alleged vote-rigging in the presidential election has demonstrated the need for forgiveness from all sides, but it is needed far more from President Alexander Lukashenko and his supporters if negotiations are to take place. Moreover, the hostility and hatred of Western governments towards Russia has prevented a speedy and effective multi-lateral negotiation to resolve the conflict, which has cost lives.

Since 1994 when the current system of presidential elections was first adopted, Lukashenko has been the president of Belarus. He has ruled with a Soviet type authoritarian style, controlling the main media channels, jailing political opponents, and his secret police is still called the KGB. Indeed, Lukashenko is known as known as 'Europe's last dictator'. Belarus retains the death penalty, and Lukashenko rarely grants clemency to the condemned when all other avenues of appeal are exhausted.

Today the young people in Belarus do not feel any nostalgia for the USSR and wish their country to be more modern and liberal. Their anger with Lukashenko increased when, as the coronavirus spread, instead of following other countries with a lockdown, he said that the way to combat the virus was through hard work, vodka and the sauna.

The country's economy has also given rise to widespread dissatisfaction because unemployment has risen with the fall in the prices of oil and potash, Belarus' main exports. It does not produce the oil but buys it cheaply from Russia to refine it. However, Russia is gradually ending this form of trade relationship causing economic insecurity.

On 9 August 2020, a presidential election was held. Before it, some of the opposition candidates had been imprisoned. The wife of one of them, Svetlana Tikhanovskaya, ran in her husband's place against Lukashenko. She was widely expected to win.

The Belarusian authorities issued an invitation to the election monitors of the Organisation for Security and Cooperation in Europe (the OSCE) far too late for

A. Wells, *The Importance of Forgiveness and the Futility of Revenge*, Contributions to International Relations, https://doi.org/10.1007/978-3-030-87552-7_9

them to witness the count. During the election, a number of witnesses reported extensive falsification of the results.

When Lukashenko's victory, claiming 80% of the votes, was announced, it was met with widespread disbelief and anger. Thousands took to the streets to protest peacefully. However, the Belarusian security services unleashed a campaign of violence and intimidation against the protesters. The weekly protests continued despite several people being killed.

The world watched in horror but seemed unable to take effective action. The EU tried to get its members to agree to impose sanctions on 40 Belarusian officials but was blocked by Cyprus, which wanted the EU to impose similar sanctions on Turkey regarding a dispute over gas-drilling in the eastern Mediterranean. However, at the beginning of October, Cyprus was persuaded to back the agreement in return for EU support over its issue with Turkey.

Meanwhile, the UK and Canada had imposed sanctions on Belarusian officials, including an asset freeze and travel ban on Lukashenko. The USA, which had already imposed sanctions on Belarus in 2006 for election fraud, also imposed further sanctions on officials it held responsible for rigging the election. However, these sanctions will probably be far less effective than international mediation involving Russia, which has the most leverage over Belarus. But the Russophobia of the West presently impedes this.

The situation was well-summed up by a former British Ambassador to Moscow, Sir Tony Brenton, in a letter to 'The Times', stating that the West and Russia have a shared interest in engineering a peaceful transition of power in Belarus, probably through a rerun of the election.

'The West should therefore be talking quietly to the Russians about how we can jointly facilitate that outcome. A Russian offer of exile to Lukashenko would certainly help, as would a western reassurance to Russia that we are not intent on using the present instability to pull Belarus into NATO or the EU—that choice will finally be for the Belarusians themselves.

Sadly, at a time when UK-Russian relations are largely reduced to name-calling and sanctions, we are not likely to contribute much to any such dialogue…' [1].

Indeed, as I have discussed in the previous chapter, Russophobia has had a very destructive effect on cooperation between Russia and the West and is based on age-old ill-founded mutual suspicion and hatred on both sides. It could be dispelled by forgiveness and empathy. Forgiveness, in this case, does not mean restraining a vengeful desire but, on the part of the West, restraining a desire to punish Russia for actions that can be best understood by empathising with that country's fear of Western encirclement. The West should be aware of its own chequered history and not take the moral high ground when judging Russia.

However, there is little sign of such an attitude being adopted and therefore of the West having a constructive influence on events in Belarus. In September 2020, during parliamentary debates on Belarus, Russophobia on all sides of the House of Commons was much in evidence. These are three examples:

Thomas Tugendhat a Conservative MP and Chair of the Foreign Affairs Committee, stated:

'The Nord Stream 2 project that is currently going through is allowing the Russian Government to salami-slice our eastern neighbours and friends one by one, and what we are seeing in Belarus could easily happen in other countries' [2].

Barry Sheerman, a Labour Co-op MP, asked:

'. . .at the bottom of all this we surely know is Russia, which is becoming almost a rogue state around the world. Russia only listens when we are tough with it. Can we not have sanctions against Russia and, in this country, clear out the nest of vipers who have taken up residence—Putin supporters and yes men and yes women-here in London? For goodness' sake, can we not take on Russia, show it we mean business and start perhaps with the owner of the Evening Standard?' [3].

Later Dominic Raab,the Foreign Secretary, answered another MP:

'The hon.Lady is right to worry about the predatory approach of Russia ,which has always regarded Belarus as a client state. We are watching that very carefully. . .' [4].

With such views in the UK parliament echoed elsewhere in the West, there seems little hope of international mediation in Belarus.

However, there could still be negotiations if forgiveness is shown by both sides. Lukashenko should stop all violence towards the protesters, ban their arrests and release all those who have been imprisoned for their part in the protests. He could offer to enter a dialogue with their leaders and even offer to step down provided that the conditions were right. He could also soften his image internationally by abolishing the death penalty, for which human rights organisations have long been campaigning.

For their part, the protesters should show clemency to Lukashenko and give up any ideas of revenge or even of bringing him to justice as this will encourage him to resist giving up power. Rather he should be persuaded to relinquish his presidency or hold another election and then possibly leave Belarus and live in exile in Russia.

If he is put on trial, of course, he may well regret not abolishing the death penalty when he had the opportunity to do so.

References

1. The Times 18th August 2020
2. Hansard Vol 680 Debate: Belarus' 24th September 2020 Col. 1173
3. Ibid Col. 1177
4. Ibid Col. 1181

Chapter 10
Sinophobia

The West has been unforgiving towards some of China's policies without trying to excuse or understand the reasons behind them, or find alternative ways of viewing them, or reflecting on their own chequered histories. Indeed, such is the judgemental hostility of the West that some commentators speak of a new cold war with China. This might turn into a hot war with all its catastrophic consequences if Sinophobia is not checked.

This chapter will look at the West's response to China's dealings with the coronavirus pandemic, China's human rights record, its policies towards the Uighurs and the Tibetans and China's economic and trade policies which have all created unnecessary tensions and growing Sinophobia.

10.1 The West's Response to China and the Pandemic

An example of the West's harsh attitude to China was demonstrated in 2020 when the outbreak of the coronavirus pandemic began there. This seems to have originated from a wet market in Wuhan in Hubei province. As the virus, Covid-19, spread to other countries some of them alleged that China had initially covered up the outbreak which had allowed the virus to spread quickly. Indeed, by May 2020 Robert O'Brien, President Trump's national security adviser, was claiming that China was guilty of a cover up 'akin to Chernobyl' [1].

As evidence for this claim the foreign media frequently cited the case of Dr Wen Liang, an ophthalmologist in Wuhan. On 30th December 2019, through his WeChat account, he told medical colleagues and friends privately that there was a new SARS virus outbreak. This was leaked and reached the ears of the police who detained him [2]. They made him sign an agreement not to spread rumours which can cause chaos in China. Probably the local Communist party did not wish to give the national authorities any reason to investigate local matters in Wuhan in view of Beijing being

A. Wells, *The Importance of Forgiveness and the Futility of Revenge*, Contributions to International Relations, https://doi.org/10.1007/978-3-030-87552-7_10

unlikely to forgive any mistakes, or it may be that the full significance of the virus escaped the notice of the local authorities.

Whatever the truth of the matter, the very next day, December 31st, doctors in Wuhan did alert the local government to the existence of the virus [3]. Therefore, there was only 1 day's delay between Wen Liang's privately informing his friends about the virus and hospital doctors officially informing the local government about it. It is debatable whether the alarm could have been raised any earlier in 2019.

What is clear is that as soon as the Beijing officials knew about the coronavirus they alerted the WHO on 1st January 2020. Chinese scientists then isolated the virus and sequenced its genome, publishing the data on 12th January [4]. Nevertheless, Western media continued harshly to blame 'China', and not the local Wuhan officials, for the delay and disregarded human error and forgiveness as part of the narrative.

On September 22 2020, the US President Donald Trump gave an address to the UN General Assembly referring to the coronavirus as the 'China' virus. He demanded that China be held accountable for 'unleashing this plague onto the world' [5].

In addition, there was in the USA an erroneous view of China's responding to the virus. According to the Pew Research Centre two-thirds of Americans believed that China had done a bad job dealing with the Covid-19 pandemic. In contrast the executive director of the WHO Health Emergencies Programme, Mike Ryan, offered 'deepest congratulations' to China for bringing the disease to 'a very low level' [6].

Indeed, the Lancet reported in October 2020 that while the world was still struggling to control Covid-19, China had managed to control the pandemic rapidly and effectively.

'As of Oct 4, 2020, China had confirmed 90 604 cases of Covid-19 and 4739 deaths, while the USA had registered 7 382 194 cases and 209 382 deaths. The UK has a population 20 times smaller than China, yet it has seen five times as many cases of Covid-19 and almost ten times as many deaths' [7].

This is partly because China has learned from the SARS outbreak of 2003 and now has a centralised epidemic response system. It responded swiftly to the virus outbreak, has an effective test and trace system and, being an authoritarian government, was able to impose severe and long lockdowns in Wuhan and other cities. Only 3% of China's elderly population live in care homes, whereas in several western countries, such facilities have been major sources of infection [8].

It is true that local Chinese officials should not have tried to cover up the disease in Wuhan initially, if this was deliberate, but the Chinese national government did not try to conceal it. China alerted the WHO as soon as it knew about it and should be given credit for its achievements in controlling it, as well as for sending medical supplies to many other countries suffering from Covid-19.

10.2 The West's Response to Human Rights in China

As with the West's relations with Russia, forgiveness here means not being harshly judgemental over a state's policies before fully understanding the reasons for them and remembering the chequered histories of Western states.

Just as China has been severely and unfairly condemned for its response to the coronavirus, so has it been unfairly judged for its human rights record by people ignorant of the fact that there are basically two kinds of human rights: the political and the socio-economic. China has excelled at the latter which it sees as a stage in its development. It has lifted millions from poverty. Democracy is for a later stage.

China is not given sufficient credit for its record on economic and social rights nor are certain Western governments, such as the USA, criticised for their own economic and social rights record. It is significant that China has signed and ratified the UN's International Covenant on Economic, Social, and Cultural Rights but it has not yet ratified (although it has signed) the UN's International Covenant on Civil and Political Rights. The USA, on the other hand, has signed and ratified the latter covenant but only signed and not yet ratified the former one (which gives the right to all of access to healthcare).

China regards itself as a developing country which must first concern itself with its economic development not with political rights. Free speech is useless if one is dying in the gutter. Moreover, the dramatic and swift reforms that the Chinese Communist Party implemented after they had restored unity and stability to China in 1949, could only have been achieved by a dictatorship since those who lost their wealth under socialism wanted to overthrow the Communists by force.

As a result of China's reforms, according to the UN Human Development Report in 2019, the life expectancy in China (76.7) is much higher than for that in India (69.4) and nearly as high as that in the USA (78.9) [9]. China's gross national income per capita is more than twice that of India where millions of people suffer from poor health, illiteracy, and miserable housing, yet India is rarely criticised for its human rights record.

China has allowed much more political liberalisation in this century in terms of freedom of speech, assembly, and travel than in the previous one, but its chief concern is still the stability of China. To this end President Xi Jinping has often been very authoritarian (probably because he and his family suffered during the Cultural Revolution and he wants to avoid chaos at all costs).

10.3 Xinjiang

Under President Xi, China has carried out a policy towards the Uighurs in Xinjiang in north-west China which the West has condemned. It may well be that China has overreacted to the two threats of separatism and Islamic extremism. The latter, over the years, has resulted in bombing attacks and mass stabbings in the region (resulting in some mosques being closed). The former is supported by Uighurs who are more moderate but still use violence. As usual when China is concerned for the stability of the country it has taken severe measures, this time of detaining thousands of Uighurs in camps for re-education and job-training. Rather than attempting to see where China is coming from, however, the West has unforgivingly criticised the camps which have been likened to the Holocaust [10]. Indeed, China has been accused of genocide. However, this allegation is extreme and most unlikely.

The United Nations Genocide Convention defines genocide as 'acts committed with intent to destroy, in whole or in part, a national ethnic, racial or religious group, as such' [11]. The key word here is 'intent'. Intentionality in such cases is very difficult to prove.

It is most unlikely that China is guilty of genocidal intent in Xinjiang. It has not pursued a policy of killing the Uighurs. The birth control measures that have been criticised as intending to destroy the Uighurs were applied throughout China and will be discussed later.

When it came to power in 1949, China used re-education camps to carry out its immense socio-economic reforms for its enormous population. Instead of killing wealthy Chinese who wanted to overthrow the Communists by force, China, traditionally believing in inculcating social values, re-educated them. China seems to have revived this method in dealing with the violence in Xinjiang. It also may have overreacted to the problems there, probably due to the particular Communist officials in charge, especially hardliner Chen Quanguo, the Communist Party Secretary of Xinjiang, who previously carried out repressive policies in Tibet. President Xi Jinping whose family suffered considerably during the Cultural Revolution is also more authoritarian than his predecessors, being determined to prevent instability. The re-education camps are nothing like the concentration camps used by Germany in the Holocaust, nor like those used by Britain during the Boer war.

An additional problem to the violent extremism and more moderate secession movement in Xinjiang is that considerable numbers of the Han Chinese (the largest ethnic group in China) have moved into the region. Usually, they lord it over the indigenous minorities in China—rather as white settlers once did in East Africa and India. This Han chauvinism has caused Uighur resentment and is probably a major cause of unrest in Xinjiang, triggering a Uighur desire for secession. It must be said, however, the Han probably do want the Uighurs to be trained to become a more efficient workforce: the Belt and Road policy will open up the area to trade through Xinjiang. When this is completed, the Uighurs may have a much higher standard of living.

A German anthropologist, Adrian Zenz, has alleged that 1 million people have been detained in the camps and that the Uighurs have been subjected to forced labour and sterilisations. However, Zenz obtained his figures from online sources and they have been heavily criticised as 'absurdly shoddy methodologies' by the journalists Max Blumenthal and Ajit Singh [12].

It is likely that, since Xinjiang is a border region of China, the Uighurs escaped the strict imposition of the one-child policy which until the Han arrived in large numbers in Xinjiang at the end of the twentieth century. When it was imposed it would have resulted in a reduced birth rate which Zeng believes is an attempt to destroy the Uighurs. Forced sterilisation and abortions were imposed throughout China during the one-child policy, not only in Xinjiang.

Adrian Zenz is a Senior Fellow at the Victims of Communism Memorial Foundation in Washington DC [13]. He was previously at an evangelical theological institute, Akademie fur Weltmission, in Germany. A far-right Christian, Zenz believes he is 'led by God' against Beijing [14]. He co-authored a book, published in 2012, with his father-in-law, Marlon L. Sias, entitled 'Worthy to Escape: Why All Believers Will Not Be Raptured Before the Tribulation' [15]. This extreme right-wing form of Christianity may have led to his being deeply biased against the atheist Chinese Communist Party. In any case his statistics should be looked at critically.

Critics of China's policies in Xinjiang might be interested to know Mao ZeDong would have heavily condemned the Han chauvinism there and demanded an investigation. In his directive 'Criticize Han Chauvinism', of March 16th 1953, he wrote:

'We must go to the root and criticize the Han chauvinist ideas which exist to a serious degree among many Party members...

Delegations led by comrades who are familiar with our nationality policy and full of sympathy for our minority nationality compatriots still suffering from discrimination should be sent to visit the areas where there are minority nationalities, make a serious effort at investigation and study and help Party and government organisations in the localities discover and solve problems' [16].

Mao even asserted:

'Moreover, the newspapers should publish more articles based on specific facts to criticize Han chauvinism openly and educate the Party members and the people' [17].

Some Western newspapers might argue that this is precisely what they have been trying to do, but 'specific facts' are hard to come by regarding Xinjiang.

A more imaginative approach to China over Xinjiang might be for Western governments to tell the Chinese government that Mao's policy on Han chauvinism seems relevant to Xinjiang and they would like to see it implemented.

However, China is unlikely to open up to outside investigation in a hostile, judgemental atmosphere. More can be achieved if Western countries appreciate that they too have erred in their treatment of ethnic groups over which they had power. They should stop taking the moral high ground and raise the issue of Xinjiang in a friendlier way with Chinese officials, perhaps through offering hospitality rather than a summons to a lecture. The West should be more forgiving of possible mistakes China has made, particularly as it is still a developing country.

China should be given credit for lifting millions from poverty which it could not have achieved through liberal democracy. Since the late 1970s, it has introduced local democracy but is above all concerned with the stability of China and avoiding the chaos that the Cultural Revolution caused for a decade. Xi Jinping's family suffered greatly during it and had to live in a cave. His father, Xi Zhongxun, a high-ranking official who ironically had been in charge of China's ethnic minorities policy which was far more liberal than his son's, was purged, humiliated by the Red Guard and imprisoned. Xi Jinping's half–sister committed suicide. This is probably one reason why Xi Jinping has clamped down on the instability in Xinjiang so heavily.

No country has so far solved the problem of dealing effectively with Islamic extremism. Rather than besmirch China's efforts to do so, the West could encourage it to share its experiences in a cooperative endeavour to solve one of the most difficult problems of our times.

The fact that Western countries have abused ethnic groups in their power should not mean they cannot criticise other countries for doing the same, but that the criticism should be made in a constructive way, understanding how China sees the problem, and aware that the West has also trespassed against the human rights of others. China is still a developing country and cannot be expected to deal with its colossal problems always correctly. The West and East should find common ground and work together on the problem of terrorism.

10.4 China and Tibet: No Need for Forgiveness?

China is often condemned by Western human rights activists for its alleged occupation of Tibet and suppression of its people and culture. Little effort is made to understand to China's viewpoint.

However, whatever the truth about China's claim to Tibet, one fact is undeniable. This is that in 1959, China ended a cruel theocracy there, liberating over 90% of the population from serfdom and even slavery. The Chinese Communists gave the Tibetans free secular education to university level and free healthcare. They built for them roads, schools, and hospitals, as well as cheap housing. No other country has ever gone into another and so dramatically improved the standard of living for most of its inhabitants.

The debate over China's right to Tibet is inconclusive. China has claimed suzerainty over Tibet for centuries. However soon after the Manchu dynasty was overthrown in 1911, China collapsed into civil war and Tibet experienced 'de facto' independence. To make it 'de jure', Tibet could have joined the League of Nations. One reason why it did not do so was because it seemed concerned that it would have to open Tibet to foreign countries' representatives who might change Tibet's customs [18]. These Tibetan 'customs' included the practice of torturing serfs by eye gouging or limb amputation [19] as well as keeping most of the population in miserable living conditions as serfs. Both polygamy and polyandry were practised.

In 1949, the Communists united China. In 1950, they took over Tibet, claiming it as part of China. For the first decade they concentrated on developing Tibet's infrastructure, introducing the telephone, a telegram, and banking system, building the first hospitals and clinics as well as providing the Tibetans with their first newspapers and radio programmes in the Tibetan language. However, as this was the period of the Cold War, the CIA gave arms and training to some of the Tibetan elite who were resisting the Chinese [Training was given in the USA at Camp Hale, in Colorado, where the local inhabitants were told it was off limits as it concerned with 'atomic related research'] [20].

In 1959, the Chinese Communists decided to liberate the majority of the Tibetan population from the misery of serfdom. This was met with fierce resistance by the serf owners armed by the CIA. Later these serf owners propagated the myth that 1.2 million Tibetans had been killed by the Chinese. However, the former head of the Free Tibet Campaign, Patrick French, has admitted that there is no evidence for this [21]. The mainly social and religious elite led by the Dalai Lama fled from Tibet to India and the West where they campaigned for Tibetan independence and continued to receive funding from the CIA.

After 1959, all Tibetans were given free secular education up to university level. They were able to study in universities in China where, like other ethnic minorities, they were admitted with lower grades than those of the Han Chinese. In 1965 China designated the area previously ruled by Lhasa as the Tibetan Autonomous Region (TAR).

Unfortunately for Tibet and China, between 1966 and 1976, the Cultural Revolution led by Mao and the Gang of Four (but opposed by leading members of the Communist Party) raged throughout China which suffered from mindless destruction by 'Red Guards'. Tibet's monasteries were also severely damaged by this hooliganism. However, China has since spent millions of dollars on the monasteries and funding monastic life.

Deng Xiao-ping's Four Modernisations, proposed in 1978, have meant the opening up of Tibet's economy to private enterprise and eventually to the global economy. The standard of living of the Tibetans has risen considerably since the 1980s [22]. However, they have been dismayed by the Chinese government's policy of encouraging hundreds of thousands of Han Chinese to settle in Tibet (as they settled in other autonomous regions such as Xinjiang). The Tibetans believe that they are discriminated against in education which is mainly in Chinese and that the Han Chinese are outnumbering them (It seems that although the population in some towns is nearing 50/50 the Han do not usually settle in rural areas. Exact figures seen impossible to obtain). Tibetans also resent the fact that the Han Chinese are generally more prosperous than they are. These are concerns that China should address.

However, China will not give Tibet independence. It believes Tibet really is part of China. Furthermore, Tibet shares a strategically important border with India and is also rich in minerals. Above all, if Tibet gains independence other ethnic minority regions such as Xinjiang, which is predominately Muslim, will probably try to break away. This will eventually lead to civil war, the breakup of China, and worldwide economic and political chaos.

The Dalai Lama today seems a remarkable spiritual leader, rejecting violence and materialism. He has said that he now wants only increased autonomy for Tibet, not independence. If he were to acknowledge the great socio-economic benefits, the Chinese have given most of the impoverished population of Tibet, China might treat him with more trust and respect.

While human rights defenders might claim it is difficult to forgive China's policies in Tibet, the truth is that China has done a lot of good there, while the West ignored the suffering of the serfs in Tibet when it was a theocracy.

10.5 A Different Perspective Can Relax Economic Tensions Between China and the West

China's Belt and Road Initiative (BRI) has aroused criticism by Western countries as a form of neo-colonialism. The Belt is short for the Silk Road Economic Belt and the Road is an abbreviation for the twenty-first Century Maritime Silk Road. It is a global development strategy that aims to improve the physical infrastructure through land corridors that roughly equate to the old Silk Road. These infrastructure corridors span some 70 countries mainly in Asia, but also stretch to Europe. The Maritime Road reaches Africa. The project is an important part of Xi Jinping's foreign policy and aims at completion in 2049 on the 100th anniversary of the People's Republic of China.

There have been criticisms of the involved countries becoming indebted to China but scholars have debated this. In any case, countries are free to decide whether they wish to participate in the project. Moreover, according to Professor Lin Chun of the London School of Economics, the state lenders also conduct periodic evaluations to reduce or even cancel debts. Furthermore, China rarely imposes IMF-type of conditionalities on borrowers [23].

There have also been scaremongering comments from Western politicians and politicians that the BRI is part of China's aim at world dominance. These ideas have been fuelled by tensions between the USA and China over China's military presence on the Spratly Islands in the South China Sea. This together with a 'tariff war' with the USA has resulted in such an increase in animosity between the USA and China that some scholars have spoken of a new Cold War [24]. Indeed, this could develop into a dangerous conflict if there is not more effort made by both sides to be friendlier and more forgiving of each others' mistakes and blind spots, while firmly standing up for their own rights.

It is important to understand how China's history has shaped its foreign policy. In the nineteenth and early twentieth centuries, the country suffered the humiliation of being carved up and exploited by mainly Western imperialist powers. Britain militarily forced the opium trade on China, resulting in much of its population to become drug addicts. China is determined it will never again be so bullied. Indeed, there is a Chinese saying: 'I am relieved by the fact that my mother country is acting as a bully to other countries' ('Kan dao zuguo zheme liumang, wo jiu fangxinle').It can best be understood by thinking of a parent, having been concerned that their child is always being bullied, is delighted when their child is reported for actually bullying. The meaning of the phrase is that that at last China is able to act to former imperialist countries as they have acted towards it.

References

1. The Guardian 24th May 2020.
2. Horton, Richard, 'The Covid-19 Catastrophe' (Cambridge 2020) p.2–3
3. Ibid p.3
4. Ibid p.3
5. www.thelancet.com, Burki, T. 'China's successful control of Covid-19' 8th October 2020 (Vol 20 Issue 11)
6. Ibid
7. Ibid
8. Ibid
9. UN Human Development Report (2019) http://www.hdr.undp.org
10. Apps, Peter, 'China's Uighur detention camps...' New Statesman, 21st March 2019
11. UN Convention on the Prevention and Punishment of the Crime of Genocide 1948 Article 2
12. https://thegrayzone.com/2019/12/21/china-detaining-millions-uyghurs-problems-claims-us-ngo-researcher/. 'Serious problems with claims by US-backed NGO and far-right researcher 'led by God' against Beijing.'Ajit Singh and Max Blumenthal, thegrayzone.com December 21 2019
13. Ibid
14. Ibid
15. Ibid
16. https://www.marxists.org/reference/archive/mao/selected-works/volume-5/mswv5_25.htm Selected Works of Mao Tse-tung 'Criticize Han Chauvinism' March 16th 1953
17. Ibid
18. Shakya, W. Tsering, 'Tibet and the League of Nations' in 'The History of Tibet, Vol 3' ed McKay, Alex (Abingdon 2003) p.324
19. Strong, Anna Louise, 'When Serfs Stood Up in Tibet' (Beijing 1960) p.54–5
20. Dunham, Mikel, 'Buddha's Warriors' (New York 2004) p.315
21. French, Patrick, 'The New York Times' 22nd March 2008
22. Tang, Didi, 'Xi's Handouts for Tibetans...' 'The Times' 24th November 2020
23. For fuller consideration of this see Chun, Lin. 'China's New Globalism' https://eprints.lse.ac.uk
24. Rachman, Gideon, 'A new cold war, Trump, Xi and the escalating US-China confrontation'. *Financial Times*, 4th October 2020

Chapter 11
Political Vengeance Has Harmed China's Development

Like most dictators, Mao Zedong could not forgive criticism: this was the source of his undoing. Forgiveness of criticism is important in politics as it can prevent policies being implemented that can cause much avoidable suffering. Initially, however, Mao was dramatically successful in carrying out socio-economic reforms in China.

11.1 The Communists' Reforms

In 1949 the Chinese Communists led by Mao, having brought peace and stability to the country after decades of civil war, implemented dramatic social and economic reforms that gave the poor, the majority of the population, secure employment, cheap housing, free education to university level, free medical care and pensions. The landlords' exploitation of the peasants was ended. Moreover, women were given equal rights with men [1]. By contrast the lives of millions of poor people in India (a comparable large developing democratic country) continued to be nasty, brutish, and short.

When the Communists came to power, over 80% of the Chinese population worked in agriculture as peasants, living miserable lives exploited by often cruel landlords who might even kill them. The Communists ended this system and redistributed the land to the peasants. However, they were soon grouped into mutual-aid teams, then cooperatives of about 100 families as private property was abolished and socialism was introduced. These cooperatives were then merged into even larger collectives by the mid-1950s for reasons of efficiency and ideology but were not so popular with the peasants.

In the towns, socialism was also implemented. The low-paid, insecure, and often starving workers were freed from their usually exploitative work as businesses were nationalised. The rich were stripped of their wealth. Some fled to Taiwan and the USA. Others were sent to labour camps for 'thought reform' in China. The

A. Wells, *The Importance of Forgiveness and the Futility of Revenge*, Contributions to International Relations, https://doi.org/10.1007/978-3-030-87552-7_11

Communists were always concerned that these potential 'counter revolutionaries' might, with foreign military help, attempt to overthrow them bloodily and regain their lands and property. Indeed, it was possible at this time of the Cold War that the USA might use its military power to help them. The Communists, therefore, cracked down on 'rightist' thinking and kept dictatorial control over the country. As in other Communist countries, force had to be used to impose social reforms as the wealthy resisted them. Inevitably mistakes were made. A socialist revolution on this scale could not be carried out through a liberal democracy.

However, the benefits that the Communists gave to the Chinese were enormous. All workers, whether in the towns or countryside were attached to work-units or 'dan-hui' which provided them with the social-welfare benefits earlier mentioned. This radical form of social security was known as 'iron rice bowl' and gave the Chinese the security and life chances of which they had never dreamed before 1949.

11.2 Mao Could Not Forgive Criticisms of the Communists' Achievements

The Chinese communists' achievements were great and no doubt Mao thought deserving of much credit. In 1956, Mao launched his 'Hundred Flowers Campaign', named after an ancient saying, 'Let a hundred flowers bloom, let a hundred schools of thought contend', in which he encouraged intellectuals to express themselves freely about the reforms. He may have wanted to hear praise for the Communists' reforms or he may have wanted to humble Communists officials who had become arrogant or to lure out the party's enemies. He may, indeed, have introduced free speech too early. What is clear is that he had not expected the severe criticisms that the intellectuals, who were mainly from the upper classes, made of the whole Communist system in the spring of 1957.

Like most dictators Mao could not forgive criticism. His response was harsh. He launched the Anti-Rightist Campaign and had the critics labelled as 'rightists' so that many of them lost their jobs and were sent to the countryside. As a result, 2 years later, when it was clear the Great Leap was disastrous, the intellectuals did not dare to criticise it openly. Nor were there the statisticians and economists available for their guidance as many had been sacked in the Anti-Rightist Campaign.

The Great Leap was a catastrophe and may have caused 30 million deaths. Had Mao been a forgiving leader and listened to his critics in the 100 Flowers' Campaign rather than sacking them, he would have been given informed criticisms and hopefully persuaded that his Great Leap was wrong.

In 'The Open Society and its Enemies', Karl Popper argued that politicians should welcome criticism of their policies just as scientists improve their knowledge through attempts to falsify their research conclusions. In this way, Popper argued, serious mistakes in policies would be avoided [2]. However, far from finding their opinions were taken seriously, Mao's critics found they were vindictively punished. As a result, fatal flaws in Mao policies went initially undetected until it was too late.

11.3 The Disaster of the Great Leap Forward and Mao's Vengeance on Critics

Criticism is important in politics since it can obviate grave policy mistakes and save lives. It should, therefore, be met not with revenge but reflection and, if it is unfair, with forgiveness, as criticism can be stifled in an unforgiving culture. This unfortunately was the ethos Mao created.

In 1958, Mao moved to implementing extreme socialism, launching the Great Leap Forward as the next step to communism. He and other Communist leaders hoped thereby to maximise the productivity of the masses and transform China's agrarian economy into a modern, but communist, industrial one.

The collective farms were forced into enormous communes where the peasants were obliged to live communally, giving up family life. But the peasants did not want to live and work this way and had no incentive to increase their productivity. Moreover, a severe drought occurred when the communes were established, resulting in low grain yields. However, the officials in charge falsified the statistics of the harvests out of fear that they would be criticised for incompetence and lose their jobs. Therefore, they took what grain was produced even that which the peasants needed for food and sent it to the cities.

As a result, the peasants began starving to death. Eventually, during the Great Leap possibly as many as 30 million peasants died [3]. It is difficult to ascertain exactly how many as the statistics for this period are unreliable. Furthermore, it is impossible to know whether the peasants would have died even if the Great Leap had not been implemented since it coincided with a severe drought. Natural disasters used to kill millions of people in China and governments prior to the Communists did not help them.

Mao also urged the Chinese to build furnaces in their backyards and make steel by melting down kitchen utensils and garden tools. The steel, however, was useless. He had vainly hoped by this method of steel production that China would catch up with the West industrially within 15 years.

Had Mao not sacked the economists and statisticians in his Anti-Rightist Campaign in 1957 they could have made informed criticisms of his Great Leap which might well have brought it to an end. His vindictive response to his critics frightened anyone who might disagree with him into silence.

The Great Leap was not Mao's responsibility alone, since other CCP leaders initially supported or did not object to it. But when they realised it was a disaster, Mao refused to listen even to them. In 1959, one of the veteran Chinese leaders, Marshall Peng Dehuai, who had been quite close to Mao, went to see him to tell him the Great Leap was not working. But Mao responded by sacking him, replacing him with Lin Biao as the Minister of Defence.

Nevertheless, in 1960, other Communist leaders, horrified by the catastrophe, managed to force Mao to give up running the economy. He had to hand over the position of Chairman of the People's Republic of China to Liu Xiao-qi who, with Deng Xiaoping the CCP Secretary-General, set about dismantling the communes and giving the peasants financial incentives instead. Liu and Deng had become convinced by the failure of Mao's extreme socialism that the way forward was more economic freedom: to allow the peasants to have their own private plots and sell part of their produce at rural markets on a private basis.

11.4 The Cultural Revolution 1966–1976: A Decade of Chaos and Revenge

Mao, however, deeply resented his loss of power and also believed that Liu Xiao-qi was putting China on a capitalist road. He was determined to remove Liu and take his revenge on him.

Unfortunately for Mao, most of the Communist party leaders supported Liu. Therefore, in 1966, Mao launched the 'Great Chinese Proletarian Cultural Revolution' which would shake from power Liu and his supporters. Mao based his Cultural Revolution on the Chinese young people who were urged to eradicate 'bourgeois influences' wherever they found them, including people senior to them, especially university staff. In this revolution Mao was supported by the 'Gang of Four' which included his wife, Jiang Qing, and three other Communists who had been rapidly promoted. Jiang Qing was a vindictive woman who seized every opportunity to take revenge on those whom she believed were her enemies [4].

Groups of students organised themselves into 'Red Guards' which first carried out big poster criticisms of staff, then dragged them out to 'struggle sessions', denouncing and humiliating them, at times forcing them to kneel on broken glass or stand in 'airplane' position with arms outstretched while they were 'struggled against'. Sometimes they were beaten to death. Their so-called bourgeois paintings, books, antiques, and any Western possessions were destroyed. Lecturers at universities were forced to attend struggle sessions daily. Some committed suicide.

It is possible that by persecuting the intellectuals who were vilified as 'stinking number 9', a very low class, just above beggars [5], Mao was taking revenge on them for their dismissive treatment of him when he was a young university librarian and tried in vain to talk to them [6].

The Chinese people were pitted against each other, criticising and accusing each other of wrong doing. There were no attempts at forgiveness or reconciliation. Forgiveness in any case has never been emphasised in China as a highly valued response as it is in the Christian-influenced West.

Mao took his revenge on Liu Xiao-qi and his supporters. This can be seen in the cruel way Liu was allowed to be treated. He was 'struggled against', beaten, tortured, and died in prison. His wife, Wang Guangmei, was publicly humiliated at mass rallies by Red Guards who forced her to wear a necklace of ping-pong balls as a way of mocking the jewellery she wore when she had travelled abroad with her husband [7].

Mao himself would make appearances in Tiananmen Square, adulated like a pop star by the Chinese young people who would wave the Little Red Book of his thoughts. The Red Guards were given free transport to go throughout China, criticising 'bourgeois' attitudes. Parading people publicly in dunce caps was one of their favourite methods. Soon most of China was precipitated into the turmoil of public criticisms, beatings, looting, smashing, and killings. Thc Communist Party was torn apart by warring factions and power struggles.

Millions of people were harmed by the chaos of the Cultural Revolution which did not end until Mao died in 1976 and the Gang of Four were arrested. Whether Mao had become ill and thus given to grandiose ideas, or whether he was in full control of his faculties may never be known. What is clear is that he destroyed much of the good work he had done in the first decade of his power. This need not have happened had he listened to his critics instead of exacting revenge on them.

11.5 The CCP's Merciless Treatment of the Pro-democracy Protesters Harmed China

It was the chaos of the Cultural Revolution as well as memories of the decades of civil war before 1949 that resulted in the Communist Party leadership's determination, after Mao's death, to avoid 'luan' (chaos) at all costs in the future. In particular, leaders such as Deng Xiaoping who had suffered considerably during the Cultural Revolution were prepared to take extreme measures to eliminate any cause of instability. When, in addition, the elderly leaders' pride had been hurt and their patience exhausted, as it was by the pro-democracy student protesters in 1989, they were merciless.

In the late 1970s, Deng Xiaoping began a policy of economic liberalisation which gradually, then with astonishing speed, took off, as the Chinese, aided by foreign investment and expertise revealed colossal entrepreneurial energy. The standard of living of the Chinese rose dramatically and millions were lifted out of poverty.

Moreover, the Chinese Communist party, while not believing that Western democracy was suitable for China at the time, did in the late 1970s, in the wake of the economic reforms, introduce local democracy so that the peasants and townsfolk could vote for their local government. This may have been the first step at introducing democracy from the grassroots upwards.

However, in December 1986, 3000 students at the University of Science and Technology at Hefei protested against the lack of any real choice in the imminent local elections. Their Vice-President, the eminent astrophysicist, Fang Lizhi, supported them. Their right to protest at all was, in fact, the result of the work of liberals in the CCP, particularly the Party General Secretary Hu Yaobang.

Students in other cities also began protesting for democracy. But the government made it clear in official publications that it condemned the protests and would use repression if they did not stop. So they stopped. The Communists then proceeded in their usual unforgiving way: Fang Lizhi was sacked from his position and expelled from the Party as was the distinguished journalist Liu Binyan who also lost his job on the People's Daily. Wang Ruowang, a well-known writer was also expelled from the Party. They were regarded as encouraging 'bourgeois liberalism'. But above all, Hu Yaobang, who was suspected of sympathising with the students and regarded by the conservatives in the Party as being supportive of the liberal intellectuals, was removed from his post as General Secretary of the Communist Party in January 1987. It was this harsh, unforgiving attitude to those who might have had constructive critical ideas that alienated many Chinese from the CCP.

Two years later, on April 15th 1989, Hu Yaobang died. Thousands of students crowded into Tiananmen Square to mourn his death, demanding that the verdict against him be reversed and demanding more freedoms such as the right to find their own jobs. Hu's funeral took place on April 22nd. Although the government had banned the public from the Square on that day, the students arrived before the police did and thousands of them crowded into the Square to honour Hu Yaobang. The student leaders then organised an Autonomous Federation to co-ordinate strikes. Some took their message to the citizens of Beijing, standing on street corners and protesting for democracy.

It is not clear exactly what form of democracy the students wanted. They did not show they understood the well-founded concern of the Communist Party that chaos could again ensue if too much political liberalisation was introduced. They did not discuss how the already established local democracy could be developed. On the other hand, some of the students' demands for an end to official corruption and nepotism were justified.

On April 26 in the 'People's Daily', an article, probably authorised by Deng Xiaoping, appeared. It called the students' protests a threat to stability and argued that the movement should be suppressed otherwise the reforms of the past decade would be lost. This enraged the students who had expressed their loyalty to the Party. On April 27, about 80,000 of them marched through Beijing.

Meanwhile the Party General Secretary Zhao Ziyang had been in North Korea. On April 30, he returned and appeared to sympathise with the students' demands that he called 'reasonable' [8]. May 4th 1989 was the 70th anniversary of the May Fourth Movement which had protested for democracy just after the First World War. Mindful that little progress had been made since then, about 300,000 people flooded into Tiananmen Square to hear speeches lauding the democratic spirit of the May Fourth. The students demanded a retraction of the People's Daily article of April 26th. Zhao supported them.

Then, knowing the world's press would be in Beijing to cover President Gorbachev's visit there, the students organised a hunger strike in Tiananmen Square

2 days before the visit took place on 15th May. In that way they ensured they would get the maximum publicity. To Deng Xiaoping's embarrassment, the welcoming ceremony for Gorbachev had to be held at the airport and not in Tiananmen Square as had been intended. Two days later, perhaps aroused by these events, Chinese citizens from all walks of life, including many teachers, journalists and, more alarmingly for the Communist leadership, industrial workers and party cadres, marched in a massive demonstration for democracy. This was too much for the elderly leadership of the Party. On 19th May, martial law was imposed. But it was not until 2 weeks later that it was implemented as the Beijing residents again supported the students by blocking the paths of the soldiers. Deng had been humiliated once more. Zhao Ziyang, who had opposed martial law but had lost out to the hardliners came to the Square to tell the students tearfully, 'I have come too late' [9].

Nevertheless, as the month of May drew to a close the Democracy Movement began to lose its momentum and the students of Beijing began to drift away. Meanwhile, students from outside Beijing were arriving and endeavouring to keep the demonstration going. A party atmosphere in some areas of the Square developed.

On May 30, a Styrofoam statue, looking rather like the Statue of Liberty, but called by the students the 'Goddess of Democracy', was erected in Tiananmen Square. This was an insult to the Communist party which had already been humiliated by not being able to give a reception for Gorbachev in the Square. In addition, the patience of the elderly leadership was no doubt exhausted. Deng Xiaoping, the paramount leader, was 2 months short of his 85th birthday at the time and the President of China, Yang Shangkun, was 83 in July of that year. Supporting the aged leaders was Premier Li Peng, who was only 61 at the time but always a hardliner.

The leaders too may have thought the Cultural Revolution was beginning again. Indeed, according to the 'Tiananmen Papers' Deng Xiaoping thought there was a real danger of civil war [10]. However, this collection of documents, claimed to be reports of the CCP leadership's decision-making during the Tiananmen crisis, secretly recorded on computer discs and smuggled out, may not be authentic. Moreover, the students were unarmed and most unlikely to start a civil war.

Exactly what happened to precipitate military action on the night of June 3rd–4th may never be known. Mistakes were made on all sides, including that of the Western mass media which encouraged the students to make inflammatory statements. Erroneous information may have been given to the elderly leadership that decided on the use of force in that volatile situation. As a result, about a thousand student protesters were killed that night.

The Chinese Communist party has often shown its heavy handedness when confronted with dissenters. However, the massacre shook the world which had looked on in horror. The CCP destroyed not only the lives of hundreds of students but also the respect and trust of many of its citizens. In addition, it also alienated other nations at a time when China was just coming in from the cold. Many Western governments strongly condemned the massacre and imposed economic sanctions on China depriving it of precious advanced technologies. The Tiananmen Square massacre did colossal harm to China's image of a normal government with which other countries could do business. Just as China could not forgive the student protesters so much of the world could not forgive China for the massacre. The people of Hong Kong were especially alarmed by it. This will next be considered.

11.6 No Mercy in Hong Kong

China's harsh authoritarian response to the protests for democracy in Hong Kong has damaged its international relations and may harm its trade benefits from having Hong Kong as part of its territory.

In 1984 China and Britain had signed the Sino-British Joint Declaration by which Hong Kong would come under Chinese sovereignty, along with the New Territories in 1997, when Britain's lease on the latter expired. Hong Kong was to be a Special Administrative Region. Its capitalist and own legal systems would be unchanged for the next 50 years and this 'one country two systems' was enshrined in its Basic Law. However, many Hong Kongers had been uneasy that their freedoms might be curtailed by China. This concern increased with the Tiananmen Square massacre in 1989.

In 2014 a so-called Umbrella Movement developed in which Hong Kongers, holding opened umbrellas, protested against the prospect of Beijing's being able to screen the candidates for the post of Chief Executive of Hong Kong. In 2019 Hong Kong erupted into a much greater mass protest against an Extradition Bill which was seen as an attempt by China to take further control of Hong Kong.

Curiously the bill would never have been introduced at that time had a young Hong Kong man forgiven his girlfriend who had told him she was pregnant with another man's baby. Instead, 19 year-old Chan Tong-kai murdered Poon Hiu-wing, also from Hong Kong and aged 20, in a hotel in Taiwan on 17th February 2018. He took her body in a suitcase outside the hotel and hid it in some bushes. Then he returned to Hong Kong [11]. When interviewed by the police there he admitted the murder. However, he could not be tried for the crime as there is no extradition treaty between Taiwan and Hong Kong. Instead he was charged with money laundering as he had stolen Ms Poon's credit card and used it. He was sentenced to only 29 months in jail in Hong Kong.

Ms Poon's distraught parents implored Carrie Lam, the Chief Executive of Hong Kong, to find a way of getting Chan extradited to Taiwan to face justice. Their appeals prompted the introduction of an Extradition Bill on 3rd April 2019.Unfortunately this bill, produced after consultation with China, covered a multitude of crimes, not just murder. Hong Kongers feared that dissidents might be extradited to China. Indeed in 2015, five booksellers had been kidnapped and taken to China as they had allegedly been trafficking banned books, critical of President Xi Jinping as well as being pornographic.

Without Chan's murdering his girlfriend the Extradition Bill would not have been introduced at this time. However, this reason received very little coverage in the mass media. It seemed to many people in Hong Kong and the West that China, without any situational prompting, was beginning to take over Hong Kong with the Extradition Bill.

On 9th June about 1 million people marched to the government headquarters to protest against the bill. On 15th June, the Chief Executive of Hong Kong, Carrie Lam, said she would delay it indefinitely. However, the protesters wanted it scrapped entirely. Their anger grew towards the police for using force. Days later they barricaded the police headquarters for 15 h demanding the exoneration of people arrested in previous protests.

On 1st July, the anniversary of Hong Kong's handover from the UK to China, the protesters stormed and ransacked the Legislative Council (LegCo) building. This was a pointless, vengeful action. The protesters were now demanding far more than the withdrawal of the Extradition Bill. They wanted greater autonomy and democratisation for Hong Kong as well as the resignation of Carrie Lam. On 21st July they defaced China's Liaison Office in Hong Kong. In August, the protests grew as the police fired tear gas and rubber bullets at them. In September the Extradition Bill was withdrawn. However, it was too late. The protesters were calling for universal suffrage and even for Hong Kong's independence. Here they were going too far. The protests continued until the pandemic in China caused them to die down in early 2020.

However, China did not forgive the Hong Kongers for their violent protests and calls for independence. As usual Beijing responded with a heavy hand. On 30th June 2020 in China, the National People's Congress Standing Committee enacted a Security Law for Hong Kong. Its main provisions were that the crimes of secession, subversion, terrorism, and collusion with foreign forces were to be punishable by a maximum sentence of life in prison. Beijing was to establish a new security office in Hong Kong which could send some cases to be tried on the mainland. The Hong Kong people feared that this new Security Law would undermine the Basic Law which was to protect certain freedoms: freedom of assembly and of speech, an independent judiciary and some democratic rights in Hong Kong. According to Article 23 of the Basic Law, Hong Kong was supposed to have enacted its own security law but because it would have been so unpopular this had never happened. Now this law imposed by Beijing sent shock waves through Hong Kong from where some of the leading pro-democracy protesters promptly fled. It is likely that many more Hong Kongers will leave as Britain took measures to give visas to the nearly 3 million British National Overseas Passport holders in Hong Kong [12].

China has harmed not only its international relations but also possibly the trade benefits of Hong Kong, since its draconian actions could drive out entrepreneurs. Hong Kong is a very important trading entrepot and shipping centre, especially for trade between China and the USA.

Meanwhile in foreign universities, Chinese students, especially those from Hong Kong, together with some academics are fearful that any criticism of China they express could make them liable to be charged with sedition when they return to China [13].

The Extradition Bill was too extreme, the Hong Kongers' reactions to it often irresponsibly violent. The Security Law is too harsh and at the moment there is little likelihood of either Beijing or Hong Kong attempting to forgive and understand each others' point of view.

In October 2019, Mr Chan was released from prison. He apologised to Ms Poon's family for the death of their daughter and to the Hong Kong people whose initial protests were against the Extradition Bill which was meant to bring him to justice over the murder of Ms Poon [14].

References

1. For studies on the Chinese Communists in power see: Meisner, Maurice, 'Mao's China and After', (New York 1999), Schram, Stuart R., 'Mao Tse-tung', (Harmondsworth, Middlesex 1970), Spence, Jonathan, 'The Search for Modern China', (New York 1999), Macfarquhar, Roderick and Fairbank, John (eds), Cambridge History of China Vols 14, 15 (Cambridge 1995) For a study of the violence involved, see Dikotter, Frank, 'The Tragedy of Liberation', (London 2013)
2. Magee, Bryan, 'Popper' (London 1973) p.75–6
3. Meisner, Maurice, 'Mao's China and After' (New York 1999) p.237
4. For excellent accounts of this period: see MacFarquhar, Roderick, 'The Origins of the Cultural Revolution' Vol 3 The Coming of the Cataclysm: 1961–66' (New York 1997) and MacFarquhar, Roderick, and Schoenals, Michael, 'Mao's Last Revolution' (Cambridge, MA USA 2006)
5. The term 'Number 9' originated during the Yuan dynasty where the Mongol conquerors identified ten "castes" of Chinese, with only beggars at a status below the intellectuals.
6. Schram, Stuart, 'Mao Tse-tung' (Harmondsworth, Middx 1966) p.48
7. 'The Sydney Morning Herald', (Wang Guangmei's obituary) October 23rd 2006
8. Meisner, Maurice, 'Mao's China and After' (New York 1999) p.502
9. Moise, Edwin E., 'Modern China' (New York 1999), p.220
10. Nathan, Andrew, and Link, Perry, 'The Tiananmen Papers' (London 2001) p.420
11. www.scmp.com/news 'Body folded in suitcase' Hong Kong 13th April 2019
12. www.bbc.com/news/UK Politics 1st July 2020 'Hong Kong: UK makes citizenship offer'
13. Lucas, Ed 'The Communist Party's malign influence on students' The Times' 17th October 2020
14. 'I'm sorry to the people of Hong Kong' by Coconuts, Hong Kong October 23rd 2019

Part III
Forgiveness Between Ethnic Groups or to an Occupying Power

Chapter 12
Mahatma Gandhi's Rejection of Revenge

I should like to begin this chapter with describing the act of revenge to which I referred briefly at the beginning of this book. It was a form of revenge that could have been multiplied many times over had not Mahatma Gandhi led the Indian people to oppose the British in a non-violent, non-vengeful way. Ironically his method was deeply influenced by Jesus Christ's teaching although he did not describe himself as a Christian, whereas the British did call their country 'Christian' yet did not practise Christ's teachings in their policies.

12.1 Amritsar India 1919–London 1940

In the late afternoon of 13th March 1940 at Caxton Hall, London, a meeting organised by the East India Association and the Royal Central Asian Society was drawing to an end. Suddenly shots rang out, killing the colonial administrator Sir Michael O'Dwyer, and wounding Lord Zetland, the Secretary of State for India, who were on the speakers' platform [1].

The gunman was Udham Singh, a Sikh, who had been deeply affected by the massacre at Amritsar in India in 1919, 21 years earlier. Like many Indians, he had held Michael O'Dwyer responsible for the bloodshed, since he had been the Lieutenant-Governor of the Punjab when Brigadier General Reginald Dyer had ordered soldiers to fire on a crowd of peaceful Indian protesters against new repressive measures by the British. (There had been no warning given of the intent to fire. Moreover, the exit to the meeting place, a public garden, was blocked for the protesters, many of whom did not know that such meetings were now banned.)

O'Dwyer had supported the shooting in which over 1000 Indians were injured and at least 379 were killed. Udham Singh was then aged 20. It seems that he may have been at Amritsar taking water to the crowds with his friends from the orphanage where he had grown up, or, as has recently been claimed, elsewhere in the Punjab, distributing seditious leaflets [2]. Whatever his whereabouts the massacre had made

A. Wells, *The Importance of Forgiveness and the Futility of Revenge*, Contributions to International Relations, https://doi.org/10.1007/978-3-030-87552-7_12

a deep impression on him. For over 20 years he had nursed a desire to avenge the deaths of his fellow Indians. As he said after his arrest for assassinating O'Dwyer:

'I did it because I had a grudge against him. He deserved it. He was the real culprit. He wanted to crush the spirit of my people, so I have crushed him. For full 21 years, I have been trying to wreak vengeance. I am happy that I have done the job. I am not scared of death. I am dying for my country. I have seen my people starving in India under the British rule. I have protested against this, it was my duty. What greater honour could be bestowed on me than death for the sake of my motherland' [3].

After Singh was arrested, he was tried, convicted, and sentenced to death. On 31 July 1940, he was hanged at Pentonville Prison and buried within the prison grounds; but many Indians hailed him as a hero. In 1974, his remains were exhumed and repatriated to India where they were received by the Prime Minister Indira Gandhi, cremated, and preserved in an urn in Amritsar.

This assassination showed the strong feelings of hatred and revenge that were held by many Indians towards the British. However, in this example, only one man was killed by one assassin. There could have been multiple deaths if the leader of the Indian nationalist movement had not been Mahatma Gandhi who believed in non-violent resistance and who therefore greatly limited the loss of life. The British were indeed lucky to have to deal with Gandhi as the leader of the opposition to their rule and not someone like Udham Singh whose act of revenge, while being that of an individual, was carried out on behalf of his people and supported by many of them. Like other such vengeful acts it was long incubated and directed against an occupying power. There is still considerable support for Singh's action in India. The day of his death is a holiday in the Punjab and Haryana. Films have been made in India celebrating him as a martyr. Mahatma Gandhi however did not see him as such. In press statements, Gandhi condemned the Caxton Hall shooting saying, 'the outrage has caused me deep pain. I regard it as an act of insanity...I hope this will not be allowed to affect political judgement' [4].

It was indeed Gandhi's great achievement to unite in India most Hindus, Muslims, and Sikhs behind him in non-violent resistance against the British. Gandhi's task was not to create forgiveness and reconciliation between two sovereign powers as was Robert Schuman's, but to get the greatest empire in the world out of India while forgiving the British for their brutality and not seeking to avenge it. He believed in 'turning the other cheek' [5] to harmful attacks while at the same time taking peaceful action to achieve independence. Although at first sight Gandhi's teachings seem concerned mainly with non-violence, not forgiveness, it is clear that he thought that the latter, denying revenge, was intrinsically part of the former. As he wrote: 'Non-violence implies love, compassion, forgiveness' [6].

Gandhi's grandson, Arun, in his book, 'The Gift of Anger', recalls:

'Bapuji taught me that being able to understand another's viewpoint and to forgive is real strength' [7].

In his writings Gandhi elaborated on this idea:

'Non-violence, therefore, presupposes ability to strike. It is a conscious deliberate restraint put upon one's desire for vengeance. But vengeance is any day superior to passive, effeminate and helpless submission. Forgiveness is higher still. Vengeance too is weakness' [8].

To Gandhi forgiving meant having the strength to restrain one's desire for revenge which one would otherwise be able to carry out:

'...forgiveness is more manly than punishment...But abstinence is forgiveness only when there is the power to punish...A mouse hardly forgives a cat when it allows itself to be torn to pieces by her...

Let me not be misunderstood. Strength does not come from physical capacity. It comes from an indomitable will' [9].

Indeed, throughout his life Gandhi showed colossal strength of willpower and self-discipline. According to his grandson, Gandhi believed:

'When we react rashly and lash out, it's as if we have shot bullets that can't be put back in the gun' [10].

To Gandhi anger was a very important source of energy for which we must train our minds to use it aright and not lethally. As he explained:

'When we channel electricity intelligently, we can use it to improve our life, but if we abuse it, we could die. So as with electricity we must learn to use anger wisely for the good of humanity' [11].

According to his grandson:

'Bapuji tried to show that we can achieve our goals through love and truth and that the greatest advances occur when we give up our distrust and look for strength in positivity and courage' [12].

Thus, Gandhi's form of resistance is intrinsically bound up with forgiveness, as it rejects revenge and demands love not hatred towards the enemy who should then be converted to the cause by such noble behaviour. Gandhi's peaceful methods indeed saved many British as well as Indian lives. These methods have been copied by protest movements throughout the world. As a result, Gandhi's leadership of the Indian nationalist movement shone as being ethically superior to his imperial masters' often brutal oppression, winning him world-wide respect.

While it was the Second World War's draining Britain's coffers that finally forced the British to leave India, Gandhi's movement did the groundwork for their departure and no doubt would have eventually obliged them to go. The need to arrest and jail thousands of Indian protestors put a huge strain on Britain's resources as did the withdrawal of the Indians' labour and cooperation on which the Raj depended. In the words of the distinguished historian of India, Judith Brown, Gandhi's protests:

'challenged the very nature of British imperialism, and were designed to undermine the implicit Indian cooperation on which imperial rule rested' [13].

Moreover, Gandhi's non-violent resistance movement united the Indians across creed, class, and caste.

12.2 Early Development of Gandhi's Thought

Mohandas Gandhi was born in 1869 in Gujarat to a merchant Hindu family. His father was a government official and his mother a particularly devout Hindu. In 1888, he went to study law at the Inns of Court in London. In that city, surprisingly, his Hindu faith was developed as well as his understanding of Christianity. There he met members of the Theosophy Society who inspired him to read the Bhagavad Gita which he had not read back home in India.

Gandhi also joined the Vegetarian Society which strengthened his Hindu beliefs on this issue. It was, in fact, at a vegetarian boarding house that he met a man who was to change his life. This nameless man was a Christian who encouraged him to read the Bible. Through him Gandhi first came across Jesus's 'Sermon on the Mount' with its exhortation to 'turn the other cheek' and not retaliate [14].

12.3 Satyagraha

In 1891, Gandhi returned to India to practise his profession but in 1893 he accepted a post with an Indian law firm in Durban, South Africa. There he was so angered at the way Indians were treated that he devoted much of his time to fighting discriminatory legislation. While he was doing so he developed his distinctive method of non-violent protest which he called 'satyagraha' or 'truth force' or 'firmness in truth' ('satya' means 'truth and 'agraha' is 'firmness of force'). It was this principle that Gandhi used later to resist the British presence in India itself. In 1909, he wrote a pamphlet 'Hind Swaraj' or 'Home Rule for India', arguing for passive resistance against the British. He explained that the object was not to make the British suffer as the Indians would suffer because:

'Passive resistance is a method of securing rights by personal suffering, it is the reverse of resistance by arms' [15].

He asserted:

'Passive resistance is an all-sided sword, it can be used anyhow; it blesses him who uses it and him against whom it is used. Without drawing a drop of blood it produces far reaching results. It never rusts and cannot be stolen' [16].

12.4 The Influence of Jesus Christ's Teaching

In developing his non-violent form of protest, Gandhi was greatly influenced by the teachings of Jesus although he would never describe himself as a Christian, since he believed other religions were of equal value if properly interpreted [17]:

'It was the New Testament which really awakened me to the rightness and value of Passive Resistance. When I read in the 'Sermon on the Mount', such passages as

'Resist not him that is evil, but whosoever smiteth thee on thy right cheek turn to him the other also', and 'Love your enemies and pray for them that persecute you, that ye may be sons of your Father which is in heaven', I was simply overjoyed, and found my own opinion confirmed where I least expected it. The 'Bhagavad Gita' deepened the impression, and Tolstoy's 'The Kingdom of God is Within You' gave it permanent form' [18].

In this quotation the intrinsic relationship between passive resistance and forgiveness can be seen.

12.5 Tolstoy's Interpretation of the Sermon on the Mount

Gandhi had read Tolstoy's 'The Kingdom of God is Within You' when it had first appeared in the English translation in 1894 [19]. In his writings Tolstoy had strongly criticised all Christian churches for perverting Christ's teachings which he believed meant total pacifism. He ignored the Church Fathers' teaching on a 'just war' and believed that in the Sermon on the Mount that Christ had condemned all violence. This made a deep impression on Gandhi.

In 1909, Gandhi wrote to Tolstoy asking for permission to translate into Gujarati his 'Letter to a Hindoo' which had been published in English in an Indian newspaper 'Free Hindustan'. A considerable correspondence developed between them, ending only with Tolstoy's death in 1910.

In his introduction to his translation of Tolstoy's 'Letter to a Hindoo' Gandhi wrote:

'Tolstoy's life has been devoted to replacing the method of violence for removing tyranny…He would meet hatred expressed in violence by love expressed in self-suffering' [20].

Gandhi explained his method of resistance:

'If we do not want the English in India, we must pay the price. Tolstoy indicates it …'participate not in evil, in the violent deeds of the administration of the law courts, the collection of taxes and what is more important, of the soldiers, and no one in the world will enslave you, …'' [21].

12.6 Practising 'Satyagraha' in South Africa

It was in this spirit that in 1909 Gandhi used his method of 'satyagraha' for the first time to protest against the new law imposed by the government of the Transvaal forcing the Indian population there to register and carry passes. Declaring they were being discriminated against, Gandhi urged Indians at a mass meeting to burn their passes or not register. As a result of their doing so, many were arrested and jailed as was Gandhi. However, so great was the public outcry at their treatment that the Transvaal government had to negotiate a compromise with him.

By the time Gandhi had left South Africa at the end of 1914, he had forced the South African government to concede to a number of his demands and had established the non-violent protest movement with which he changed the thinking of the world, not so much by writings but by a practical flesh and blood example of what could be achieved. It was because of this that the poet Rabindranath Tagore called him 'Great Soul'.

12.7 'Satyagraha': No Violent Revenge for Amritsar Massacre

In 1915, Gandhi arrived back in India where he organised some local peaceful protests on socio-economic issues in Bihar and Gujarat which encouraged him to believe that 'satyagraha' should be used to achieve Home Rule [22].

In 1919, as I discussed at the opening of this chapter, the British troops opened fire on a demonstration of unarmed Indians amassed in Amritsar to protest against the Rowlatt Acts that allowed the British to imprison them without trial. The demonstration was illegal, but the Indians may not have been aware of it. The British troops, led by General Dyer, opened fire on the unarmed crowd repeatedly, killing 379 persons and injuring about 1137 more. The general had already angered the Indians by ordering all the men who wanted to use a certain road to crawl along it on all fours because an Anglican missionary had recently been attacked on it. The Indians' fury at their treatment by the British reached boiling point throughout the country. The Nobel prize-winning Indian poet, Rabindranath Tagore, who had been knighted by Britain, angrily renounced his knighthood in disgust at the massacre.

Gandhi took the lead of the Indian nationalist movement and of its vehicle, the Indian National Congress which was demanding Home Rule. In contrast to the ugly responses of those around him he urged the Indians not to use violence against the British, not be enslaved by hatred of the imperialists. Here Gandhi was showing forgiveness by restraining the desire to avenge. But he also had the difficult task not of reconciliation with the enemy but of driving it out of India. Therefore he asked his fellow countrymen to follow him by practising 'satyagraha' by peaceful non-cooperation in order to convert the British to his cause and get them to leave.

At this time, not all Indians agreed with Gandhi's methods and wanted revenge for the Amritsar massacre, such as Udham Singh, who later assassinated Michael O'Dwyer, the Lieutenant General of the Punjab. The fact that Singh's action had considerable support in India shows the difficulty of Gandhi's task.

It was indeed Gandhi's great achievement to persuade so many Indians against the easier path of violence and to conduct their protests in a dignified peaceful way so that they did not harm the enemy. The British government never realised how fortunate they were to be opposed by such a peace-loving, non-vengeful nationalist leader. Instead, the British foolishly jailed him for alleged conspiracy to overthrow their government in India. He was sent to prison in 1922 for 6 years but released in

1924 after an operation for appendicitis. Meanwhile, his followers had given up on his non-cooperation movement and Hindus and Muslims were fighting each other. Gandhi fasted until they stopped.

In 1925, Gandhi was elected president of the Indian National Congress. He campaigned against the British in India, and in addition against child marriages, against the treatment of the Untouchables and for village democracies together with a simple life based on home-made products.

12.8 No Revenge for Britain's Crushing the Salt March

In 1929, the Indian National Congress declared that complete independence, not just Home Rule, was its goal. As part of their non-cooperation movement, Congress members decided not to pay taxes to the British. The Salt Tax, imposed by the British in the nineteenth century had always been deeply resented by the Indians. Therefore, in March 1930, Gandhi led his famous Salt March against the tax. After over a month's walking, joined by thousands of Indians, he reached the sea at Dandi. There he gathered a handful for evaporated salt and held it symbolically aloft in defiance of the British Empire. His supporters followed him and 'salt madness' swept India as contraband salt was made. Hundreds of Indians were imprisoned, including him. Nothing daunted he asked his son to organise a march on the Dharansana salt works. Two and a half thousand Indians, in wave after wave, marched to the works to be confronted by hundreds of policemen who beat them bloodily, killing two of them. Most leaders of independence struggles at this point would have been calling for revenge. But Gandhi did not. As usual he and his supporters won the moral argument since they had not sunk to using violence as had the British: international respect for Gandhi increased.

Because of the outcry on Gandhi's behalf the British had to release him and furthermore invited him to the Second Round Table conference in London in 1931 on the constitutional future of India. However, the conference failed partly owing to the religious and social divisions among the Indians. In Britain Gandhi wanted to win over the British people rather than the government and this he certainly did. Everywhere he went he was mobbed by admiring crowds, although Winston Churchill dismissively referred to him as 'posing as a fakir. . .striding half-naked up the steps of the Viceregal Palace' [23].

In 1934 Gandhi resigned his seat in Congress and political leadership was now taken over by Jawaharlal Nehru. Gandhi travelled around India like a holy man looking at social ills. He published a newspaper, 'Harijan', commenting on social and economic problems and also explaining the spiritual dimension of 'satyagraha'.

12.9 'Satyagraha': A Spiritual Discipline Against Revenge

For Gandhi the 'satyagraha' the protester aimed at converting, not coercing, the oppressor by example:

'. . .it is never the intention of a Satyagrahi to embarrass the wrongdoer. The appeal is never to his fear: it is, must be, always to his heart. The Satyagrahi's object is to convert, not to coerce, the wrongdoer. He should avoid artificiality in all his doings. He acts naturally and from inward conviction' [24].

Gandhi's methods did convert many British people to support his cause although not, as we have seen, Winston Churchill.

In 'Harijan' Gandhi explained the rules for those who wanted to participate in his movement and thus be 'satyagrahi'. It is obvious that by these rules revenge is not possible:

'1. He must have a living faith in God, for He is his only Rock.

2. He must believe in truth and non-violence as his creed and therefore have faith in the inherent goodness of human nature which he expects to evoke by his truth and love expressed through his suffering.

3. He must be living a chaste life and be ready and willing for the sake of his cause to give up his life and his possessions' [25].

In addition, he thought that fasting was important to eliminate 'self' in order to 'listen to the voice of God'. Gandhi also believed in the importance of prayer:

'. . . in all my trials. . .I can say God saved me. When every hope is gone, 'when helpers fail and comforts flee,' I find that help arrives somehow, from I know not where. Supplication, worship, prayer are no superstition. . .I have not the slightest doubt that prayer is an unfailing means of cleansing the heart of passions. But it must be combined with the utmost humility' [26]. (The quotation 'when helpers fail and comforts flee' is from Gandhi's favourite hymn 'Abide With Me'.)

Gandhi's process of 'Satyagraha' was, therefore, a long, inward process of deep spiritual and moral discipline which trained a person to go through life never even contemplating using violence or hating one's enemy. For some people forgiveness is a lengthy internal process after they have been wronged. Gandhi's was a process whereby any ideas of revenge or hatred are ruled out by 'truth and love' even before a wrong has been done.

Gandhi was exceptional in exemplifying this behaviour. Indeed, Einstein once said of Gandhi:

'Generations to come, it may be, will scarcely believe that such a one as this ever in flesh and blood walked upon this earth' [27].

12.10 Second World War–India's Independence–Gandhi's Death

Gandhi had done the groundwork for Indian independence, making the British realise that they would have to cede it, but it was the Second World War that acted as a catalyst and forced them to leave India.

Gandhi and the Indian National Congress opposed Britain's declaring war on Nazi Germany about which they had not been consulted. Gandhi would have opposed the violence of war anyway. In 1942, he began a 'Quit India' campaign against the British for which they imprisoned him. In contrast, Jinnah and the Muslim League supported Britain's war effort so that their demand for a Muslim state was sympathetically received.

After the war Britain's coffers were drained. It could no longer afford to control the growing nationalist movement in India. Moreover, the Labour party with its decolonisation policy had come to power in Britain and the USA was pressing for India's independence. This was granted in 1947, when Lord Mountbatten went out to Indian and swiftly divided it into two states, India and Pakistan. A bloody conflict between the Hindus and the Muslims then broke out as they fled to the countries where the majority of the population was of their religion. Gandhi fasted for peace which was eventually restored. However, in 1948, Gandhi's life was ironically ended by violence. He was shot by a Hindu fanatic who disagreed with the creation of Muslim Pakistan.

12.11 Gandhi's Achievements

Gandhi played a vital role in India's independence for which the Second World War was only the catalyst. His non-violent methods of protest and rejection of revenge, hatred, and bitterness towards the British saved many lives, British as well as Indian. Gandhi was exceptional in exemplifying this behaviour. Later, out of admiration for his outstanding example, some of the most distinguished leaders of resistance movements have adopted his form of protest. Among them have been Martin Luther King and the civil rights movement in the USA, Nelson Mandela and the early resistance movement to apartheid in South Africa (before civil resistance itself was made a criminal offence), Chief Albert Luthuli, the anti-apartheid activist who won the Nobel Prize for peace in 1960, Aung San Suu Kyi and the opposition to the of Burmese dictatorship, Vaclav Havel and the Czech Velvet Revolution, and many more.

Gandhi may not have said an 'eye for an eye will make the whole world blind' (there is no evidence for this) but his message was certainly a rejection of revenge. The fact that he is often attributed with this saying shows how he is perceived as an essentially forgiving person. His 'satyagraha' was a world-transforming example of what a disciplined human being can rise to in the ugliest of situations. Perhaps the 'inherent goodness of human nature' of which he wrote (see quotation 25) enables others to recognise his nobility and want to emulate it rather than reach for the gun. Gandhi showed that 'turning the other cheek' to one's enemies did not preclude taking non-violent action which could not only be effective and win international respect but could above all save lives.

Forgiveness does not mean toleration of oppression but does mean using the most effective and least lethal means of resistance. Gandhi's methods of non-violent resistance might not work in all situations (as against the Nazis or Japanese Fascists, for example) but in many cases of resistance they are worth trying to save lives. While violent conflicts are taking place in many countries, Gandhi's peaceful methods of protest look particularly superior and civilised. Their appeal to the noblest instincts in humankind is both global and timeless. At the time of writing (2020) the attempts of the Palestinians to resist Israel's occupation has dragged on bloodily for 70 years with revenge seeming to be the default position of both sides. Indeed, al-Qaeda's attack on the USA in 2001, which provoked the USA's vengeful assaults on Afghanistan and Iraq, was inspired by the desire to avenge the fate of the Palestinians. However, some Palestinians have now turned to Gandhi for inspiration. It is, therefore, the issue of Israel and the Palestinians that will be considered in the next chapter.

References

1. *Revolutionary Democracy*, Vol V, No 2, Sept (1999)
2. Anand, Anita, 'The Patient Assassin A True Tale of Massacre, Revenge and the Raj' (London 2019) p.112
3. CRIM 1/1177, Public Record Office, London, p.64
4. *Harijan*, 15 March 1940.
5. Nanda, BR, 'Mahatma Gandhi: A Biography' (New Delhi 1981) p.95
6. CWMG Vol. 32, (9th Aug.1925) p.273 That forgiveness was one of Gandhi's core values has been well-argued by A. Hunter and A. Rigby in their interesting study: 'Gandhi and the virtue of forgiveness.' Gandhi Marg. Vol 30 (4)421–47 (2009)
7. Gandhi, Arun, 'The Gift of Anger' (London 2017) p.22
8. Gandhi, M.K. *Young India* 12th August 1926
9. Gandhi, M.K. *Young India* 11th August 1920
10. Gandhi, Arun, op.cit. p.23
11. Ibid p.20
12. Ibid p.8
13. Brown, Judith M, p44 'Gandhi and Civilian Resistance in India 1917-47', in Roberts, Adam and Ash, Timothy Garton, 'Civil Resistance and Power Politics' (Oxford 2009) p.44
14. Gandhi, M.K. 'An Autobiography', (London 2001), p.76–78
15. Gandhi, M.K. 'Hind Swaraj', at: http://www.mkgganhi.org/swarajya/ch017.htm, 'Passive Resistance' p.2
16. Ibid p.4
17. Nanda, op.cit., p.67
18. Ibid p.95
19. Parel, Anthony J, 'Gandhi and Tolstoy', in Mathai, M.P, 'Meditations on Gandhi', (New Delhi 2002) p.97

20. Tolstoy, Leo, 'Letter to a Hindoo', (Natal 1910 reprint) p.3
21. Ibid p.4
22. Brown, op.cit. p.44
23. '*The Times*', July 27th 2013, *Saturday Review*, p.12
24. Gandhi, M.K. '*Harijan*', p.64
25. Ibid p.64
26. Gandhi, M.K., 'An Autobiography', (London 2001), p.80
27. Nanda, op.cit. p.7

Chapter 13
Israel and the Palestinians: The Futility of Violent Revenge

On 12 June 2014, three Israeli students at 'yeshivas' (religious schools) on the West Bank were kidnapped by some Palestinians who were not members of Hamas which was nevertheless blamed for the deaths. Some Israeli extremists promptly kidnapped and burned alive a Palestinian teenager in revenge, to the outrage of the Palestinians. Meanwhile, Israel, searching for the murderers of the three Israelis, arrested hundreds of Hamas officials in the West Bank and closed their offices. In Gaza, militants began firing rockets at Israel which, on 8th July, responded by launching 'Operation Protective Edge'. This involved the disproportionate and indiscriminate shelling of buildings in Gaza including many private homes, as the Israeli Defence Force claimed that rockets were being fired from them or kept there.

Thus, began yet another cycle of revenge attacks between Israel and the Palestinians resulting in unnecessary deaths and destruction. Ever since its foundation in 1948, Israel and the Palestinians have been in a state of intermittent conflict over land which each side believes is rightfully theirs. Much of the time has been wasted on violent vengefulness rather than constructive actions.

It is perhaps ironic that the region that produced Jesus Christ should be in such need of his teaching on the importance of forgiveness. Both a Mahatma Gandhi and a Robert Schuman are needed here: a Gandhi to guide the Palestinians on how to resist Israel's occupation non-violently and a Schuman, perhaps with a love of both Israeli and Arab cultures, to encourage forgiveness and economic cooperation between Israel and its Arab neighbours, including the Palestinians who should be given their own state, unless they agree to a unitary state solution with Israel.

13.1 Brief Background

When in November 1947, the UN voted to partition Palestine, creating a Jewish state, an Arab state and a UN administered Jerusalem, the Jews accepted the plan but the Arabs did not, believing it to be unfair as it allocated 56% of its land to the Jews

A. Wells, *The Importance of Forgiveness and the Futility of Revenge*, Contributions to International Relations, https://doi.org/10.1007/978-3-030-87552-7_13

who comprised only a third of its population. Conflict intensified between the Arabs and Jews in Palestine, ending with the Jews triumphing.

13.2 Palestinians Forced to Leave Homes

On 14 May 1948, when the British mandate expired, Israel declared its independence. The next day neighbouring Arab states attacked Israel on behalf of the Palestinians. As the Arabs had less troops, were disunited and incompetent, they lost to Israel. In 1949, when the UN secured armistice agreements between Israel and Egypt and the Arab states, almost half of the Palestinian Arabs, that is 725,000 people, had become refugees. This was the result partly of force as well as of fear. In the 1980s, the research of Israeli historians such as Benny Morris demonstrated that many Palestinian villagers had been forced out of their homes by the Israeli high command while others fled on learning of Israeli attacks [1]. Some of the Palestinians fled to other Arab countries, others to the unconquered areas of Palestine, the West Bank and the Gaza Strip which came under the control of Jordan and Egypt, respectively. Palestine disappeared, but not in the minds of the Palestinians who call the events at this time 'al-Nakba', or 'the disaster', while the Israelis call it the 'war of independence'. Although the UN recommended that the refugees who wished to return to their homes and live in peace with their neighbours should be permitted to do so, Israel would not allow this, seizing the land and property of the Palestinian refugees. For their part, the Arab states refused to recognise Israel which, although extending its territory, felt the need to remain on a war footing, constantly feeling vulnerable.

13.3 Palestinian Exodus 1967–UN Resolution 242

There then followed three wars with the Arab states. After the last, the 'Six Day War' in 1967, Israel greatly extended its borders, taking control of the Sinai Peninsula from Egypt, the Golan Heights from Syria, a strip of land on the Jordanian frontier, together with the territories populated with Palestinian refugees: the West Bank, the Gaza Strip, and East Jerusalem which became known as the Occupied Territories. The UN, therefore, tried to resolve the situation. In November 1967, the Security Council agreed on its Resolution 242 which basically proposed 'land for peace': that Israel would get peace in exchange for the Arab lands it had taken. However, the Resolution still has not been implemented. After 1967, thousands of Israelis went to settle in the Occupied Territories, often bulldozing the homes of the Palestinians and taking away their lands. To make matters worse, many Palestinian farmers found they could no longer make a living through farming as they were denied the subsidies enjoyed by Israeli farmers who flooded the Palestinian market with their cheap agricultural produce. Furthermore, restrictions on land-use and access to the

Israeli markets destroyed the livelihoods of the Palestinian farmers who were often forced to travel each day to take low-paid manual jobs in Israel.

13.4 Palestinian Revenge for 1967: 9/11

After the Israeli military occupation of the West Bank in 1967, many Palestinians left to live as refugees in Jordan. Among them was one Abdullah Azzam who later became a distinguished Islamic scholar. He went to Afghanistan where he set up al-Qaeda with Osama bin Laden and no doubt helped to feed his hatred of the USA as a supporter of Israel. Azzam's desire for vengeance was realised eventually in the 9/11 attack on the USA [2].

13.5 The PLO

In 1964, the Palestine Liberation Organisation (PLO) had been formed from the guerrilla groups which had been attacking Israel since its foundation. Dominated by the Al-Fatah group led by Yasser Arafat, the PLO refused to recognise Israel because the latter would not recognise the Palestinians' right to their own state. After the failure of the Arab states to defeat Israel in 1967, the Palestine Liberation Organisation committed itself to armed struggle, resulting in attacks on Israeli targets throughout the world.

13.6 Mossad

Israel responded with revenge assassinations by its national intelligence agency, Mossad, which only increased Palestinian hostility and retaliatory actions. In 1972, for example, during the Olympic Games held in Munich, a Palestinian terrorist organisation, Black September, took hostage 11 Israeli athletes, demanding that Israel releases hundreds of Palestinian prisoners. Tragically, nine of the Israelis were killed as the authorities tried to free them. In revenge, during the following years, Israel's Mossad tracked down and assassinated 16 members of Black September involved in the Munich killings. No good came of these cold blooded-killings [3].

13.7 Hezbollah, Hamas

The likelihood of the cycle of violence ending was diminished further after the Iranian Revolution in 1979 when Iran gave financial support to two pro-Palestinian organisations. The first was the Shia Islamist Hezbollah, ('Party of Allah'), which was founded in 1982 when it helped drive Israeli forces from Lebanon where it is based and from where it has periodically launched rocket attacks on Israel. The second was the Sunni Islamist Hamas, whose name is an Arabic acronym for 'The Islamic Resistance Movement' and was founded in 1988. Both Hezbollah and Hamas have gained considerable popular support partly because they provide the Palestinians with free medical care, education, and social services.

13.8 The First Intifada/Israel's Vengeful Response/Hamas' Goal

In 1987, after 20 years of Israeli oppression, including extrajudicial killings, mass detentions, house demolitions, and forced relocations, Palestinians rose up in the 'Intifada' (Arabic for 'shaking off') against Israel's rule in the Occupied Territories (The actual event triggering the Intifada was the colliding of an Israeli army truck with a civilian car, killing four Palestinians). Mainly young Palestinians pelted armed Israeli patrols with stones and petrol bombs. Arab workers went on strike and Arab traders closed their businesses. The Israeli army was sent in to restore order, but it was not until 1991 that the Intifada died down.

Israel acted often vengefully and brutally against the protestors. This no doubt encouraged Hamas, when it drew up its charter in 1988, to retaliate in the same spirit by making the destruction of Israel its goal. This has remained a stumbling block regarding negotiations between Israel and Hamas ever since. Had Israel responded with more compassion and forgiveness, Hamas's constitution may well have been different.

13.9 Gandhi-Style Resistance on the West Bank During the Intifada

Nevertheless, at this time, some Palestinians on the West Bank rose above the desire for violent revenge. In 1989, villagers in Beit Sahour (where most of the population is Christian) engaged in 6 weeks of civil disobedience, publicly burning their Israeli identity cards and refusing to pay taxes to the Israeli authorities. One of the leaders of civil disobedience at this time was Mubarak Awad, a Palestinian Christian youth worker and therapist, originally from the USA, who had studied the writings of Gandhi, Martin Luther King, and Gene Sharp, translated them into Arabic and left them on village noticeboards and at bus stops across the West Bank, encouraging Palestinians to resist the Israeli occupation non-violently. He urged them to refuse to carry their Israeli identity cards, defy curfews and the law against flying Palestinian flags. He also promoted the civil rights movement of mass arrest, resulting in thousands of Palestinians filling the jails. Awad believed that by involving the whole population in non-violent resistance to the Israeli army, the latter would realise the harm it was doing to the Palestinian people more than if facing armed attacks. In 1988, Awad was deported from Israel and went to the USA [4]. Unfortunately, much of the civil disobedience of the Palestinians was under-reported internationally by the mass media which concentrated on the violence, no doubt because it was more dramatic. Peaceful resistance needs to be widely reported to arouse sympathy for the cause. Nevertheless, as the media photographed the vindictiveness of the Israeli soldiers beating children and firing on crowds of young Palestinians, Israel lost the support of world opinion which swung in favour of the Palestinians.

In addition to the non-violent resistance there was another faint ray of hope for peace when, in 1988, the PLO announced the independent state of Palestine and recognised Israel's right to exist. However, Israel treated this with cynicism. Indeed, the Israeli author David Grossman recalls being sacked by Israel's national broadcasting service for refusing to bury the news of the PLO'S announcement [5]. Meanwhile, Israel and the USA continued to regard the PLO as a terrorist organisation.

13.10 Likud

Israel's harsh policy towards the Palestinians has usually been determined by Likud, one of the two main political parties, the other being the Labour party. Most members of Likud hold that the Occupied Territories were part of Biblical Israel and that the Israelis have a right to build settlements there. Likud has been unforgiving of Palestinian violence, and rigid in its stance. This attitude has always been a major impediment to peace.

13.11 The Oslo Peace Accords 1993

In contrast, the Israeli Labour party has constantly been more open to negotiations with the Palestinians. In 1992, it came to power, led by the courageous Yitzhak Rabin, after Likud had been governing Israel for most of the 1980s. Greatly helped by skilful Norwegian and American diplomacy, Rabin agreed to negotiate the Oslo Peace Accords which were signed in the USA by Rabin and Arafat in September 1993. This was the first official agreement between Israel and the PLO and was to be the framework whereby Israel traded 'land for peace'. Israel recognised the PLO as Palestine's official representative, while the PLO recognised Israel's right to exist and renounced the use of violence. Both sides agreed to Palestinian self-rule in Gaza and the Jericho area of the West Bank by 2000.

13.12 Peace Hopes Fade as Revenge Cycle Resumes

However, the leaders of Likud together with rabbis of the religious right vehemently opposed what they saw as a renouncing of lands to which Israel had a Biblical right. In 1995, an ultra-nationalist Israeli student, who espoused this view, shot and killed Rabin as he left a rally in support of the Oslo Peace Accords. Shimon Peres took over as prime minister and called for elections the following May.

Unfortunately, the familiar cycle of revenge between the Palestinians and Israelis then resumed. On January 5 1996, Shin Bet (the Israeli Security Agency) killed Hamas's chief bomb maker, Yahya Ayyash, with a booby-trapped mobile phone [6]. He was a Palestinian, who was known as 'the Engineer' and who, as a member of the Qassam Brigades (an armed wing of Hamas), had been responsible for organising bombing attacks on Israel. In revenge for his death, the next month Muslim suicide bombers detonated pipe bombs in Jerusalem and Ashkelon, killing 25 people and wounding 77. A fax sent from 'the cells of Martyr Engineer Ayyash' declared that the bombings came as a 'promise to the blood of the Engineer, who fell 50 days ago' [7].

The bombings no doubt influenced the result of the general election in the following May when Benjamin Netanyahu came to power. The Israelis have usually voted for Likud after violent attacks by the Palestinians [8], despite the fact that the use of military force against the Palestinians does not give Israel the security it longs for but only perpetuates the tragic cycle of vengeance. After this the Oslo peace process lost its momentum.

While one might blame Hamas for the bombings that damaged the peace process it is also clear that Israel need not have killed Ayyash and should have been aware that this would trigger revenge killings on the part of Hamas.

Since 1996, Israel has had only one other Labour government. This was led by Ehud Barak from 1999 to 2001. He offered generous concessions to Arafat. But the latter, probably thinking the new Palestinian state would be divided by Israeli bypass and checkpoints, rejected his offer, especially as the settlement building had continued in the Occupied Territories.

13.13 The Problem of the Smaller Parties: Hard Line and Unforgiving

The situation has been aggravated by the fact that Likud is usually supported in government by small ultra-nationalist parties that push it to take an even harder line towards the Palestinians. Forgiveness and compromise are far from the thinking of these nationalist parties which can and often do impede any peace settlement between Israel and the Palestinians. The Israeli system of proportional representation involves a low electoral threshold which, although raised from 2% to 3.2.5% in 2014, is still too low. It ensures that the governments in Israel will always consist of coalitions involving the smaller parties which can threaten to bring the government down if their demands are not met. This is at the heart of Israel's problems with the Palestinians and its security.

In the Likud government that won the 2009 election, for example, Avigdor Lieberman had considerable influence. He founded and led the Yisrael Beiteinu party, which is supported by Soviet immigrants in Israel (of whom he is one) and takes a hard line towards the Palestinians. He was both Minister of Foreign Affairs and one of the four Deputy Prime Ministers which meant he was central to policy making. During the conflict in Gaza in 2014, Lieberman was pushing Netanyahu to be even harder on the Palestinians, arguing during the ceasefire that Hamas must be defeated, even at the cost of an escalation of the war [9].

Clearly Israel needs to raise its electoral threshold to limit the power of the smaller parties which are usually the most unforgiving and uncompromising, in order to increase the likelihood of peace with the Palestinians.

13.14 Ariel Sharon

A step towards ending the conflict then came from an unexpected quarter, showing that even the most hard line politicians can change their minds.

In 2002 Likud, led by Ariel Sharon came to power in coalition with ten other parties. Sharon at first seemed a major threat to peace. He had triggered the Second Intifada in 2000 by claiming the Temple Mount complex, containing the al-Aqsa Mosque, would always be controlled by Israel. The Second Intifada then erupted and, unlike the first one, involved suicide bombing attacks on Israel.

In order to stop the violence, the USA, EU, UN, and Russia had formed themselves into the 'Quartet Powers' and agreed on the 'road map for peace' (a two-state solution) to settle the Israeli–Palestinian problem. However, in 2002, Sharon disrupted the peace process by building a 'separation wall' on the West Bank to prevent Palestinian terrorists from entering Israel. The 'wall' separates some Palestinians from their agricultural land and from the rest of their people on the West Bank.

13.15 Sharon's Surprise

Then very surprisingly, in 2005, Ariel Sharon took one of the most courageous and dramatic actions in the whole peace process when he withdrew all the Israeli settlements from the Gaza Strip and four from the West Bank, despite the bitter opposition of his Likud party. Altogether about 8000 Israelis were forced to leave the Occupied Territories, while Israel remained in control of most of Gaza's land borders, territorial waters, and land space. Moreover, there were still nearly 400,000 Israeli settlers living on the West Bank where 2 million Palestinians also lived.

13.16 Hamas in Power, Israel's Blockade of Gaza (2007)

Unfortunately, Israel had left concessions too late, since the Islamic militant Hamas had now developed its electoral strength in Gaza. In 2006, Hamas won the Palestinian Authority legislative elections, refusing to recognise Israel and to eschew violence. Hamas foolishly did not return the generosity of Sharon's government with a similar gesture of its own, such as recognising Israel and thus missed a great opportunity for renewed negotiations.

At first Hamas and Fatah formed the Palestinian Authority national unity government. But in 2007, claiming Israel and the USA were bolstering Fatah against it, Hamas took control of the Gaza Strip, seized government institutions, and replaced Fatah with its own officials. Fatah retained control of the Palestinian National Authority in the West Bank.

Israel responded with a land, sea, and air blockade of Gaza, only allowing limited humanitarian aid into it. Israel claimed this was necessary to stop Hamas from obtaining more weapons to fire at Israel. Egypt also sealed its border to the Palestinians who nevertheless dug tunnels to aid the passage of supplies.

13.17 Gaza Under Siege

At the time of writing (2021) Israel's blockade of Gaza is continuing. As a result, the Palestinians' living conditions have been steadily worsening as they struggle to find work, feed their families, and provide them with drinkable water.

Power cuts and fuel shortages have caused hazardous hospital operations, while some Palestinians have resorted to dangerous eating and cooking methods which have resulted in their suffering from serious burns [10].

Because of the Israelis' blockade on the Palestinians in Gaza, hemming them in by land, sea, and air, in 2010, the then British Prime Minister, David Cameron, called it a 'prison camp' [11].

When, in their frustration, the Palestinians periodically have fired missiles such as rockets from Gaza into Israel they have been met with a disproportionate response of bombing from the Israelis. Moreover, the blockade meant that the Palestinians could not obtain the construction materials needed to rebuild their homes, public buildings, and facilities destroyed by Israel. Thus, Israel has vindictively imposed a collective punishment on the innocent majority of Palestinians for the sins of a violent few. In Gaza, half of the suffering population are children. It is they who are being punished by Israel.

By 2010, there were about 1.5 million Palestinians living in the Gaza Strip and about 2 million on the West Bank and in East Jerusalem [12]. The Palestinians cannot freely leave these Occupied Territories nor move easily between them for work, medical treatment, or visiting relatives as they need permits for doing so and have to pass through checkpoints. This results in humiliation and frustration. Moreover, they can be stopped, searched, and arrested at any time.

Furthermore, there is scant work available in the Territories and therefore little hope of a prosperous future for the young people. In addition, the Palestinians are without adequate medical, educational, or social services and sometimes lack even food, clean water, and proper sanitation. Israel actually draws off water from Palestinian aquifers beneath Gaza and the West Bank, leaving an inadequate supply for the Arabs.

13.18 The Problem of Hamas

In March 2009, Netanyahu became prime minister again and in June of that year announced for the first time that he would accept a Palestinian state. However, he simultaneously rejected a settlement freeze which is the main Israeli requirement under the 'road map'. He claimed he had to meet the needs of the 'natural growth' of the population, and thereby showed that peace was unlikely while he was in power [13].

Since then, Israel's refusal and that of the Quartet (the USA, EU, UN, and Russia), to attempt to negotiate with Hamas has resulted in more violence. Unfortunately, the three members of the Quartet other than Russia have three principles with which a negotiating partner has to comply before joining the Middle East peace talks. They are the recognition of Israel, the renunciation of violence, and adherence to previous diplomatic agreements (although most of them were never concluded). Russia does not agree with this and does not designate Hamas as a terrorist organisation. Moreover, it has tried to get it to recognise Israel and renounce violence [14].

Had it been invited to the negotiations, Hamas might have altered its stance, especially as its leadership is not a monolithic bloc and the people in it change. Moreover, it is here that forgiveness and empathy is important. As earlier mentioned, Hamas's charter was drawn up in 1988 during the First Intifada and naturally the organisation took a hard line of seeming intransigence. However, the charter is not written in stone. It is surely important to extend the hand of friendship and not raise the fist of hostility in attempting to get Hamas leaders to reconsider their stance in exchange for concessions.

The urgent need for Israel and Hamas to begin to talk in the spirit of forgiveness was shown in June 2014 when the cycle of bloody revenge broke out again between Israel and the Palestinians. By the end of the conflict in August of that year the death toll according to the UN had risen to 2104 Palestinians killed, including 1462 civilians, of whom 495 were children and 253 women, while 66 Israeli soldiers, 6 Israeli citizens, and a Thai national also lost their lives [15]. In addition, thousands of houses, hospitals, and clinics were destroyed and thousands of Palestinians made homeless. The situation was made worse by the fact that, as mentioned earlier, the blockade prevented the necessary construction materials into Gaza. During the war Hamas' rockets generally missed their targets or were intercepted by Israel's defence system, the American-funded 'Iron Dome' so that Israel was clearly overreacting although Hamas was unnecessarily provoking it.

In 2015, the Israeli people elected again to office the Likud Party led by Benjamin Netanyahu, probably because they wanted their government to take a hard line with the Palestinians, Hamas in particular. Nevertheless, in October 2017, there was some hope that Hamas's policy and also life in the Gaza strip would change as the two main Palestinian factions, Fatah and Hamas signed a deal brokered by Egypt to end the rivalry and ease life in Gaza. Hamas agreed to relinquish sole control of Gaza and sit in a unity government alongside the secular Fatah which is based on the West Bank.

However, any hope of peace was soon crushed the next year. In March 2018, the Israelis shot dead 16 Palestinians who were protesting, mostly non-violently near Gaza's border with Israel. Thousands of Palestinians flooded onto the streets in the Gaza strip for the funerals, demanding revenge [16]. The protests continued, culminating, on May 14th 2018, the 70th anniversary of the founding of Israel, with a massive march to the border/barrier with Israel. The Gazans were protesting against the USA's moving its embassy from Tel Aviv to Jerusalem, and were commemorating the 70th anniversary of the Palestinians' 'Nakba' or disaster, when they lost their homeland to Israel. They also demanded the right of Palestinians to return to their country.

The march was mainly by young Palestinians who were unarmed although some threw stones and Molotov cocktails, while others pushed burning tyres to the wire fence. But the Israeli army opened fire, killing 58 Palestinians and injuring over 2700 more. Israel claimed the soldiers felt threatened and blamed Hamas for organising the protest. Whatever, the truth of this Israel was condemned by many countries for its reaction which seemed vengeful and disproportionate. It is clear that Israel will have to forgive its enemy Hamas for its actions and words against it. It will have to welcome Hamas into peace talks. Hamas for its part will have to recognise the state of Israel and discourage the Palestinians from taking reprisals. Rather than take revenge for the past, both sides should see the benefits in forgiving each other and beginning negotiations to ensure a peaceful future for the generations to come.

13.19 The West Bank Under the Palestinian National Authority: Non-violent Protest

Israel under Netanyahu continued to build settlements on the West Bank (which is under the Palestinian National Authority controlled by Fatah), but some Palestinians showed a positive way forward by not retaliating with violence. Since 2004, in the Palestinian village of Bilin on the West Bank, Palestinians have been gathering to protest peacefully at the Israeli barricade that cuts across their land [17]. Sometimes boys do throw stones and the Israeli military fires teargas in response. A few people have been killed and more injured but generally the protest is non-violent. In this way the Israeli military have to look at and hear the protests of the non-combatant Palestinian people whose lives Israel is harming. In 2006, this practice was adopted by another village, Nilin, and there have been attempts to extend it further [18]. This is surely the way forward to win support for negotiations internationally and from the Israelis, some of whom feel they gave 'land for bombs' in Gaza. But before these negotiations take place the Palestinians may need to take further measures. Forgiveness means giving up violent revenge but it also allows for taking up peaceful constructive action against the enemy where pressure is needed. Such non-violent actions will now be considered since they should depress the desire for revenge.

13.20 The Way Forward

Israel's defiance of international law and opinion in continuing to build settlements on the West Bank is largely due to the financial and military backing of the USA. In January 2020, President Trump revealed a peace plan whereby Israel would be allowed to 'incorporate' its settlements on the West Bank. The Palestinians saw this as annexation and destroying their hopes of a Palestinian state comprising the West Bank and the Gaza Strip. However, in August 2020, Israel and the UAE signed a peace agreement whereby Israel agreed to 'suspend' its plans to annex parts of the West Bank. Fortunately, in 2020, Donald Trump lost the presidential election in the USA to Joe Biden and these plans were abandoned.

To counter the USA's support for Israel, the Palestinians should try to build up support for their cause in the USA by buying up or establishing a media outlet that puts over their point of view, such as an American newspaper or television station, or establishing a strong presence using the social media. A boycott of Israeli goods would probably not be as effective owing to the international Jewish presence in commerce.

In addition, the Palestinians could do well to increase the funds of the Jewish lobby 'J Street' in the USA. It might, therefore, become more influential than AIPAC, the American Israel Public Affairs Committee (made up of mainly Jews but some other people such as Christian Zionists) which contributes considerably to the campaigning funds of both Republican and Democrat politicians, greatly influencing Congressional voting and thus determining the USA's strong and largely uncritical support for Israel.

'J Street' is formed by Jews who disagree with the policies of AIPAC, believe in a 'two-state solution' and that Hamas should be brought into the negotiations. It is however short of funds which the Palestinians could greatly increase by getting rich Arabs to contribute generously to it (through third parties in the USA). 'J Street' could then out-lobby AIPAC resulting in the USA forcing Israel to compromise in negotiating with the Palestinians. Furthermore, the Palestinians could try to encourage more Muslims and Arabs (particularly from Palestine) in the USA to enter Congress and fight for the Palestinian people from there.

Al-Qaeda's attack on the USA on 11th September 2001 was due to America's support for Israel, as well as the presence of American troops in Muslim countries. The destruction of the World Trade Centre was an extreme and spectacular example of the long-nursed desire for revenge [19] that many Palestinians shared, as was shown by reports that they were celebrating the news on the West Bank, although the PLO condemned the attack [20]. However, the destruction of the twin towers achieved nothing for the Palestinian cause. The money could have been better spent on building up constructive support for the Palestinians in the USA using the methods considered above. Such funds should in future be so used. At the same it is in the USA's best interests to focus on creating a just and lasting peace settlement for Israel and the Palestinians. With such a settlement, America's own security is intrinsically linked.

Whether ultimately the solution to the conflict between Israel and the Palestinians lies in a 'two state' or unitary solution, it is clear that both the Israelis and the Palestinians must stop retaliating with violence and realise their future lies in negotiations and forgiveness of the harm they have done to each other. Hatred and a desire for revenge are inimical to the creativity and compromise needed for successful peace negotiations. While forgiveness is not stressed in Judaism or Islam as much as in Christianity it should not be beyond the comprehension of the Israelis and Palestinians that it is their interests to demonstrate it.

It is now time for Israel to show the magnanimity and nobility of gesture that is fitting for a people that want to be seen as 'chosen' to be a moral example to the world. If the Palestinians were not so intermittently violent, there would not be an opportunity for Israel to show that it can forgive and rise above the desire merely to retaliate. Perhaps more Jews, especially rabbis, internationally will call for Israel to lift the blockade on Gaza, stop building settlements on the West Bank, and negotiate generously with the Palestinians. Perhaps the voice of the Old Testament prophets, through the rabbis, will be heard again rebuking Israel for its behaviour.

Meanwhile, Christians in other countries could ask American Christians to lobby their government to put pressure on Israel to negotiate with the Palestinians and stop its expansion. Muslims worldwide could also lobby the Palestinians against using violence and understand the historic causes of Israel's insecurity.

In addition, more countries could recognise Palestine as a state and support Palestine's application to the International Criminal Court for it to investigate Israel's occupation.

Moreover, Israel could look to the future and consider, as did Robert Schuman with the age-old enemies of Germany and France, establishing a sort of common market with the Palestinians and the surrounding Arab states (most of which have been officially boycotting trade with Israel since 1945). The way to developing prosperity in this region lies in peace and cooperation.

Above all Israel and the Palestinians need outstanding leaders, of the calibre of Robert Schuman, Mahatma Gandhi, or Nelson Mandela to lead their peoples into the ways of peace and mutual forgiveness. However, all three men were profoundly influenced, as I have attempted to show in this book, by the teachings and example of Jesus Christ. It is this that the peoples of the region that produced him have ignored at a colossal cost to themselves.

Postscript: There could be no better illustration of the futility of revenge than that of the conflict which erupted in May 2021 between the Palestinians and Israel. It began over the possible eviction of Palestinians, after a lengthy legal process, from their homes in East Jerusalem where their families have lived for generations. To the Palestinians this symbolised Israel's gradual encroachment on Palestinians lands, preventing, perhaps, the two-state solution from being practicable. Hamas rained rockets down indiscriminately on Israel which was largely protected by its Iron Dome defence. Israel retaliated by blowing up not only alleged Hamas buildings but also Palestinian homes. After 11 days of conflict a ceasefire was negotiated by Egypt. The death toll was 219 people in Gaza of which at least 63 were children. Of the 10 people killed in Israel 2 children were among the dead. For this high price nothing was clearly gained by either side. It is to be hoped that at least the international community will feel prompted to call for peace talks with more urgency.

References

1. Morris, Benny 'The Birth of the Palestinian Refugee Problem 1947-9' Cambridge (1988)
2. Halliday, Fred, 'Two Hours the Shook the World' (London 2002) p234, for Azzam's role see Audrey Wells, 'The Rule of Reverse Results' (London 2016) p43
3. www.bbb.co.uk, Shalev, Noam, 'The hunt for Black September' 24 January 2006
4. Shahid, Waleed, Lessons in NonViolent Palestinian Resistance From the First Intifada', inthesetimes.com/article/palestine-israel-nonviolence (26 October 2015)
5. Cooke, Rachel, 'David Grossman 'I cannot afford the luxury of despair." *The Guardian* (29 August 2010)
6. Cockburn, Patrick, 'How the Phone Bomb Was Set Up', *The Independent* 9 January 1996
7. Schememann, Serge, 'Bombings in Israel' *The New York Times* 26 February 1996
8. Professor Colin Schindler of SOAS, London University, Guest Lecture at University of Notre Dame (London) 1 December 2011
9. www.theguardian.com/world/2014/aug/13/gaza-conflict
10. Baroness Morris of Bolton, Hansard, House of Lords, 27 2014; Vol 751, c.978-80
11. *The Guardian,* 27 July 2010
12. PLO Information Politics Dept., London
13. www.aljazeera.com/news, 24 May 2009
14. Eke, Steven 'Moscow risks anger over Hamas visit' BBC News 3 March 2006

15. www.bbc.co.uk/news/world-middl-east-28439404, 1 September 2014
16. The Sunday Times, April 1st 2018
17. Garcia-Navarro, Lulu, 'Palestinians Practice Non-Violent Resistance in Bilin,' 29 Dec 2009, NPR transcripts, www.npr.org/templates/story
18. Ibid
19. Halliday, Fred, 'Two Hours the Shook the World' (London 2002) p234
20. *The Times,* 11 September 2001

Chapter 14
Forgiveness and the Irish Conflict

14.1 Home Rule

By the end of the nineteenth century nationalism in Ireland had become widespread and violent in its attempts to throw off the oppressive English yoke. In the 1880s, the leader of the Liberal Party, William Gladstone, became convinced that Home Rule for Ireland was the only way forward. His policy split the Liberals but two Home Rule bills did pass the House of Commons, only to be defeated in the House of Lords. In 1912, Home Rule looked more likely as the powers of the House of Lords had been limited the year before, and the Liberal government needed the Irish Nationalists' votes; but the outbreak of the First World War led to an agreement to postpone the matter until the end of the war.

14.2 The Easter Rising

This was too much for some Irish nationalists who decided to organise an uprising for independence from Britain even though many other Irish were fighting for Britain against Germany. In 1916, a schoolteacher and barrister, Patrick Pearse and James Connolly, a socialist activist, led over 15,000 republicans, the Irish Volunteers, and the Irish Citizen Army in the Easter rising which lasted from 24th to 30th April. Key installations in Dublin were seized and independence was proclaimed from the General Post Office.

Most Dubliners were bemused by the revolt and did not join it. Nevertheless, the British responded with brutal repression, sending a firing gunboat up the River Liffey and thousands of soldiers to crush the rebellion. Over 200 Irish civilians were killed as well as over 60 of the rebels. Fifteen of the leaders of the Rising were rounded up and executed. Connolly was so badly wounded that the British tied him to a chair in order to be able to shoot him. Pearse asked to say farewell to his mother

A. Wells, *The Importance of Forgiveness and the Futility of Revenge*, Contributions to International Relations, https://doi.org/10.1007/978-3-030-87552-7_14

and brother but was refused his request. It is true that the Easter Rising was tainted by an attempt to buy arms from Germany. (Roger Casement, a retired British consul and Irish patriot, tried to arrange this but the ship carrying the weapons was intercepted by the British. Casement was arrested and executed for treason.) Nevertheless, the British foolishly and mercilessly overacted to the revolt with vengeance. The bloody crushing of the Easter Rising enraged the Irish who had previously been apathetic to it. They flocked to join the republican party, Sinn Fein. In the General Election of 1918, Sinn Fein won 73 out of 100 seats with a policy of independence.

14.3 Britain's Vengeance Leads to the Irish Free State

In 1919, Sinn Fein convened its first Dail or parliament and proclaimed the republic of Ireland. The British refused to accept this. Therefore, a violent struggle for Irish independence broke out. This ended in 1921 with negotiations for the independence of Southern Ireland. In 1922, the Irish Free State (which became Eire in 1937) was established in Southern Ireland but the northern six counties where the Protestants were in the majority remained part of the UK.

The Irish Free State would probably never have occurred had Britain not engendered so much hatred and desire to be free from its rule by vindictively bloodily crushing the Easter Rising. Certainly, the Irish generally during the war had been supportive of Britain and were prepared to fight on its behalf themselves.

Britain did not make southern Ireland's independence inevitable but highly probable by its cruel and excessively punitive treatment of the Irish nationalists, shocking their fellow countrymen into a determination to be rid of British rule entirely and forever. Had Britain shown forgiveness and mercy to the rebels this would not have happened.

14.4 Britain Drove the Irish to Support the IRA

Southern Ireland gained independence in 1922, becoming first the Irish Free State then Eire in 1937. It made its laws in accordance with Catholic teachings. The six provinces in the north (Ulster) were dominated by the Protestants who formed 60% of the population and controlled the parliament at Stormont. In Ulster there was a semi-secret Orange Order that was modelled on the Freemasons and was dedicated to maintaining Protestant supremacy. This ensured, through its influence in local government, that the Catholics were discriminated against in jobs and education. Moreover, the fact that owners of more than one house had more than one vote gave the Protestants, usually the house-owners, an even more unfair electoral advantage.

14.5 The Troubles in Northern Ireland

In the late 1960s, the new, educated Catholic middle class organised peaceful civil rights protest marches, but the Stormont government responded with repression rather than reform, using their paramilitary police force, the 'B-Specials'. This resulted in more inter-communal violence as the Catholics turned to the Provisional Irish Republican Army for support. The Protestant Unionists controlled the government and asked Britain to send troops to keep the peace. Britain agreed provided that the Unionist government made reforms. The latter responded with dismantling the 'B-specials' but other reforms were just window dressing.

In 1970, the Conservative Party, led by Edward Heath, came to power at Westminster. The party, bearing the full name of 'The Conservative and Unionist Party', had always been more sympathetic to the Ulster Unionists than had the Labour Party. The Unionist government told Heath and his Cabinet that it would continue with reforms but in order to stop the violence it needed to use the policy of internment without trial. Heath's government foolishly agreed to this, resulting in a wave of arrests. Catholics, appalled at the injustice of the policy, therefore flocked to support the Provisional IRA. Britain, instead of following a forgiving, understanding policy that addressed the grievances of the Catholics, had again driven them to support an independence movement.

On 30th January 1972, a protest march was organised in Derry to demonstrate against internment. The Unionist government banned the march which nevertheless took place. Tragically, British paratroopers shot dead 13 unarmed protestors on what later became known as 'Bloody Sunday'.

14.6 Internment

Faced with the continued unrest, the British government finally suspended the Stormont government and imposed direct rule from London in March 1972. This had certainly not been the intention of the Conservatives when they had come to power at Westminster in 1970, but their policy of internment had resulted in the last thing they had wanted: renewed support for the IRA.

Twenty-five years of inter-communal conflict followed with unnecessary loss of life fuelled by decades of inherited hatred and desire for revenge handed down through families.

14.7 Forgiveness and Reconciliation

But there were a few who pointed the way to forgiveness and reconciliation by refusing to give into feelings of hatred and revenge even when seriously harmed by the enemy. Unfortunately, these were actions by ordinary innocent people caught up in the tragedy, not actions by politicians who could lead the people to peace.

14.8 Gordon Wilson

One man who set an outstanding example of forgiveness was Gordon Wilson. He was a Northern Ireland Protestant who in 1987 immediately forgave the IRA bombers who had just killed his daughter, along with ten other people, by a lethal explosion at a Remembrance Day ceremony in Enniskillen. The Queen later remarked in her Christmas broadcast that he had impressed the whole world with the depth of his forgiveness. The point about Wilson's immediately forgiving the murderers is that he thereby discouraged violent reprisals. Had he delayed such a statement while he ruminated about the matter and discussed it with other people, revenge attacks would probably have taken place. Wilson's was no swift cheap statement, but the agonised costly expression of a man determined to take a stand on what his faith required of him. No doubt he reflected deeply on the event forever afterwards.

14.9 Betty Williams

Earlier an outstanding example of one woman's determination to stop the cycle of revenge occurred in 1976. Betty Williams was a receptionist in Belfast. Her mother was a Catholic and father a Protestant. She joined an anti-violence campaign in the early 1970s headed by a Protestant priest. In August 1976, Betty Williams witnessed the deaths of three children when they were hit by a car whose IRA driver had been shot by a British soldier in return for being fired on. The mother of the three children later committed suicide.

Betty Williams first led a peace march to the graves of the three Maguire children. It was composed of 10,000 Protestants and Catholics but was disrupted by the IRA who accused the protestors of being dupes of the British. The next week she organised a successful march of 35,000 people and then began The Community for Peace People which focussed on creating peace groups composed of former opponents and developing a grassroots peace process. Together with her friend Mairead Corrigan, the aunt of the dead children, Betty Williams received the Nobel Peace for their colossal effort to prevent violent revenge from taking place and to bring the warring sides instead together.

14.10 Father Alec Reid

In mid-1980s Fr Alec Reid, a Catholic priest, became a go-between Sinn Fein and the SDLP in an effort to encourage a peace process, after discussing the matter with Gerry Adams whom he visited in prison. In 1988, he attended a funeral of IRA member when he saw two British soldiers being dragged from their car and lynched by a mob. This had assumed them to be members of the SAS which had recently killed three IRA members in Gibraltar. Fr Reid went to help the soldiers as they lay on the ground, but the soldiers were taken away and shot. However, a chance photo by a journalist of him kneeling besides the soldiers as he administered the last rites shocked the world and helped galvanise the fledgling peace process in which Fr Reid played a courageous pivotal part [1]. Reid later revealed that the blood from one of the soldiers got on to correspondence in his jacket, probably from his hands. In Reid's jacket was a letter for John Hume, the leader of the SDLP, from Sinn Fein's president Gerry Adams, outlining the latter's proposals for a political solution to the Troubles. When he delivered it to Hume's messenger he said 'It's got British blood on it'.

14.11 Colin and Wendy Parry

Since the early 1970s, the IRA carried out attacks both in Northern Ireland and England in order to pressure Britain to withdraw from Northern Ireland. In March 1993 in Warrington, England, two bombs exploded in a crowded shopping centre, killing 3-year-old Jonathan Ball and 12-year-old Tim Parry, while injuring 54 other people. This resulted in public outrage. At the scene of the killings, flowers and wreaths were left, the message accompanying one read 'May God forgive them because we can't' [2]. Some people however could. Showing enormous magnanimity, Colin and Wendy Parry, Tim's parents, set up a Foundation for Peace to educate young people in non-violent resolutions of conflict. This centre remains active today.

14.12 Susan McHugh

Outraged by the deaths of the two children in Warrington, thousands of Irish attended a peace rally in Dublin organised by a housewife, Susan McHugh, who then founded a group called 'Peace 1993' which was another enterprising action by a member of the public calling for peace and reconciliation.

These are four examples of civilians urging forgiveness instead of revenge. Obviously, they could not make the same impact as a leader of the Catholic republicans or the Ulster Unionists would have done, demanding the same noble response.

However, one politician did stand out as a peace campaigner. John Hume, a Catholic, who briefly trained for the priesthood, became the leader of the Social Democratic and Labour Party in 1979 and was often a lone voice for non-violence when all around wanted violent revenge. It was largely due to his efforts that the Anglo-Irish agreement of 1985 between the British and Irish governments was made [3], establishing regular meetings between them and allowing Dublin to raise matters which affected the nationalists of the North. In that year Hume's home was firebombed by the IRA which saw him, a different kind of nationalist, as an electoral threat. Instead of taking revenge, Hume attempted to set up secret meetings with its political party, Sinn Fein. In 1988, he succeeded and despite several setbacks, Hume eventually persuaded Sinn Fein and the IRA that peaceful politics was better than bloody violence.

This helped, in 1993, the Conservative Prime Minister John Major to negotiate, with the Taoiseach of the Republic of Ireland, the Downing Street Agreement which affirmed the right of the people of Northern Ireland to self-determination and that Northern Ireland would only become part of the Republic of Ireland when the majority in the former agreed. The next year the Provisional IRA agreed to a ceasefire. This was largely due to John Hume's secret and persuasive meetings with its leaders.

14.13 The Good Friday Agreement

Peace at last was achieved in 1998 when Prime Minister Tony Blair's government, with the help of the former US Senator George Mitchell negotiated the Good Friday Agreement between the British and the Irish governments and the political parties of Northern Ireland.

John Hume was largely the architect of the Good Friday Agreement between the British and the Irish governments and the political parties of Northern Ireland in 1998. He realised that it was important for it to be agreed by Westminster, Dublin, and Belfast. For his work in bringing about a lasting peace, John Hume was jointly awarded the Nobel Peace Prize with the Ulster Unionist leader David Trimble in 1998.

The American negotiator, George Mitchell, played an important role in the actual negotiations of the Agreement. As another great mediator, Lord John Alderdice, later explained:

'The approach of Senator George Mitchell as chairman of the multi-party talks that led to the Belfast Agreement in 1998 was vital for its success. He did not bring his own solutions to the talks. He listened patiently and carefully for a very long time to all the different parties to the problem. He excluded no-one, and created a process where the parties brought their proposals to him in the presence of each other. They did not reach agreement in this way but he built such trust that when the parties had exhausted the process of talking, they asked him to bring forward proposals. This work of building a process, rather than conjuring up a solution, was the heart of the conflict resolution. It required skill and stamina and like the preparatory phase took some years. There were many aspects to the negotiations. The careful use of deadlines, gradual building of respectful behaviour...I must however emphasise again that the key was coming to an understanding that it was the process, and not any specific formulae or propositions which enabled us to make real progress' [4].

This process of building up respectful behaviour was not, of course, the same as forgiveness, but was a courageous step towards it in denying its opposite: revenge. Obviously, many on both sides no doubt never actually forgave their enemies. The next step was a dialogue with those who had been involved in the violence. Lord Alderdice observed:

'Engagement with people that you have hated and who have hated and tried to kill you demands a degree of moral courage and emotional containment that I can promise you does not come easy to any of us' [5].

This too was not the same as forgiveness but a further step towards it. While the participators in the dialogue might have still hated each other, their face-to-face respectful talks might well have changed their feelings or lessened their intensity, encouraging peace and the eventual the elimination of hatred and the desire for reprisals.

By the Good Friday Agreement the majority of the people of Northern Ireland at that time wished to remain as part of the United Kingdom while a substantial section of the people of Northern Ireland and the majority of the people in the whole of Ireland wanted a united Ireland. Both views were legitimate and it was for the people of Ireland as a whole, by agreement between North and South, to exercise their right of self-determination.

The agreement committed the participants to partnership, equality, and respect and to exclusively democratic and peaceful means of resolving differences on political issues. The people of Northern Ireland could decide their future while the Irish government was to be consulted on governmental action in Northern Ireland. The decommissioning of arms and release of prisoners was arranged. The peoples in both Northern and Southern Ireland agreed to the provisions in a referendum.

The peace was greatly helped by both sides being in the EU which meant that the border between them effectively disappeared: those who wanted a united Ireland could think they were almost in one.

14.14 Forgiveness: The Release of Prisoners

The release of the prisoners was both an act of forgiveness and an important step in securing concessions from both sides of the conflict (the Republican IRA and the Loyalist UVF). To maintain the ceasefire both the Irish and the UK governments agreed to release prisoners whose crimes related to the conflict. Some of these had committed mass atrocities and it was very difficult for the other side to accept that they were pardoned. But this was a governmental form of forgiveness that had to be accepted and it seems to have worked. Since the Good Friday Agreement there has been peace in Northern Ireland with occasional outbreaks of violence from a few extremists.

In 2004, a study was published on intergroup forgiveness among 340 young adults in Northern Ireland [6] ('Intergroup' as opposed to 'interpersonal' meant there was a shift from the personal to a social identity and an emphasis on the ingroup rather than the self). The study found overall levels of forgiveness were low. It suggested that, as in other areas of conflict, this might be because harbouring feelings of revenge and anger could be regarded as keeping faith with the dead, by not allowing the injury to be forgotten or trivialised. The report also found that a predictor of a low level of forgiveness in an interviewee was found to be the perceived degree of hurt rather than the actual hurt caused by the injury. Some of this related to verbal abuse within the previous 5 years, that is, after the cessation of violence. It seems, therefore, that there was still a lot of hatred bubbling under the surface ready to be released by verbal provocation. The study quotes Robert D. Enright's definition of forgiveness: 'Forgiveness is defined here as a forswearing of negative affect and judgement, by viewing the wrongdoer with compassion and love, in the face of the wrongdoer's considerable injustice' [7]. This was Jesus Christ's teaching but the Catholic and Protestant communities understandably have yet to fully follow it.

14.15 Brexit

Postscript: In 2020, Britain left the EU which had encouraged those who wanted a united Ireland to believe they were almost in one. The Northern Ireland Protocol introduced the Irish Sea border to avoid the need for a hard border on the island of Ireland. The Protocol means that Northern Ireland remains in the EU single market for goods, so products being moved from Great Britain to Northern Ireland undergo EU import procedures. It avoids the need for checks on the Irish border, as customs rules are enforced at Northern Ireland's ports instead. However, Unionists claim the Protocol damages trade and threatens Northern Ireland's position as part of the UK.

The resulting simmering tensions gave way to Loyalists rioting in Northern Ireland in April 2021.Whether this was partly the result of pent up frustration with the lockdown imposed to prevent the spread of the pandemic remains to be seen. However, it is clear that skilful navigation of issues arising in a forgiving, peaceful environment is the only constructive way forward.

14.16 Truth and Reconciliation Commission?

The long conflict in Northern Ireland has left bitterness in the hearts of many of involved, particularly those whose loved ones were killed by the British army. This sometimes has resulted in litigation and meant that soldiers were accused of committing atrocities for which any evidence had long disappeared in the passage of time. In May 2021, the acquittal of two former paratroopers on charges of murdering an IRA commander in Belfast in 1972 forced the government to rethink the process. At the time of writing (May 2021) it was considering replacing such prosecutions with a South African style truth and reconciliation commission. No soldiers or terrorists would be prosecuted for incidents up to the Good Friday Agreement of 1998 save for war crimes, genocide, and torture. People on all sides would be encouraged to come forward to talk about historical events without risks of prosecution. If implemented, hopefully this will be a more positive step towards forgiveness and reconciliation.

References

1. McGarry, Patsy, 'NI peace process began with question from Fr Alec Reid to Gerry Adams', Irish Times, June 7, 2017
2. *The Independent* 22nd March 1993
3. Frayling, Nicholas, 'Pardon and Peace: A Reflection on the Making of the Peace in Northern Ireland' (London 1996) p.158
4. Alderdice, Lord John, 'Risks, Rights and Respect-Essential Elements of the Irish Peace Process' The 11th Dudley Senanayake Memorial Lecture, Colombo, Sri Lanka, 24th September 2008
5. Ibid
6. McLernon, F. and Cairns, E. Hewstone, M. and Smith R., The Development of Intergroup Forgiveness in Northern Ireland (Journal of Social Issues, Vol 60 No 3, 2004) p.587–601
7. Enright et al., 'The Moral Development of Forgiveness' in Kurtines, William and Gerwitz, Jacob, 'Handbook of Moral Behaviour and Development' (New Jersey 1991) p.123

Further Reading

Coogan, Tim Pat, The IRA, (London) 1980
O'Leary, Brendan and McGarry, John, The Politics of Antagonism Understanding Northern Ireland, (London) 1994

Chapter 15
Nelson Mandela: Faith, Force, and Forgiveness

Forgiveness between separate states which have been at war is clearly a different matter from that between two ethnic groups who have to live with each other in the same state after a conflict. Nelson Mandela showed how to avoid the bloodshed of revenge that is usually present in such a situation. His outstanding leadership of forgiveness and reconciliation in South Africa after apartheid resulted in his becoming the most admired and loved political leader in the world. He wrote in his autobiography:

'I knew people expected me to harbour anger towards whites. But I had none. In prison, my anger towards whites decreased, but my hatred for the system grew. I wanted South Africa to see that I loved even my enemies while I hated the system that turned us against one another' [1].

Mandela's leadership after apartheid led to the setting up of the Truth and Reconciliation Commission which was later copied by other countries as a way to restore peace between previously warring groups. After his release from 27 years in jail (when he was not even allowed to attend the funerals of his mother and eldest son) he also set a personal example of forgiveness and reconciliation with his enemies. Much of this was due to his Christian faith which he held throughout his life.

15.1 Mandela's Christian Faith

As Mandela remarked to his close friend and former fellow inmate on Robben Island, Ahmed Kathrada,

'I never abandoned my Christian beliefs' [2].

Yet he never said much publicly about them. In a letter to his daughter Maki from his prison cell on Robben Island, he wrote that he thought it was better to keep religious beliefs to oneself:

A. Wells, *The Importance of Forgiveness and the Futility of Revenge*, Contributions to International Relations, https://doi.org/10.1007/978-3-030-87552-7_15

'As you know, I was baptised in the Methodist Church and was educated in Wesleyan schools—Clarkebury, Healdtown and at Fort Hare. I stayed at Wesley House. At Fort Hare I even became a Sunday School teacher. Even here I attend all church services and have enjoyed some of the sermons. . .from experience, it's far better, darling, to keep religious beliefs to yourself. You may unconsciously offend a lot of people by trying to sell them ideas they regard as unscientific and pure fiction' [3].

It was Mandela's mother who gave him his faith. He was born in 1918 into the Thembu tribe in a small village in the Transkei, on the Eastern Cape of South Africa. His mother was one of a Thembu chief's four wives and uneducated. Nevertheless, she was a devout Christian, had Mandela baptised and sent him, in 1925, to a primary Methodist mission school where his teacher gave him the name 'Nelson'.

Two years later, when Mandela was 9 years old, his father died. The regent and chief of the Thembu people became his guardian. Mandela went to live with him in the royal household where he was given a Christian upbringing with the crown prince. He went regularly to church with the royal family and was sent to Wesleyan schools and later to Fort Hare College.

15.2 The African National Congress

In 1941, at the age of 23, Mandela arrived in Johannesburg to train as a lawyer. Having spent his early, privileged life among mainly black Africans, he was shocked to see fully for the first time the degrading treatment that the whites meted out to them, having seized their land and forced them to work in exploitative, degrading conditions. He, therefore, joined the African National Congress in 1944 to work for a fully democratic South Africa, the black people having no vote.

The ANC used only peaceful methods of protest at that time, as it followed the ideas of Gandhi who had campaigned for fellow Indians against racial discrimination in South Africa during the first decade of the twentieth century.

However, after the Afrikaner Nationalists came to power in 1948 and imposed 'apartheid' in South Africa, anyone even just criticising the laws of segregation could be arrested as a Communist according to the Suppression of Communism Act of 1950.

Mandela soon felt the ANC's response was not adequate. He became deputy president of the ANC, leading peaceful protests against the apartheid laws and being jailed briefly. He also qualified as a lawyer and set up the first all-black law firm with Oliver Tambo, helping to get opponents of apartheid out of jail.

15.3 Mandela Turns to Violent Resistance

Then in 1960, two events occurred that made Mandela decide that the ANC's principle of non-violence must be changed. The first was the shooting in Sharpeville of 69 peaceful protestors against the pass laws by young, inexperienced policemen. The second was the subsequent banning of the ANC. This meant that even peaceful protests under the auspices of the organisation could result in jail sentences.

Mandela had decided that Gandhi's ideas were not effective when dealing with the Afrikaners: 'In India, Gandhi had been dealing with a foreign power that ultimately was more realistic and far-sighted. That was not the case with the Afrikaners in South Africa' [4].

Mandela's espousal of violence did not mean that he no longer believed in forgiveness or wanted revenge, but that he thought that selective violence, such as blowing up railway lines, could help lead to the collapse of apartheid. In 1961, Mandela persuaded the ANC to agree to an organisation to be set up as the military arm of the ANC but be separate from it. This would not to jeopardise the legality of unbanned organisations which supported the ANC but not the use of force.

The organisation was called 'Umkhonto we Sizwe', (MK for short) or 'The Spear of the Nation' and Mandela was to be its Commander-in-Chief. The form of violence to be used was sabotage since, according to Mandela, it did not involve loss of life and therefore would make reconciliation between the races easier afterwards [5]. However, it was obvious that loss of life was likely to occur.

In December 1961, the MK started its campaign with leaflets distributed over the country and bombs exploding at electric power stations. Mandela, meanwhile, secretly left South Africa to ask governments in Africa and the West for support, and to undertake military training. But on his return in 1962, he was arrested and eventually sentenced to life imprisonment, with other members of the MK, for sabotage.

15.4 Prison and Forgiveness

He remained in jail for 27 years, serving 18 of them on bleak Robben Island. Had he died there he would not have been remembered as such an international hero, for it was his leadership of reconciliation after his release and the collapse of the apartheid system that won him the world's admiration.

From his prison cell Mandela wrote movingly to his family and friends in letters which have fortunately been preserved. One such was to his wife, Winnie, when she was also in prison, in fact, in solitary confinement in Pretoria Central Prison where she was humiliated by the guards [6]. The letter shows the depths of Mandela's faith, and how, instead of promising her that her humiliation will be avenged, as might a lesser mortal might do, he reminds her of Jesus's humiliation and suffering, recalling a consideration of it in a book by the Afrikaner writer CJ Langenhoven, 'Shadows of Nazareth':

'to you and I, it raises issues of a contemporary nature. I hope you will find it significant and useful, and trust it will bring you some measure of happiness' [7].

In 1982, Mandela was transferred from Robben Island to Pollsmoor Prison on the mainland. There he kept a desk diary which often had only one short phrase for each day's entry. Some of them show his concern with spiritual matters. There is one entry for 19th August 1986: 'Rev Peter Storey on Forgiveness' and then for the next day: 'The Rev Peter Storey on The Lord's Prayer' [8]. Peter Storey was Chaplain to Nelson Mandela, and later the President of the Methodist Church of South African and of the South African Council of Churches.

15.5 Freedom

Indeed, it was Mandela's forgiveness of his enemies after he was freed in 1990 that won him the world's admiration and avoided much bloodshed in South Africa. We cannot know for certain whether Mandela's use of violent protest made a significant contribution to the ending of apartheid, as other factors, such as foreign disinvestment, internal peaceful protest, the collapse of the Soviet Union, and De Klerk's personality as well as Mandela's, all helped to end the system of institutionalised racism.

But we do know that it was Mandela's desire to show forgiveness and encourage reconciliation, extending the hand of friendship to his white oppressors, that enabled him to lead South Africa to democracy peacefully. His example sent a powerful message to his black followers that no doubt prevented civil war.

15.6 The Truth and Reconciliation Commission

Even before Mandela was elected president of South Africa in 1994, he worked with Archbishop Desmond Tutu and others on the idea of the Truth and Reconciliation Commission (TRC), which was set up in 1996, to investigate the truth about alleged human rights abuses and attempt to dispense restorative justice.

The TRC was a court-like body that heard and recorded witness statements from victims of gross human rights abuses who were offered reparation and rehabilitation. Some of the cases were heard in public. The perpetrators (white and black) of crimes under apartheid could confess their crimes and ask for amnesty from civil and criminal prosecution. This in most cases was not given unless the crime was clearly politically motivated and proportionate. The perpetrators were not asked to show remorse (otherwise it would be not necessarily be freely volunteered) but to tell the truth about their deeds, if they were to be granted amnesty. In addition, a register of reconciliation was set up so that South Africans could express their remorse for actions taken during apartheid.

The Rev Peter Storey was asked by Mandela to help in selecting the members of the TRC. He gives this account of one of its hearing, in a township community hall, before an audience (and a TRC panel) of mainly black but some white South Africans. A black woman in tears describes seeing the tortured, almost unrecognisable body of her son who was killed after being interrogated by the security police:

'The remembrance overwhelms her and affects both the panel and the audience. Some weep quietly while she struggles with her grief. 'I do not know if I can forgive', she says, 'I must know who did this to my son. When I see the face of the one who killed him, and he tells me why, then perhaps I can forgive'' [9].

Storey noted:

'Victims do seem to have been helped by telling their stories. Many have said that they now feel able to move forward with their lives. Most important has been the 'reverencing' of their suffering. 'Today', said an old Black man, 'the nation cried my tears with me'' [10].

Clearly this procedure was of value to the victims who could not be expected to forgive immediately those who had harmed their loved ones, but might do so later after listening to the confessions of the perpetrators. As Richard Holloway reflected:

'The act and its consequences *cannot* be undone, but confession may change the psychological reaction of the victim to the event and interrupt the expected sequence of revenge' [11].

Holloway has credited to the 'powerful influence' of Christians like Archbishop Desmond Tutu, the inclusion of the amnesty in the procedure, calling it 'the political equivalent of forgiveness and absolution' which was 'extended to those who admitted or confessed their trespasses during the bitter years of apartheid' [12]. However, as I earlier mentioned, remorse, essential for absolution, was not required for the amnesty. Moreover, it was not freely given: only 849 applications for amnesty were granted but 5392 were refused in 2001 [13].

Although there was some disappointment among the black Africans that there was not more wealth redistribution after the end of apartheid, the TRC has been a courageous venture that played an important part in holding the nation together. It is probably responsible for the fact that further conflict has not broken out in South Africa and has therefore been copied by other countries facing similar situations. It was replaced in 2000 by the Institute for Justice and Reconciliation.

15.7 Mandela Encourages Forgiveness

Nelson Mandela also personally showed his determination to prevent the nation being torn apart by hatred when in 1993 his probable heir apparent, the charismatic Chris Hani, was assassinated by a white supremacist. Mandela calmed the nation by pointing out that it was an Afrikaner woman who called the police and gave them the car's licence-plate number. His handling of the situation no doubt helped his election to the presidency of South Africa in 1994. Further examples of his desire for reconciliation were his invitation to four of his former prison guards to his inauguration ceremony to share 'in the joys' of the day [14]. Even more imaginative was the luncheon for the widows and wives of the leaders, black and white on both sides of the apartheid struggle [15].

In 1995, Mandela made a dramatic gesture of reconciliation. At the World Cup rugby final, where the white Afrikaner Springboks team was playing, he strode onto the pitch wearing their green and gold jersey and cap. This had been a hated symbol of apartheid to black Africans who used to cheer the opposition team from their pen in the stadium. But now they and the Afrikaners together cheered Mandela as one.

Mandela showed how well he understood the need to resist the temptation of taking revenge on one's enemies after gaining power. In 1997, in his final address to the ANC congress, when he handed over the baton to Mbeki, he departed from his prepared speech to warn:

'One temptation of a leader elected unopposed is that he may use that powerful position to settle scores with his detractors, marginalise them and in certain cases get rid of them and surround himself with yes men and women' [16].

He went on to comment that he was sure that Mbeki would never do such a thing, but he was obviously concerned to prevent reprisals.

Nelson Mandela has indeed shown how a strong leader's ethics can transform the society he or she leads. In a world of bloody cycles of revenge, he has demonstrated what a human being can achieve through forgiveness. By doing so he has won the applause of the world.

References

1. Mandela, Nelson, 'Long Walk to Freedom', (London 1995) p.680
2. Mandela, Nelson, 'Conversations with Myself,' (London 2011) p.53
3. Ibid, p.235
4. Mandela, 'Long Walk to Freedom', p.182
5. Ibid p.336
6. For full account of her humiliating treatment see: Mandela, Winnie, 'Part of My Soul' (Harmondsworth, 1985) p.99
7. Mandela, 'Conversations with Myself', p.227
8. Mandela, 'Conversations with Myself', p.298
9. Storey, Peter, 'A Different Kind of Justice: Truth and Reconciliation in South Africa', *The Christian Century*, Sept 10–17, 1997 (http:gbgm-umc.org/nwo/99ja/different.html)
10. Ibid
11. Holloway, Richard, 'On Forgiveness' (Edinburgh 2015) p.66
12. Ibid p.65
13. http://www.justice.gov.za/trc/amntrans/index.htm
14. Frost, Brian, 'Struggling to Forgive; Nelson Mandela and Reconciliation' (London 1998) p.5
15. Ibid p.12
16. 'Mandela hands the baton to Mbeki', 20th December 1997, www.bbc.co.uk

Part IV
Forgiveness During or After Civil War

Chapter 16
The Relevance of Forgiveness and Revenge to the Syrian Civil War

The conflict in Syria, which began in 2011, has already lasted (at the time of writing) for a decade, causing about half a million deaths, including hundreds of thousands of civilians and displacing millions more as refugees. It began with a series of vengeful actions and could have been stopped by early forgiving and proportionate responses, but these were not forthcoming.

It is also possible that the war could have been ended before it ever gained moment by the decisive intervention of the UN Security Council. This, however, did not happen because Russia and China, having agreed not to veto Resolution 1973 on Libya, were outraged when the USA, the UK and France took revenge on Gaddafi and overthrew him. Consequently Russia and China did not trust the intentions of USA, UK and France over Syria. As a result, the UN Security Council has been paralysed throughout the Syrian civil war.

Moreover, one of the results of Presidents Bush's ignorantly thinking he could avenge the 9/11 attack by invading Iraq was the rise of ISIS. This went into Syria, where it formed a nefarious opposition to the Assad government, complicating and compromising the West's support of the rebels. Had the USA shown forgiveness for the 9/11 attack and the Western powers forgiven Gaddafi for Lockerbie, they would have probably been able to work with Russia and China to end the civil war in Syria.

Thus, the above two vengeful actions by the West in Libya and Iraq had disastrous effects on the Syrian civil war. Moreover, within it, extreme revenge on a personal basis was also wreaked by a Syrian leader, Maher Assad, the younger brother of the Syrian president, as will be discussed later. However, there were also leaders who worked for and showed forgiveness, such as Ali Haidar, who has been Syrian Minister for National Reconciliation since 2012 and who will also be discussed later in this chapter.

A. Wells, *The Importance of Forgiveness and the Futility of Revenge*, Contributions to International Relations, https://doi.org/10.1007/978-3-030-87552-7_16

16.1 The Civil War Begins

When the civil war broke out in Syria against the background of the 'Arab Spring', there was already political and economic discontent in Syria. The USA had imposed tough economic sanctions on Syria in 2004 for allegedly supporting terrorism. This had aggravated the already struggling economy. In addition, the hopes that President Bashar al-Assad would relax his dictatorship were fading. Moreover in 2006, there was a severe drought causing the failure of agriculture and the movement of farmers and their families into the cities where they could scarcely scrape a living. Climate change played a part in causing the Syrian war.

The actual conflict was sparked in 2011 surprisingly by a teenage schoolboy in the southern city of Daraa, who, egged on by other boys, sprayed an anti-Assad slogan on a wall: 'It's your turn Doctor Bashar al-Assad' referring to the fall of the Egyptian and Tunisian governments in the 'Arab Spring'. Instead of forgiving this prank, which would have been the wisest response, the Syrian security forces arrested and tortured the boy to find out who had encouraged his actions. They then arrested and tortured the other boys. As a result, there was a public protest in Daraa to which the security forces responded by opening fire and killing four people.

16.2 Maher

The vengeful, cruel response of the Syrian government was the responsibility of General Maher Assad, President Bashar Assad's violent and unstable younger brother. The USA reacted by placing sanctions on him and two other Syrian officials [1]. Known for his violent temper and brutality, Maher, the de-facto commander of the army's Fourth Armoured Division and of the Republican Guard, is likely to have been responsible for many of the atrocities attributed to 'Assad's regime'. Prime Minister Erdogan of Turkey (as he was in 2012) later publicly denounced Maher's 'savagery' and urged President Bashar Assad to remove him from power. However, Bashar Assad is probably trapped by his father's old regime, of which Maher Assad is part [2]. Maher was well-entrenched in it and held military power long before Bashar returned from his medical career in London to become president of Syria in 2000.

Probably because he realised Maher was unstable, his father, President Hafez Assad, chose Bashar as his successor after his eldest son, Bassel, was killed in a car accident in 1994. Bashar was indeed older than Maher, but he did not have the latter's political ambition or military experience. Instead, he chose to study ophthalmology in London.

When Bashar Assad became Syrian president in 2000, he encouraged open political debates and freed many political prisoners. However, within a year, no doubt due to Maher's pressure, the government resumed its iron grip. Any disagreement with Maher could be dangerous. He was rumoured to have shot his own brother-in-law, Assef Shawkat, in the stomach during an argument. (Emergency surgery in Paris saved him.) [3]. Both Maher Assad and Assef Shawkat are cited in the UN's Mehlis Report as the suspect assassins of President Hariri of Lebanon in 2005 [4]. Maher's actions show how much lethal harm can be caused by one vindictive man with military power.

16.3 The Conflict Develops

Inspired by the 'Arab Spring', protests grew in 2011, calling for an end to the Syrian dictatorship. The Syrian rebels no doubt thought that NATO would intervene on their behalf as it had done in Libya. But it did not, despite the Assad government's bloody attempts to crush the rebellion which was formed initially by defectors from the Syrian army who had set up their Free Syria Army.

16.4 Russia and China Distrust the West Because of Its Revenge on Gaddafi

When the NATO powers had taken revenge on Gaddafi in 2011 and overthrown him, Russia and China, veto-holding members of the Security Council, were outraged. They, therefore, would not support any UN resolution on Syria, believing that the West would also aim for regime change there. As a result, the UN Security Council has been paralysed throughout the Syrian civil war, which, by 2021, has dragged on for 10 years.

It is true that Russia has a long-standing trade relationship with Syria and values the deep-water port of Tartus as its only Mediterranean naval base for its Black Sea Fleet. For that reason, it would not want to support regime change. But if it had trusted the West, it might well have been willing to back measures that stopped short of that to end the bloodshed, especially if China had done the same. Russia indeed could have used its influence with Assad's regime to force it to cooperate with any UN resolutions. However, suspicion of the West's true intentions prevented this or at least gave Russia and China an excuse not to cooperate. As Alexander Kramarenko, the Minister Counsellor of the Embassy of Russia to Great Britain and a member of the Ministry of Foreign Affairs of Russia explained: Russia had felt its trust had been betrayed by the West's actions in Libya and therefore was less willing to cooperate with Western initiatives over the Syrian conflict [5].

On 6 February 2012, the British Foreign Secretary, William Hague, attempted to blame Russia and China for the failure of the international community to act over the Syrian war. In a statement to the House of Commons on Syria he regretted the fact that Russia and China had vetoed an Arab League plan, supported by Britain, the USA, France and other countries. While some MP's joined him in deploring the actions of Russia and China, others strongly disagreed, such as Sir Edward Leigh and David Winnick [6], pointing out that had NATO not extended the resolution on Libya to regime change, Russia and China might have been more supportive over Syria.

If the USA, Britain and France had admitted to Russia and China that they had gone further than the UN Security Council had agreed over Libya, had apologised for their actions and aroused some trust and forgiveness from Russia and China, they could probably have worked together to end the Syrian civil war earlier.

16.5 Islamic Extremism: The Effects of the USA's Revenge in Iraq

In addition, the civil war was later complicated by the arrival in Syria of ISIS, which could not have happened if President Bush had not attacked Iraq in misplaced revenge for 9/11. Thus because of the USA's revenge on Iraq and Libya, there could be no joint UN intervention to stop the bloodshed in Syria.

The Sunni Muslim rebels in Syria were later joined by Sunni Muslim extremists who were against the Alawite government but not demanding democracy as were the original rebels. In April 2013, al-Qaeda in Iraq announced it was allied to al-Nusra in Syria, where it was fighting with the rebel forces and had been responsible for car bombing and suicide attacks. This new group called itself the Islamic State of Iraq and al-Sham-or ISIS ('Sham' being Arabic for Levant). Conflicts later developed between groups opposing the Assad government. This created difficulties for Western countries sending military and logistic support to the non-extremist rebels.

The original rebels were mainly from the Sunni Muslim majority in Syria and supplied with weapons chiefly from Saudi Arabia and Qatar and Turkey. The Alawite government was supported by the Shias, Christians and Druzes domestically and externally by Russia and Iran as well as Hezbollah and the Syria-based Palestinian group the PFLP-GC. The war became increasingly complex, sectarian and a geopolitical war between Shia Iran and Sunni Saudi Arabia.

16.6 Maher and Poison Gas

By August 2013, the Syrian conflict had claimed over 100,000 lives and descended into even further depravity by the mysterious use of gas in Damascus to kill nearly 1500 civilians, including children. Both sides blamed each other. The evidence shows that the culprit was probably again President Assad's vindictive brother, Maher, who acted without consulting Bashar Assad [7]. Had the UN been able to intervene earlier, it could have stopped this from happening.

16.7 Assad Persuaded to Hand over Chemical Weapons

Then in September 2013 in Moscow, at a conference of the G20, which was not meant to be about Syria, the leaders of Russia, the USA, the UK and other states discussed the USA's proposed punitive airstrikes against the Syrian regime for the alleged chemical weapons attack. The suggestion was made that Assad could hand over the chemical weapons to an international authority to avoid the airstrikes. However, the idea was not taken further. The US Secretary of State, John Kerry, then casually mentioned this suggestion at a press conference in London, as if it were an impossible idea, but Russia took it up and got President Assad to agree to it, thereby avoiding a possible further conflagration in the Middle East. As no talks had been arranged on Syria at that time, the G20 meeting of the world leaders played a pivotal role in bringing people together to find a solution to the impasse.

Consequently, the international community was able not only to pressure President Assad to agree to give up his give up his chemical weapons for destruction but also to arrange talks between his government's representatives and those of the opposition. This belated cooperation shows just how much could have been achieved earlier if the USA, Britain and France had made an effort to regain the trust of Russia and China and agreed not to aim for regime change in Syria.

16.8 Peace Talks

The peace talks on Syria began in Geneva in January 2014 with the main mediator being Lakhdar Brahimi, who was a former Algerian foreign minister and envoy to the United Nations. By this time, the death toll had reached 130,000 and the number of refugees nearly a 2.5 million. They had fled mainly to the neighbouring countries of Turkey, Jordan, Lebanon and Iraq, putting a strain on the resources and stability of those countries.

However, the talks came to nothing, and military action increased. In 2015 Russia began bombing rebel strongholds, particularly those of ISIS, at the request of the Syrian government. Turkey meanwhile took military action against further expansion of the Syrian Kurdish forces along its border. In 2017 peace talks were opened in Astana, Kazakhstan, sponsored by Russia, Iran and Turkey to try to obtain a ceasefire between the Syrian government and the opposition. But these talks so far have not been productive.

During the 9 years of war in Syria, about 500,000 people have been killed and millions wounded or become refugees. Had the Western powers been able to work with Russia and China to stop the war from escalating in its earlier stages all of this might have been avoided. This could have happened if the NATO states had admitted the error of their ways in Libya, apologised for their breach of trust to Russia and China and earned their forgiveness and respect. Now, if any peace talks are to be successful, forgiveness on all sides is needed, and for that, they may need leaders of the calibre of Mandela, Gandhi, or Robert Schuman, but such leaders are rare.

16.9 Forgiveness: The Ministry for Reconciliation

There are, however, some people in the Syrian government who clearly show they understand the value of forgiveness. Ali Haidar, who was once a fellow student of ophthalmology with Bashar Assad at Damascus University, has been Syrian Minister for National Reconciliation since 2012. As the leader of the Syrian Social Nationalist Party, he was a member, in the Syrian parliament, of the official opposition which proposed to President Assad the idea of the Ministry for National Reconciliation, to which Assad agreed [8]. Haidar is now one of two non-Baathists ministers in the Syrian government. As Minister for National Reconciliation, his goal is to search for a pluralistic political solution through reconciliation, involving all moderate parties while excluding extremists. At the same time, his ministry's job is to encourage Syrian terrorists to cut all ties with foreign terrorists, lay down their arms and engage in the 'reconciliation process', after which they can return to their previous jobs without persecution [9]. As other Syrian terrorists see their former comrades-in-arms doing this without being harmed, they also follow suit. It is too early yet to see if this campaign is successful, but Haidar claims it is with thousands of terrorists laying down their arms, especially in Homs, the Damascus suburbs and Latakia.

In 2012 Haidar's 21-year-old son, Ismail, a medical student, was murdered by terrorists who ambushed his car. Haidar has said that he has forgiven his son's killers [10]. Whether or not he can persuade other Syrians to forgive those who have killed their loved ones in the civil war remains to be seen, but at least he has set them a very good example. Syria's Grand Mufti, Dr. Ahmad Badreddin, whose son, Sarya, was assassinated in 2011, has also done so. At his son's funeral, sobbing, he forgave his son's killers and called for forgiveness and reconciliation [11]. It is this kind of response that can surely heal Syria.

References

1. www.washingtonpost.com>world>2011/04/29 USA imposes sanctions on Syria's intelligence service, security officials
2. www.bbc.co.uk/news/world-middle-east/ 'Bashar al-Assad's inner circle' 30th July 2012
3. 'Middle East Intelligence Bulletin' Vol 2 No 7 5th August 2000
4. The UN Mehlis Report (paragraph 96 2005) October 2005 (Microsoft Word edition)
5. Kramarenko, Alexander, Minister Counsellor of the Embassy of Russia to Great Britain, Lecture to the Great Britain-Russia Society, 30th October 2013
6. (http://www.publications.parliament.uk/pa/cm201212/cmhansrd/cm120206/debtext/12) Col 32,35

7. Jones, Brian, 'Bashar Al Assad's Brother May Have Ordered Last Week's Chemical Weapons Attack' Aug 28 2013 www.businessinsider.com Chulov, Martin, 'What do we know about the regime's use of chemical weapons in Syria?' *The Guardian*, 30th June 2017 See also: nationalpost.com>news>maher-al-assad-accused-of orchestrating-deaths 25Aug 2013 uk.reuters.com>article>uk-mideast-crisi-syria-chemical weapons 13 Jan 2017
8. Taliano, Mark 'Syria's Minister for National Reconciliation', www.globalresearch.ca/ 16th September 2016
9. Taliano, Mark and Bartlett, Eva, 'As Foreign Insurgents Continue to Terrorize Syria, the Reconciliation Trend Grows', https://dissidentvoice.org August 22nd 2014
10. www.bbc.co.uk/news/archive.org/details/Ali Haidar,bereaved father/ 5th July 2018
11. Taliano, Mark and Bartlett, Eva op.cit.

Chapter 17
Forgiveness After Civil War: Yugoslavia, Rwanda, Sierra Leone, Colombia and South Sudan

17.1 Yugoslavia

When Yugoslavia collapsed into civil war in the 1990s, some of the different ethnic groups, which had co-existed peacefully for generations, committed atrocities against each other, often because rumours had reawakened ancient, deeply-rooted vendettas. The Serbs caused the most bloodshed. Afterwards there were attempts at forgiveness and reconciliation, but these came to nothing. However, as the warring peoples had by then (with the exception of Bosnia) formed themselves into separate states, there was not the danger of civil war breaking out.

17.1.1 Background

After the break-up of Yugoslavia, Bosnia had followed Croatia and Slovenia in declaring independence in 1992 against the wishes of Serbia. The Serb government, led by its president Slobodan Milosovic, had aimed bloodily to ethnically cleanse the Muslims and Croats from the areas in Bosnia that it had wanted for a 'Greater Serbia' which would unite all other Serb areas in former Yugoslavia. The Serbs, using the federal army, seized most of the land they wanted and evicted the people living there. Atrocities were committed on all sides, but the worse was by the Serbs in Srebrenica and Sarajevo.

17.1.2 The Srebrenica Massacre

In 1993 Srebrenica was declared a UN safe area. In 1995 the UN Protection Force (UNPROFOR) in the city was a Dutch battalion (Dutchbat) armed with personal

A. Wells, *The Importance of Forgiveness and the Futility of Revenge*, Contributions to International Relations, https://doi.org/10.1007/978-3-030-87552-7_17

weapons and machine guns, which they could only use for self-defence. They had to count on air support from the French for backup. In July 1995, the Serbs under the command of General Ratko Mladic shelled the city mercilessly. The Dutch commander repeatedly asked the French for airstrikes, but they were occupied with bombing the Bosnian Serbs besieging Sarajevo.

Thousands of Muslims then fled for protection to the Dutchbat's compound in the suburbs where they were surrounded by Serb soldiers. Mladic promised them safe passage by bus to a safe city. The women and children were allowed to go, but the men and boys were separated from them ostensibly in a search for war criminals. They were then taken to places of execution such as fields, farms, or football grounds. About 7500 were shot in cold blood.

The final straw for NATO (which was not fully aware of the extent of the massacre) was the killing of nearly 40 people in an open-air market in Sarajevo by a Serb mortar bomb which also injured 90 more civilians at the end of August. This was the second time the crowded marketplace had been shelled.

NATO then carried out airstrikes against the Serb troops, which eventually led to peace negotiations and the arrest of Serb leaders who were charged with war crimes and genocide. By the Dayton Peace Agreement of 1995, Bosnia was divided into a Croat-Muslim Federation (for Bosnian Croats and Muslims) and the Republika Srpska (for Bosnia Serbs).

In Kosovo, a province of Serbia, the Serbs led by Milosovic had tried to cleanse the Albanians from the region ethnically. This was stopped by NATO with a bombing campaign in 1999. But by the war's end, 10,000 civilians had been killed, and hundreds of thousands had become refugees. Serb leaders were charged at the Hague with crimes against humanity. In 2008 Kosovo declared itself an independent state and had been recognised as such by over half the members of the UN.

17.1.3 The Commission of Truth and Reconciliation in Yugoslavia

In 2001 the Commission of Truth and Reconciliation in Yugoslavia was set up by Yugoslav President Kostunica. It was to report, within 3 years, on the causes of the conflicts in former Yugoslavia. However, in 2003 Yugoslavia formerly dissolved and became Serbia and Montenegro. This meant the end of the Commission as it relied on a mandate from the defunct Yugoslav presidency. It seems not to have held any hearings, nor made reports, nor been in any way beneficial for the people, unlike the Truth and Reconciliation Commission in South Africa. Indeed, one of the problems emerging from Yugoslavia as it broke up, after the death of Tito, is that it lacked any leaders of the stature of Nelson Mandela who could reconcile the different ethnic groups with a leadership of forgiveness. Adem Demaci, an Albanian Kosovar writer, human rights defender and politician who died in 2018, was known as the 'Balkan Mandela', but he could not lead the people of his region in forgiveness and reconciliation as did Nelson Mandela. However, as a writer, Demaci did highlight the problem of blood vendettas in the Balkans with his most famous novel 'The Snakes of Blood'.

17.1.4 Serb and Croat Leaders Apologise

Some Serb and Croat leaders did attempt to apologise for the past aggression of their countries. In 2010 the Serbian parliament passed a resolution condemning the 1995 Srebrenica massacre. The Serbian President Boris Tadic declared, 'silence is no longer acceptable, and neither is hiding behind outdated wartime rhetoric. The era of accountability in our part of the world has begun, and it is here to stay' [1].

However, critics have pointed to the omission of the word 'genocide' in the resolution, the tabling of a second resolution condemning all crimes in the former Yugoslavia, the failure to apprehend General Mladic and have suggested that Serbia's primary motivation was improving its EU-membership prospects [2].

Similarly, the Croatian President Josipovic, in an address to the Bosnian parliament, expressed his deep regret 'that the Republic of Croatia...has contributed to the suffering of people and the divisions that still burden us today' [3].

He visited Ahmici, a village in central Bosnia, where over 100 Bosniak civilians were killed by Bosnian Croat forces in 1993. However, the Croatian prime minister, Jadranka Kosor, condemned the president's gesture and remarked, declaring:

'Croatia was never the aggressor...the war was just and of a defensive character'.

Kosor was joined by several former Croatian prime ministers expressing similar indignation [4].

The attempts of Serbian and Croat leaders to apologise for the atrocities their peoples committed in the Yugoslav conflict show how difficult it is ever to do so on behalf of a group of people without their full support. Moreover, it certainly does not earn the forgiveness of those who have been wronged. Indeed 'The Snakes of Blood' that Demaci wrote about are no doubt still lurking in the Balkans.

While most of the different ethnic groups of former Yugoslavia are now living in separate states without much forgiveness of, or reconciliation with, each other, the people in Bosnia have a different experience. It seems that the Bosniaks and Croats are prepared to co-exist, but the leadership of the Serb Republika Srpska (part of Bosnia) wants to be independent and eventually join with Serbia. The international community has blocked its attempts, fearing bloodshed if the borders are changed. It is possible, however, that if more Balkan states join the EU, founded to end the enmity between Germany and France, their mutual hatred could end.

In Bosnia, the tripartite divisions of the Dayton Peace Agreement may have helped to preserve ethnic differences while preserving the peace. It seems that bitterness over past atrocities, particularly of the Serbs, still bubbles under the surface. The Christian churches of all denominations across Bosnia, with international ecclesiastical support, perhaps could surely do more to encourage forgiveness here.

17.2 Rwanda: The Gacacas and the Churches

In Rwanda, a group of Hutu genocidal killers (the Interahamwe) in 1994 set out to exterminate the Tutsis who had once held power under Belgian imperial rule. The massacre was sparked by the shooting down of the plane of the Rwandan president, Habyarimana, who was a Hutu. Armed with machetes, the Hutus killed an estimated 800,000 Tutsis and moderate Hutus in 100 days: the biggest killing spree the world has ever known. The UN was unable or unwilling to prevent it. The Hutus were finally defeated by the Tutsis' Rwanda Patriotic Front.

Yet the Tutsis have not emerged as reigning supreme over the Hutus, for both sides seem now to work together. This is partly because a government of national unity was formed after the conflict, but most importantly because of the use of the traditional Rwanda village-based 'gacaca' court system where respected elders endeavoured to dispense some kind of truth and justice. These courts were held outdoors with the judges sitting at a table with the accused standing before them while the public sat on the grass under trees. The term 'gacaca' means 'justice on the grass': sitting down and talking about an issue.

The decade-long work of the 'gacacas' was mainly to dispense restorative justice (such as the rebuilding of a home or making a convicted person work in the fields for the victim).In addition, the courts also could sentence the accused to long prison sentences. The system was set up to deal with the huge number of genocide-related crimes committed in 1994, but it has been criticised for not being suitable for work that requires a high level of forensic enquiry. Nevertheless, the courts, which worked alongside the International Criminal Tribunal for Rwanda, seem to have encouraged confessions, forgiveness and healing for lesser crimes.

How far the Catholic Church in Rwanda could lead the country in forgiveness is difficult to ascertain. During the conflict, some priests and nuns showed bravery, offering people shelter from the massacre. However, the bishops were disproportionately Hutus, while the priests were mainly Tutsis. When the conflict broke out some of the bishops condoned or even participated in killing the Tutsis [5]. As a result, in the last weeks of the genocide in 1994, the Tutsis' Rwanda Patriotic Front killed three Catholic bishops as well as some priests in revenge. In 2016 the Catholic Church in Rwanda apologised for the fact that its members planned and took part in the genocide:

'Forgive us for the crime of hate in the country to the extent of also hating our colleagues because of their ethnicity. We did not show that we are one family but instead killed each other', the statement said [6]. It was timed to coincide with Pope Francis' 'Holy Year of Mercy'. In 2017 Pope Francis himself asked the Rwandan President Paul Kagame for forgiveness for 'the sins and failings' of the Catholic Church during the 1994 Rwandan genocide [7]. Nevertheless, many Catholics moved their allegiance to the Pentecostal churches [8].

The Anglican church fared no better. Its Archbishop of the Episcopal Church in Rwanda, Augustin Nshamihigo, instead of condemning the actions of the Hutus (to which he belonged), blamed the Tutsis for the genocide. (He had earlier been a military chaplain and retained links to the army). Later the then Archbishop of Canterbury, George Carey, told him to resign unless he returned to Rwanda from Kenya to where he had fled. Therefore, Nshamihigo agreed to resign [9].

The genocide in Rwanda is an appalling example of how ethnic groups can descend to hatred and barbarism, despite their whole profession being dedicated, if they were priests, to love and forgiveness.

Another Anglican Bishop, Jonathan Ruhumuliza, a Hutu, came to Britain after the genocide in Rwanda and served as a parish priest in Worcestershire. However, as the British government believed he was complicit in the genocide, he was refused legal permission to stay. He appealed and found forgiveness coming from an unexpected quarter. In 2016 an Immigration Appeal Tribunal declared, regarding his case, that:

'Redemption is possible and therefore what the bishop has done since 1994 is relevant and carries weight'. It added: 'It is not necessarily the case that somebody involved in a crime against humanity in 1994 is an undesirable immigrant in 2015' [10].

In 2018 the Court of Appeal upheld the decision. Neither the Tribunal nor the Court concerned itself with whether or not the bishop had been complicit in the genocide [11]. Whatever the truth of the matter (he himself expressed regret for not strongly condemning the genocide when it was taking place), the Church of England, which did carry out checks on him [12], reinstated him as a bishop in Rwanda in 2020 [13].

17.3 Sierra Leone: The Truth and Reconciliation Commission

In 1999, after an 11-year brutal civil war in Sierra Leone that left 50,000 people dead, a Truth and Reconciliation Commission was set up as a condition of the Lome Peace Accord with the assistance of the international community. It operated for only 2 years, from November 2002 to October 2004. One of its aims was to promote healing and reconciliation. Another was to determine whether the violations and abuses of the civil war were the results of deliberate planning, policy or authorisation by any government, group or individual. It also sought to avoid the atrocities happening again, to respond to the needs of the victims.

The first phase of its work consisted of statement-taking, the second of public hearings. However, these hearings have been criticised as not being effective since it has been argued, the people of Sierra Leone would have preferred to 'forgive and forget' rather than revive past memories of suffering [14]. How far this criticism is justified is difficult to tell. Obviously, for some people recounting their stories of torture publicly could be cathartic, depending on the response they receive.

The Commission made its final report, including the names of perpetrators and recommendations for the government moving forward, to both the government of

Sierra Leone and the United Nations Security Council in 2004. It would seem that it may have been more successful in getting a record of what happened in the civil war rather than encourage forgiveness and reconciliation.

17.4 Colombia: FARC and Forgiveness

In Colombia, a low-intensity conflict dragged on for over 50 years between the governments and right-wing paramilitary groups, criminal syndicates and the Marxist guerillas such as FARC (the Revolutionary Armed Forces of Colombia) which had been fighting for peasants' land rights and been financed by drug-trading and kidnapping. In 2016 the government and FARC, at last, signed a peace agreement that provided some agrarian reform. In 2017 Pope Francis visited Colombia and urged forgiveness and reconciliation. In response, the former FARC leader Rodrigo Londono (alias Timochenko) asked for forgiveness from the Pope for the pain and suffering caused by his group (up to 220,000 people were killed in the war) [15]. In May 2018, the widow of Guillermo Gaviria, the former governor of Antioquia in Colombia, showed she realised the enormous danger of avenging deaths when she agreed to Londono's request for forgiveness for killing her husband;

'What would've happened in Colombia if the 8.6 million victims decided to take revenge'? she asked rhetorically' [16].

In 2018 at a tribunal established under a truth and reconciliation system, Londono apologised to the victims of the kidnappings and forced disappearances for which FARC (now a political party) would provide details and pay compensation. The tribunal, 'Special Jurisdiction for Peace' or 'JEP' was set to run for 15 years and was based on government investigations and victims' accusations. It was not clear whether there would be an amnesty for those who confessed their crimes [17]. But in any case, President Santos granted an amnesty in 2017 to all FARC members who had not committed serious crimes [18]. As a result, over 7000 rebels were granted amnesty or freed from prison in order to reintegrate them into society. They handed in their weapons to the UN mission in Colombia.

The alleviation of poverty and the need for rural reform (infrastructure, land redistribution, schools and medical services) were the major causes of the unrest. Therefore, lasting peace and reconciliation are unlikely to be achieved unless the government tackles the issues of poverty and lack of life chances in Colombia, together with the persistent drug trafficking.

However, in order to overcome the immediate hatred between groups that have been fighting each other, further methods of promoting reconciliation in Colombia have been proposed. A human rights lawyer, Felix Mora, for example argued that football could be the way forward. The sport is like a religion in Colombia. Mora suggested that a football team could be created consisting of both ex-FARC members and their victims. In this way, they would work with each other literally to achieving a common goal.

In 2017 Mora formed this team [19] and 2 years later founded the Football and Peace Foundation, from where he managed the training of the players and the team matches. The Foundation has the support of public and private organizations as well as the former president Juan Santos. In June 2019, in the framework of the Second Normandy World Forum for Peace, in which five Nobel peace prize winners and delegates from 132 countries participated, Mora's La Paz team played against the Bayeux and Normandy teams, showing how through sport and dialogue, peace and reconciliation are possible [20].

Football could be a way of introducing forgiveness as the previously warring sides share an enjoyable activity together. They get to know each other in a different way, especially as players often warmly hug each other after a goal. It must, however, be mentioned that the game does not always promote forgiveness. In 1994, at the football World Cup, a Colombian player, Andres Escobar, scored an own goal which meant his team did not go through to the next round. He was murdered when he came home, probably by drug-fuelled gangsters who had lost a lot of money on the game or thought he was trying to fix it for another gang. Arguably this unusual situation took place against a background of a country already torn apart by bloody conflict. This would not have happened if peace had been formally established.

Obviously, all sports, cultural activities and work opportunities that bring previously warring groups together in a friendly way could be encouraged to overcome vindictiveness and hatred. In Medellin, the second-largest city in Colombia, the building of a public transport system, including a metro and cable cars, that enables the impoverished in the rural areas to travel easily into the city to find work, has greatly reduced the level of crime in a city which was once of the most violent in the world. Education and medical services for the poor have greatly improved their life chances. The removal of the injustices that have caused a conflict is essential to promote reconciliation between previously warring groups, as forgiveness by itself is not enough.

17.5 South Sudan

The civil war in South Sudan between the supporters of President Kiir, who belongs to the Dinka ethnic group, and supporters of the leader of the opposition, Riek Machar, who is a Nuer, began in 2013. In 2018 a ceasefire was signed between the combatants, by which time over 300,000 people had been killed, many of them civilians and horrific atrocities committed. As part of the peace agreement of 2018, the South Sudan government was to set up truth and reconciliation commissions or tribunals. However, it was not until February 2021 that it announced it was developing the mechanism for this [21].

Meanwhile, the of the country's Episcopalian church, Justin Badi, had been courageously leading the churches to try to get the hostile groups to get together, talk about their experiences and to forgive each other. He had seen his own mother and aunt killed by bombing but could speak about it without bitterness [22]. He thus set a very good example to those working towards forgiveness. The hope of the church leaders is that reconciliation at local level between the groups will strengthen peace at the national level.

17.6 The Truth and Reconciliation Commissions and Forgiveness

How far the TRC commissions considered above have been effective in encouraging forgiveness and reconciliation is difficult to ascertain. The public recounting of suffering during the conflicts may not be cathartic for everyone, depending on the sensitivity of the questioners. The victims may have found they are able to forgive those who admit wrongdoing and express remorse. However, this would be a personal matter and often take a long time. What is important is that members of the conflicting sides actually meet. This can be an opportunity for forgiveness. Above all, when these TRC's are convened, it seems that further revenge and bloodshed are then avoided.

Obviously, other factors are also important in uniting a country. A strong leader who sets an example of forgiveness greatly helps the victimised group to follow suit. Sports and cultural activities which engage both victims and their perpetrators in enjoyable experiences can also help to encourage forgiveness. Indeed football teams composed of members of previously hostile groups may break down the barriers of enmity when a goal results in much hugging and praised by the rest of the team. It is, however, very important to redistribute wealth to the disadvantaged and encourage a thriving economy where all citizens can look forward to a better life.

References

1. Bancroft, Ian, 'The Dynamics of Apology and Forgiveness in the Balkans,' April 27th 2010 RadioFreeEurope https://www.rferl.org/
2. Ibid
3. Ibid
4. Ibid
5. Sherwood, Harriet. 'Pope Francis asks for forgiveness for the Church's role in the Rwandan genocide' www.theguardian.com/ 20th March 2017
6. www.catholicherald.co.uk/bishops-apologise/ 21 Nov 2016
7. Sherwood op.cit.
8. Ibid
9. www.episcopalarchives.org (press release 95089)
10. Brown, David 'Bishop accused of genocide can stay in UK, court rules', The Times, June 2nd 2018
11. Ibid
12. Ibid

13. McGreal, Chris and Sherwood, Harriet, 'Church welcomes back Rwandan bishop accused of defending genocide,' The Guardian, 31 May 2020
14. Shaw, Rosalind 'Rethinking Truth and Reconciliation Commissions, Lessons from Sierra Leone', The United States Institute of Peace Special Report, February 2005, www.usip.org
15. www.irishtimes.com/ 8 Sept 20172
16. www.telesurtv.net/.../Timochenko-Asks-Victims-Widow-for-Forgiveness
17. Murphy, Helen, https://uk.reuters.com/.../colombia seeks to heal war wounds/ July 13 2018
18. 'Colombia: President Santos grants FARC members amnesty' www.bbc.co.uk/news/world-latin-america-40564577
19. Worswick, Carl, www.theguardian 11th Oct 2017/ 'Colombia's FARC guerillas turn to football as route back into society'
20. Bocanegra, Juan Gabriel, La Paz F.C.: 'The reconciliation in Colombia through football', Latin American Post, 6 Jun 2019
21. https://news.un.org›story›2021/02 'South Sudan: UN rights commission welcomes 'first steps' 1st Feb 2021
22. Badi, Archbishop Justin; 'Peacebuilding in South Sudan: Linking Local and National Approaches' Panel Meeting at Chatham House, The Royal Institute of International Affairs, Chatham House, 7th September 2018

Further Reading

Glenny, Misha, 'The Fall of Yugoslavia (London 1996)

Glenny, Misha, 'The Balkans Nationalism, War and the Great Powers 1804-1999' (London 1999)

Judah, Tim, 'The Serbs History, Myth and Destruction' (Yale1999)

Melvern, Linda 'Conspiracy to Murder: the Rwandan Genocide', (London 2004)

McGreal, Chris, 'Rwanda's genocide and the bloody legacy of Anglo-American guilt', www.theguardian.com/ 2th December 2012

Gourevitch, Philip, We Wish to Inform You That Tomorrow We Will Be Killed With Our Families (London 2015)

Part V
Further Aspect of Forgiveness in Politics

Chapter 18
A Leadership of Forgiveness

Here I shall consider the concept of leadership of forgiveness. Such a leader will show by their actions and words that they are not vindictive, and they will be compassionate to wrongdoers and accept and, indeed, value criticism. They will be aware that everyone, including themselves, makes mistakes that should be dealt with sympathetically to discourage their concealment. A political leadership of forgiveness will also seek to understand, not punish, foreign hostility. In his study of transformational leaders, 'The Art of Forgiveness: Differentiating Transformational Leaders' Manfred FR Kets de Vries argues that:

'leaders are responsible for creating a culture of forgiveness (Fehr and Gelfand 2012), and creating such a culture has many advantages. To begin with, forgiveness builds loyalty and good citizenship. In organizations with a forgiveness culture, people are more likely to make an extra effort. If people feel that they will not be forgiven for the mistakes they make, they are not going to be at their most productive; they will not take risks. People are more likely to be open and less likely to hide mistakes, transgressions, and wrongdoings, when they operate in a forgiving environment' [1].

There have certainly been dramatic examples of the reverse of this environment under dictatorships. Although Kets de Vries did not mention this disastrous event, it is relevant to recall here that in China during Mao's Great Leap (1959–1961), the Chinese cadres did not have the courage to say the plan was not working. They were terrified of being accused of poor work and sacked if their grain production was insufficient, so they sent to the towns grain seized from the starving peasants who consequently died in their millions.

A similar situation occurred in the Soviet Union under Stalin when, during the famine in Ukraine from 1932 to 1933, the officials in Ukraine took grain from peasants for the towns and let them starve to death rather than admit they could not harvest enough grain. About 4 million people died from starvation.

Lysenkoism in the USSR is another example of people too frightened to openly speak out about a process clearly erroneous. Trofim Lysenko was a Soviet biologist whose ideas that plants could be altered by their treatment, such as

A. Wells, *The Importance of Forgiveness and the Futility of Revenge*, Contributions to International Relations, https://doi.org/10.1007/978-3-030-87552-7_18

toughening them by planting their seeds in winter, were officially supported in the USSR from the early 1930s to the early 1960s. The experiment was a failure, but those who criticised it were sacked or imprisoned. As a consequence, the USSR's food production was harmed, and its people suffered.

These tragedies could have been averted had there been a forgiving culture in the USSR where criticisms of policies and also mistakes were not responded to harshly and vindictively.

I have argued in the chapter on Russia and the West that President Gorbachev transformed Soviet society by introducing a forgiving culture with his policies of 'glasnost' and 'perestroika'. He became even more determined to implement these reforms when he realised that officials were initially feeding him misleading information about the Chernobyl disaster which occurred in April 1986. In order to cover up their mistakes, they tried to minimise the colossal harm the meltdown of the nuclear reactor caused, but soon over 300,000 people had to be evacuated from the Chernobyl area, and untold numbers of people died or were stricken with cancer because of the explosion.

China is no longer a dictatorship but still very much an authoritarian regime which often remains unforgiving towards those who make mistakes. As a result, there serious cover ups still occur, as happened at the end of 2019 when it was probably the local Communist party in Wuhan that concealed the outbreak of Covid-19 causing delays in response to stop it spreading.

Six months after the initial outbreak of the virus, in June 2020, the Covid-19 virus started spreading again from the Xinfadi market in Beijing, the city's largest wholesale food market. The general manager of the market was immediately dismissed along with other officials, yet it was not clear whether they were in any way responsible for the outbreak nor whether it was simply a matter of human error [2]. The Chinese Communist Party thus showed, by its harsh and perhaps unjust punishments, how the Chinese Communist Party encouraged workers to cover up rather than own up to their mistakes.

Kets de Vries argues: 'truly effective leaders need to be at peace with themselves and past and present events in their life, which include forgiving others for transgressions, and not bearing grudges. When we let go of our grudges, we build collaboration, reduce conflict and release a lot of pent up energy that can be used to move countries. . .and individuals forward' [3].

Unfortunately, the motivation of many politicians is power, prestige, and money instead of public service. In dictatorships, the revenge of leaders on those who have criticised them can be bloody and massive. Very often, such leaders are narcissistic and megalomaniac, not tolerating blows to their vanity. Even in democracies, too much energy is wasted by politicians criticising each other and indulging in vindictive behaviour.

As Kets de Vries points out that

'Unfortunately, the default model of too many people in leadership positions, when they feel wronged, is righteous indignation, the urge for revenge and/or avoidance behaviour towards the transgressor' [4].

He cites Nelson Mandela as an outstanding exception to this default model and contrasts his leadership with that of another African leader, Robert Mugabe, whose vindictiveness towards the white population of Zimbabwe has led to their being ousted from their farms and fleeing the country, resulting in an economic and political disaster:

'Exceptional transformational leaders recognize that holding grudges is a form of arrested development; it holds people back. Like Mugabe, they will get stuck-along with everybody else; in the case of Mugabe, a whole country has become stuck. In contrast, as Mandela has demonstrated, forgiveness by a leader is not a sign of weakness but a sign of strength'.' [5].

Gandhi was another transformational leader. He transformed the people he led so that they did not want to use violence against the British. Unfortunately, such leaders are very rare. Both Gandhi and Mandela were deeply influenced by Jesus Christ's teachings, as was Robert Schuman who played a major part in ending the revenge cycle between France and Germany. Obviously, the world needs more such leaders but how it can produce them is a very difficult problem. One method could be to encourage the establishment, wherever possible throughout the world, of colleges providing courses on good leadership. These would emphasise the positive outcomes of being a forgiving leader. The examples of Mandela, Gandhi, and Schuman could be heavily drawn on.

There are, indeed, in the West, already some courses in leadership for Chinese citizens. One such is organised by the Cambridge China Development Trust and consists of 2 weeks of seminars on leadership and strategy and day trips to the Foreign Office in London. It is for senior Chinese business executives and Communists officials [6]. If such programmes also included courses on the importance of being a forgiving leader and leading in an anti-authoritarian way, these values might be transferred to the political environment in China.

References

1. Kets de Vries, Manfred, 'The Art of Forgiveness: Differentiating Transformational Leaders' (April 18, 2013) INSEAD Working Paper No. 2013/52/EFE, p.10
2. www.bbc.co.uk.›news›world-asia-china-53046454/ 15th June 2020
3. Kets de Vries op.cit. p.10
4. Ibid p.11
5. Ibid p.10
6. Parker, Charlie, Dunning, Sam, Morgan-Bentley, Paul, 'Cambridge fellows tutor Beijing elite in art of leadership.' The Times June 12 2021

Chapter 19
Political Apologies, Forgiveness and Reparations

This book is primarily to show how forgiveness can stop wars from breaking out either by restraining a desire for revenge or by not being too harsh and judgemental. However, when atrocities have already been committed, there is usually later a need for apologies to enable forgiveness, or at least a lessening of hostile feelings, to take place. In such circumstances, a public apology by a national leader may facilitate such a process.

19.1 Willy Brandt's Apology in Poland

Such a gesture was made by the German Chancellor, Willy Brandt, in what was then the Communist People's Republic of Poland on 7 December 1970, when he visited a monument to the victims of the Warsaw Ghetto Uprising. After laying a wreath, he unexpectedly went down on his knees before the monument for a short time, as the surprised crowd of officials and media surrounding him fell silent. It seems it was a spontaneous, sincere gesture, apologising for the Nazi atrocities and asking for forgiveness and reconciliation. It was later called the 'Kniefall von Warschau', the 'Warsaw genuflection'. In his memoirs, he later wrote:

'At the abyss of German history and burdened by millions of murdered humans, I acted in the way of those whom language fails' [1].

On the same day as his genuflection, Brandt signed the Treaty of Warsaw, which acknowledged the Oder-Neisse-Line as the German border with Poland. The powerful, memorable image of Brandt's genuflection was thought by some commentators to symbolise his Ostpolitik or policy towards the East. The next year Brandt received the Nobel Prize for Peace. It may be that his gesture of apology, as well as his policy towards the East, resulted in this prize which was because he had 'stretched out his hand to reconciliation between countries that have long been enemies' [2].

A. Wells, *The Importance of Forgiveness and the Futility of Revenge*, Contributions to International Relations, https://doi.org/10.1007/978-3-030-87552-7_19

However, Brandt's agreeing to Germany's Oder-Neisse Line border with Poland did anger some Germans as it meant Germany had lost lands in the East. Perhaps for that reason, 'Der Spiegel' reported that only 41% of Germans interviewed said that Willy Brandt should have gone down on his knees before the monument and 48% disapproved of his doing so [3]. Nevertheless, his gesture made a great impact in the West and Time magazine named him as 'Man of the Year' [4]. How far Brandt's gesture induced forgiveness in the hearts and minds of the Jews and Poles, it is, of course, impossible to say. Willy Brandt personally was not guilty of any Nazi crime, since not only was he a Resistance fighter, but he lived in Norway and Sweden during the Second World War.

Willy Brandt's apology raises the question of whether apologies on behalf of a nation can be made to another, when most of the people in the guilty nation were not involved in the crime nor even born at the time. This argument was countered in 1985 by the President of Germany, Richard von Weizsacker:

'The vast majority of today's population were either children then or had not been born,' he said, 'But their forefathers have left them a grave legacy. All of us, whether guilty or not, whether old or young, must accept the past. We're all affected by its consequences and liable for it.' [5].

19.2 President Clinton's Apology to Guatemala

The apology from President Bill Clinton to the people of Guatemala in 1999 was of a very different order from that of Willy Brandt's in Poland. In 1954 the USA had been instrumental in overthrowing the democratically elected government in Guatemala led by Jacobo Arbenz whose land reforms threatened the interests of the United Fruit Company in which prominent Americans had a financial interest. A 36-year civil war followed the USA's intervention.

When visiting Guatemala in March 1999, President Bill Clinton made an apology for the human rights abuses committed during the war there in which 200,000 people died. 'It is important that I state clearly that support for military forces or intelligence units which engaged in violent and widespread repression of the kind described in the report was wrong,' Mr Clinton said. 'And the United States must not repeat that mistake. We must and we will instead continue to support the peace and reconciliation process in Guatemala' [6].

The remarks came as the USA declassified thousands of documents made available to the independent Historical Clarification Commission, which concluded the USA was responsible for most of the atrocities committed during the civil war which it had initiated. The USA then helped the Guatemalan security forces to sustain that war for 36 years against civilians suspected of aiding left-wing guerrilla movements.

It would seem that President Clinton's apology was prompted by the revelations of the documents and not something he was longing to say. Neither did Clinton make a physical gesture such as Willy Brandt's falling onto his knees. The apology may have been sincere, but its effectiveness is difficult to evidence.

Besides apologies, reparations and bringing the perpetrators to justice are also important factors in creating an ethos of forgiveness and reconciliation. Reparations were made to the victims of the Holocaust by Germany and some of the chief perpetrators of the atrocities brought to justice. The Guatemalan government has also paid compensation to some of the victims of the civil war and brought some of those who committed atrocities to justice.

19.3 The Issue of Reparations

In 2010 President Obama apologised to the Guatemalan president Alvara Colon, and all those affected, over a 1940s study by the USA in which 696 Guatemalans were infected with syphilis. However, no reparations were made. An apology without reparations is unlikely to improve relations, as can be seen in the relations between Japan and South Korea.

During the Second World War, an estimated 200,000 women, mostly Koreans, are estimated to have been forced to serve the Japanese army in front-line brothels. They are euphemistically called 'comfort women'. In 1965 Japan apologised to South Korea for its use of them. However, the former comfort women had to fight for compensation which by 2018 was still regarded by a United Nations panel as inadequate. The panel stated that Japan should ensure that all victims of wartime sexual slavery should receive adequate compensation. Such was the bitterness of a support group for the women that they erected a statue of a comfort woman outside the Japanese consulate in Busan in South Korea.

The USA's record of paying reparations is selective. It has paid reparations to Japanese Americans interned during the Second World War and compensated Native American tribes for seizing their lands. However, it has not made any reparations for slavery.

The widespread movement of protest for 'Black Lives Matter' caused by the killing of George Floyd in May 2020 in Minneapolis (by a policeman kneeling on his neck) showed the need to improve relations between the black and white Americans in the USA. The Afro-Americans have never been compensated for slavery. In 2019 a bill (HR40) was introduced into the House of Representatives for a Commission to Study and Develop Reparations for Afro-Americans Act. It was to look at the state's involvement with slavery, subsequent forms of discrimination, and the lingering negative effects of slavery on living African-Americans and society.

Such compensation, together with a sincere apology and a gesture like Willy Brandt's kneel might go a long way to reconcile the descendants of American slaves with the descendants of American slave owners.

19.4 Time Lapses

There could, of course, be an issue with the amount of time allowed to elapse before apologies seem irrelevant.

In January 2019, President Andres Obrador of Mexico wrote to King Felipe 1V of Spain and Pope Francis to ask them to apologise for Hernan Cortes' invasion of Mexico in 1519. He asked them to seek the 'forgiveness of indigenous peoples, for violations of what are now known as human rights' [7]. His demand was ignored and, when leaked to the press merely opened him to ridicule. As 'The Guardian' newspaper observed:

'A demand for an apology for a nation's actions 500 years earlier is hardly likely to improve relations between countries' [8].

19.5 PM Tony Blair's 'Apology' for the Potato Famine

However, Prime Minister Tony Blair did express regret for an event that happened 150 years earlier. In June 1997, he issued a statement of regret, which was interpreted as an apology by the media, for the British government's inaction during the Irish potato famine during a festival to commemorate it in County Cork.

He said: 'The famine was a defining event in the history of Ireland and Great Britain. It has left deep scars. That one million people should have died in what was then part of the richest and most powerful nation in the world is something that still causes pain as we reflect on it today. Those who governed in London at the time failed their people' [9].

The Irish Prime Minister, John Bruton, commented: 'While the statement confronts the past honestly, it does so in a way that heals for the future' [10].

Blair's statement did indeed own up to Britain's culpability. As Wendy R. Sherman, a former US Undersecretary of State for Political Affairs and a senior fellow at Harvard's Belfer Centre wrote:

'Apologies . . .are not ends in themselves. . .The most powerful agent of forgiveness seems to be remembrance: because it forces the perpetrator to acknowledge and own the crimes it has committed, victims are likely to find that admission more sincere than a brief apology' [11].

19.6 The Apology of the Australian Prime Minister, Kevin Rudd, to the Aboriginal People in 2008

Kevin Rudd's acknowledgement of the wrongs committed by the white Australian settlers to the aborigines was certainly no 'brief apology'.

Between 1910 and 1970, the Australian government forcibly took aboriginal children away from their families and put them into white settler institutions such as orphanages, children's homes or foster homes in order to encourage 'assimilation.' This was done through federal and state government agencies and church missions. The children were frequently prevented from contacting their families or staying connected with their community. The aim was to strip from them their culture, language, land and identity in the hope that their aboriginal culture would die out.

In addition, the settlers drove the aborigines from their lands and gave them new diseases as well as alcoholism and mental health problems. The effects of this oppression could be seen in terms of the aborigines' employment, education, health, and low self-esteem. By the end of the twentieth century increasing concern was being expressed over the fate of the aborigines.

In 1995 the Australian Federal Attorney-General, Sir William Deane, launched the *National Inquiry into the Separation of Aboriginal and Torres Strait Islander Children from Their Families*. This Inquiry was conducted by the Human Rights and Equal Opportunity Commission (HREOC).

In 1997 the Commission published its report called 'Bringing them Home', recommending that apologies were to be made to the aborigines by officials on behalf of their predecessors, to heal the effects of the forced removals and other laws and policies, as well as providing financial reparations and rehabilitation. The Australian parliaments and police forces were to acknowledge their roles in the creation and enforcement of the policies [12].

The Report quoted Sir William Deane, who said that true reconciliation between the Australian nation and its indigenous peoples could not be achieved without the nation acknowledging it had wrongfully dispossessed, oppressed, and degraded them. He added:

'That is not to say that individual Australians who had no part in what was done in the past should feel or acknowledge personal guilt. It is simply to assert our identity as a nation and the basic fact that national shame, as well as national pride, can and should exist in relation to past acts and omissions, at least when done or made in the name of the community or with the authority of government' [13].

However, the Prime Minister at the time of the release of the report, John Howard, did not agree with this and refused to make an apology to what became known as the 'Stolen Generations'. He felt that a formal national apology was inappropriate. He told parliament, 'Although in a personal sense many Australians will feel sorrow and regret in relation to past injustices suffered by sections of the Australian community, it is the view of my government that a formal national apology, of the type sought by others, is not appropriate'. He said that the government believed that the most appropriate way to help the 300,000 or so Aborigine community was to address their disadvantage in areas of health, housing, and education [14].

His statement was condemned by the Labour opposition and the smaller parties.

'If you are a person who has become aware of a great injustice and that you are part of a process which has assisted in producing those injustices it's a pretty poor, weak character who can't actually come out and say 'sorry'', the opposition leader Mr Kim Beazley declared [15].

In the federal election of November 2007, however, Kevin Rudd swept to power, replacing John Howard. As the new Prime Minister of Australia, Rudd promised to make the apology to the 'Stolen Generations' early. This he did in the Australian Parliament in Canberra on 13 February 2008.

The apology was accompanied by much fanfare across Australia. Big screens were set up in parks and communal areas to broadcast Kevin Rudd speaking of the wrongs that governments had inflicted on Aboriginal and Torres Strait Islander peoples across Australia. His speech brought much applause and tears of relief. Rudd's apology was more than a lone national leader apologising for past governmental actions: he had much of the nation publicly supporting his apology and the aborigines appreciating it [16].

However, in 2017, 20 years after the Bringing Them Home Report was released, the Healing Foundation published another report called 'Bringing Them Home 20 years on an action plan for healing'. The report showed that the majority of recommendations made in the report of 1997 had not yet been implemented, and the effects were still being felt. Furthermore, the trauma felt by the Stolen Generations because they did not grow up in a healthy family structure had affected their children, grandchildren, and great grandchildren. This was termed 'intergenerational trauma' [17].

It is clear that Kevin Rudd's apology was a significant event in Australia's history and that it was welcomed by the aborigines. It authenticated Sir William Deane's assertion (quoted earlier) that a full acknowledgement of wrongs done to the aborigines by the white settlers is important for true reconciliation. His assertion also that national pride and national shame (he did not say 'guilt') based on past acts can be felt by an individual who had made no contribution to either is evidenced by experience. It justifies a person in an official capacity apologising for the past acts of an institution for which they work, although they personally were not involved.

Just as an apology can restore a harmed person's dignity, so a dominating settler people apologising for past wrongs to the aborigines must do something to restore the latter's self-pride. However, it may not prompt forgiveness in the sense of ending their bitterness. This is more likely to occur when there is evidence of the sincerity of the apology in the form of reparations. These would materially relieve the aborigines' distress and encourage forgiveness and reconciliation. Whether any of them actually did forgive those responsible for harming them can never, of course, be known [18]. What surely has happened is that some aborigines have been made more comfortable and happier. When that happens to people they usually become more forgiving.

This is not a case of a mighty nation which, when attacked, should forgive and not yield to the desire of revenge because of the bloodshed unleashed (which was the concern of the opening chapters of this book), but of a powerful, white settler people apologising to a vulnerable, smaller, black ethnic people whose forgiveness and lack of hostility is important for national reconciliation.

19.7 Germany Asks Namibia for Forgiveness for Genocide in 2021

In May 2021, it was reported that the President of Germany, Frank-Walter Steinmeier, was planning to go to Namibia, stand in front of the parliament and ask for forgiveness for genocide committed in South West Africa by Germany in the early twentieth century. This apology again raised issues of how long can be the time lapse between an atrocity committed against a people and an apology made for it, together with reparations.

In the 1880s German traders arrived in South West Africa, which Germany claimed as a crown colony in 1890. The Germans took control of the region, seizing the land and cattle of the native people, who were used as forced labour.

Between 1904 and 1908, the Herero and Namaqua tribes rose in rebellion against the Germans whose troops crushed them, driving them out into the Kalahari desert, where they died from starvation and dehydration. The Germans also forced the natives into concentration camps where at least half died from malnutrition, disease, overwork, beatings, and executions. About 75,000 natives died in this way. This is sometimes known as the first genocide of the twentieth century [19]. It is curious that the Lutheran church did not protest loudly about the genocide in Germany since its missionaries were working in German South West Africa and it must have heard about the atrocities.

The Germans sent the skulls of some of the natives whom they had killed back to Germany for eugenics research and display in museums vainly to show the alleged superiority of the white race. In 2018 the last of the natives' skulls were returned to Namibia [20].

In 2004 the German Minister for Development, Heidemarie Wieczorek-Zeul, apologised for the mass murders, but negotiations for the settlement with Namibia (as German South West Africa now called) took longer. They were begun in 2015, but there was much disagreement over the terms, including the terminology for the payments to be made. Germany had ruled out the terms 'financial reparations' or 'compensation', forming part of the formal apology for fears such payments could set a precedent for further claims. Instead, Angela Merkel's government has since 2014 negotiated with Namibia 'to heal the wounds' with Namibia [21].

In May 2021, it was reported that the sum that Germany agreed to pay Namibia was 1.1 billion euros (£940 million) in what the German government called a gesture of reconciliation but not legally binding reparations [22]. Germany was to make additional aid payments towards infrastructure, healthcare, and job-training programmes in areas where the descendants of the massacred tribes now live, as well as help with building affordable housing and expanding Namibia's renewable energy capacity [23].

While Germany has not admitted to paying compensation for fear of further legal claims (despite a time lapse of over 100 years), it has admitted to genocide, perhaps partly because the Genocide Convention of 1948 cannot be applied retroactively. Germany's liability is therefore political and moral rather than legal.

'Our aim was and is to find a joint path to genuine reconciliation in remembrance of the victims', the German foreign minister, Heiko Maas, said in a statement. 'That includes our naming the events of the German colonial era in today's Namibia, and particularly the atrocities between 1904 and 1908, unsparingly and without euphemisms. We will now officially call these events what they were from today's perspective: a genocide' [24].

Some of the leaders of the Herero and Namaqua have expressed dissatisfaction with the agreement (with the amount and the omission of word 'reparations'), claiming it is a public relations coup for Germany [25].

But despite the cynicism, the financial agreement must do some good for the Namibian people. Whether it will arouse a sense of forgiveness in them is another matter.

It could be argued that there is a problem here regarding Germany's president asking for forgiveness when he and the present day German people had nothing to do with the genocide which was committed over a century ago against tribes people in German South West Africa who have long since died. However, some of the descendants of these tribes were party to the negotiations with the present day government of Germany. They would have been told by their elders about the atrocities. Moreover, the comments quoted earlier in this chapter of the then President of Germany Richard von Weisacker in 1985 regarding the Holocaust are relevant. He observed that the forefathers of the present day Germans had left them a grave legacy for which they were liable [26].

19.8 Germany and Israel: Reparations But the Israelis Deny Forgiveness

For some people involved, the century between the genocide in South West Africa and the German government's apology was too long a time lapse for it to be meaningful, although the reparations were welcome. But with regard to Israel's receiving reparations from Germany after the Holocaust, the situation was very different.

In 1951 the Israeli government, being nearly bankrupt, approached West Germany to ask for reparations. However, this move angered other Israelis as the genocide was too recent, the memories too raw, for many of them to want anything to do with Germany. Regardless of the needs of Israel's economy, they thought the reparations might be regarded as an act of atonement for the Holocaust. Israel's acceptance of them might then be seen as forgiveness for the genocide. Israel erupted into a furious debate about the issue. Opposition to the agreement came from both the right (Herut and the General Zionists) and the left of the political spectrum (the Mapai and Israeli Communist parties).

In a heated debate in the Knesset on whether to open negotiations for reparations with Germany in January 1952, Menachem Begin, the head of the Herut party (and later the founder of Likud), expressed the hatred that many Jews felt towards Germany and their outrage that Israel might directly negotiate with that country. He himself had lost his parents and brother in the Holocaust. His speech condemned all the German people as Nazis and the Israeli Prime Minister for negotiating with them:

'The fact that Western Germany is a democracy nowadays does not exonerate it from its Nazi past.

You may say that [Chancellor] Adenauer's Government is a new German Government, not a Nazi one... I ask: Who are Mr. Adenauer's assistants? The answer: Half of the employees at Adenauer's Foreign Office are members of the Nazi Party. And with these people you are going to negotiate... with the murderers who laid down the ground for the annihilation of millions of our brethren while telling the whole world that the persecution of Jews is 'horrendous propaganda?' [27].

For Begin all the Germans were guilty:

'...From a Jewish standpoint there is not a single German who is not a Nazi, and there is no single German who is not a murderer. And to these people you go to receive money from?' [28].

MK Elimelech Rimalt (General Zionists) objected to the direct negotiations and queried why the German government wanted to pay:

'And what are their motives? Why do they want to pay? Perhaps the better ones amongst them seek to salve their consciences? Perhaps through compensation they seek peace and quiet, nights without nightmares of remorse? We should leave them to their nightmares, to their shattered consciences, to their mark of Cain. We must not relieve them of these horrors!' [29].

Like many members of the Knesset, Rimalt was concerned that the Germans would assume they had been forgiven for the genocide. He argued:

'But if we conclude a deal and say... we have taken the money but have not forgiven denying the Holocaust what will they say? They won't believe us. And the gentiles are familiar with the old rule: where there is trade, there are relations' [30].

He was also appalled at the idea that it seemed that Germany was paying Israel for the Jewish lives lost in the Holocaust and asked:

'And what shall we say to our youth, to our children... in whom we have inculcated moral values, whom we taught that there are situations in which what might seem worthwhile can also be morally unacceptable? Can we prevent them from translating the money we shall receive into a per capita figure? My young son asked me: 'How much will we get for Grandpa and Grandma'? for both of my parents were murdered. This is too grave and too painful for us.' [31].

It was to avoid the idea that Israel was receiving compensation for Jewish lives lost in the Holocaust, or that the money could be regarded as an atonement for it, that Prime Minister David Ben-Gurion and other members of the government based their reparations demand on recovering Jewish property and financing the resettlement of Holocaust survivors in Israel. When the Knesset finally voted on the matter, it agreed by 61 votes to 50 to endorse Ben-Gurion's policy of direct negotiations with the Federal Republic of Germany.

On 10 September 1952, in Luxembourg, the State of Israel and the Federal Republic of Germany signed the reparations agreement, which emphasised it was for the material damage done to the Jews and for their resettlement:

'Whereas unspeakable criminal acts were perpetrated against the Jewish people during the National-Socialist regime of terror and whereas by a declaration in the Bundestag on 27th September, 1951, the Government of the Federal Republic of Germany made known their determination, within the limits of their capacity, to make good the material damage caused by these acts and whereas the State of Israel has assumed the heavy burden of resettling so great a number of uprooted and destitute Jewish refugees from Germany and from territories formerly under German rule and has on this basis advanced a claim against the Federal Republic of Germany for global recompense for the cost of the integration of these refugees' [32].

In accordance with the agreement, West Germany paid Israel a sum of 3 billion marks over the next 14 years; 450 million marks were paid to the World Jewish Congress. Initially, a Jewish agency in Germany was paid the money and bought goods and machinery with it and shipped it to Israel.

Chancellor Konrad Adenauer was willing to pay the reparations. As a devout Christian, he knew that his country morally had to help Israel. As a politician, he knew that Germany needed to do so to win the trust of other countries with which it would have to deal.

However, according to Hanns Maull, one of Germany's leading academic foreign policy analysts, the German people themselves were not then concerned with 'reconciliation and atonement'. They were suffering from the 'collective trauma' of being devastated by the war which they lost and finding their country was partitioned. Indeed for many Germans, only the Nazis were guilty of the genocide, not the whole German population [33].

There was then from Germany no apology to the Israelis. They certainly did not want one either. There was also understandably no forgiveness from Israel at that time. But did it matter? No lives would be lost because of this. The Holocaust was too near in time, the memories too fresh for forgiveness and reconciliation to be appropriate. Moreover, the Israelis did not live with the Germans in one state where revenge would be easy.

Some Jews did want revenge. At a discussion of the Mapai (Socialist Party) Central Committee, Meir Dvorzhetsky, a Holocaust survivor who succeeded in escaping from the Vilnius Ghetto declared:

'If you ask me what is my wish regarding the German people, I would say, A mother for a mother, a father for a father, a child for a child. My soul would rest in peace if it were possible to kill six million Germans for six million Jews' [34].

But his idea was rejected by Mapai member, Haim Yahil:

'I do not believe we are psychologically capable of taking revenge. No revenge proportional to what has been done to us is possible at all... We cannot take this road. Our only historical revenge is to be found in the survival of our people and in the establishment of a sovereign Jewish entity after the Holocaust. Our revenge lies in our very existence...'

But it seems to me that another historical revenge is also possible. It must be hoped that it will be attained when, at some time in the future, a German generation arises that will be appalled by the evil deeds perpetrated by its ancestors' [35].

Indeed, this generation did arise, helped by German faith groups who were prepared to consider that it was not only the Nazis who were responsible for the genocide and who reached out to Israel. The Auschwitz Frankfurt trials of the early 1960s in which Germany, not the Allies, pursued those who had worked in the camp helped raise German awareness of what had gone on in Auschwitz [36].

In December 1970, Germany's Chancellor Willy Brandt did make the sort of gesture that people like Haim Yahil (quoted above) seem to have been longing for when, on an official visit to Poland, Brandt went down on his knees and knelt in silence when laying a wreath before a monument to the victims of the Warsaw Ghetto Uprising. This has been described at the opening of this chapter.

Whether Brandt's action aroused forgiveness in the hearts of the Jewish people can never be known, but it seems that most of the world has forgiven Germany. Through a policy of acknowledging, with reparations, its moral debt to countries it has harmed and making an effort with reconciliation programmes, it has won international respect.

Israel, meanwhile, has been illegally annexing lands from the Palestinians, who have been precipitated into immiseration. If later on there is a peace settlement, Israel may be called upon to pay reparations and apologise to the Palestinians who, it is hoped, will forgive their close neighbour.

19.9 Political Apologies Conclusion

It is clear that, just as an apology can on a personal level sometimes restore the dignity of a person who has been harmed and make them feel better, so a government's apology may have that effect on a people at a national level. Certainly, it will do no harm, and it may help the healing process between ethnic groups. However, if a nation does not want it, it is pointless to give it and certainly no guarantee of forgiveness or an end to hatred on the part of the injured members of a nation. A full apology accompanying reparations can raise the process above the merely financially transactional and help with the healing process. A nation will never know how far the people it has harmed have forgiven it, but this is no reason for a country not to attempt to say it is sorry and to try to make amends. The apology will be a marker on the accounting side of its history. While there is a problem with ascertaining how far back in its history a country can be held responsible for its past deeds, arguably if the harm done in the past remains significantly in the present, the guilty state should endeavour to compensate, with an apology to restore the dignity of the harmed.

The peoples from whom forgiveness was hoped in this chapter were small, weak ones. Here were not situations in which more powerful nations, to avoid war, should exercise restraint over their desire for revenge, but the smaller ethnic groups which hopefully will forgive and be reconciled with more powerful peoples who have harmed them.

Today there is much resentment in the former colonies of Western imperialist powers over the latter's treatment of them. It is surely time not only for apologies but for compensation to be paid to them is. It will also be wise to treat them generously because, still impoverished, many African states are turning to Islamic extremism, which does not respect forgiveness and many other cherished Western values. This subject will be dealt with in the next chapter.

References

1. The Warsaw Genuflection, Willy Brandt's Historic Gesture-Deutsches Historisches Museum, www/dhm.de/blog/2016
2. Ibid
3. Ibid
4. Ibid
5. Timsit, Annabelle, https://qz.com/1915185/'How Germany Paid Reparations for the Holocaust'
6. The Guardian 12th March 1999
7. The Guardian 11th April 2019)
8. Ibid
9. Marks, Kathy 'Blair Issues Apology for Irish Potato Famine', The Independent, 2nd June 1997
10. Ibid
11. Policy Brief (June 2016), Sherman, Wendy R., Former US Undersecretary of State for Political Affairs and a senior fellow at Harvard's Kennedy School Belfer Centre.
12. Australian Human Rights and Equal Opportunity Commission Report 'Bringing them Home' Report of the National Inquiry into the Separation of Aboriginal and Torres Strait Islander Children from Their Families April 1997
13. Ibid
14. The Irish Times 'Howard refuses to join in apology to Aborigines' Wed May 27 1998
15. Ibid
16. 'Apology to the Stolen Generations' https://www.deadlystory.com>page>culture>apology
17. 'Bringing Them Home 20 years on', https://healingfoundation.org.au
18. Tom Bentley has written an interesting article on whether colonial setter-state apologies such as Rudd's could obtain forgiveness:'Settler state apologies and the elusiveness of forgiveness: 'The purification ritual that does not purify', Tom Bentley, Contemporary Political Theory, Volume 19, pages 381–403 (2020)
19. Moody, Oliver, 'Germany ready to atone for colonial-era 'genocide 'in Namibia' The Times' 19th May 2021
20. Ibid
21. Oltermann, Philip, 'Germany Rules out Reparations' The Guardian, 21st May 2021
22. Oltermann, Philip 'Germany agrees to pay Namibia E1.1bn' The Guardian 28th May, 2021
23. Moody, Oliver, op.cit.
24. Oltermann, Philip 'Germany agrees to pay Namibia E1.1bn' The Guardian 28th May, 2021
25. Moody, Oliver, op.cit See also Crossland, David, 'Namibians reject €1 bn for Genocide' The Times June 3rd 2021
26. Timsit, Annabelle, https://qz.com/1915185/ 'How Germany Paid Reparations for the Holocaust'

27. Sharett, Yaakov (Ed) The Reparations Controversy: The Jewish State and German Money in the Shadow of the Holocaust 1951-1952, (Berlin 2011) Knesset Debate. "Reparations from Germany," Sitting 38, 7 January 1952 p.179
28. Ibid
29. Ibid p170
30. Ibid
31. Ibid p171
32. 206 United Nations — Treaty Series 1953 No. 2137. Israel and the Federal Republic of Germany'
33. Rienzi, Greg, 'Other nations could learn from Germany's efforts to reconcile after WW11 hub.jhu.edu/magazine/2015/summer/germany-japan-reconciliation
34. Sharrett op.cit. Mapai Central Committee, 13.12.1951, p.114–5
35. Ibid p.120–21
36. Rienzi Greg op.cit.

Chapter 20
The Limits of Forgiveness (1): Islamic Jihadism in Africa

There are some situations in international politics where forgiveness seems irrelevant. At the time of writing (May 2021), it seems that Africa is becoming a fertile ground for Islamic jihadism, which does not value or warrant forgiveness.

In my chapter on the invasion of Iraq by the USA and UK, I argued that if this had not happened, ISIS would never have arisen. If President Bush had forgiven the attack of 9/11, not responded with a military onslaught on Afghanistan but issued international arrest warrants for the perpetrators of the crime, then turned his attention to stopping the harm American support for Israel was doing to the Palestinians, the world would have been a more peaceful place. Moreover, there was no reason for Bush to go on to attack Iraq, which had nothing to do with 9/11. The invasion allowed al-Qaeda to enter Iraq from where it went into Syria and metamorphosed into ISIS. Today its terrorising of Iraq and Syria has subsided.

However, in Africa, both al-Qaeda and ISIS are now resurging and have links with their movements in Syria. Neither al-Qaeda nor ISIS shares with the West the values of the Enlightenment, such as tolerance and the authority of reason; neither are the two movements influenced by Christian teaching of the importance of forgiveness which they would regard as weakness. The aims of the movements (an extremist Islamic state or a caliphate that most Muslims do not want) as well as the jihadists' brutal methods do not warrant a forgiving, empathetic response to their attacks. Moreover, the horrific atrocities carried out by ISIS have not been followed by the remorse of the perpetrators and thereby warrant forgiveness.

It is true that many Africans join movements linked to al-Qaeda and ISIS because they have no job and no other means of support. Certainly, the international community must do more to develop that continent's economic well-being and remove the financial need for its people to support Islamic jihadism.

However, unfortunately at the time of writing in 2021, the international response must also be military support to the African states which are trying to protect their peoples by defeating the Islamic jihadists. None of this would have happened had President Bush responded with enlightened forgiveness after the USA was attacked in 2001. I shall now consider the African states most affected by Islamic extremism.

A. Wells, *The Importance of Forgiveness and the Futility of Revenge*, Contributions to International Relations, https://doi.org/10.1007/978-3-030-87552-7_20

20.1 Somalia: Al-Shabab

Al-Shabab, which means 'the Youth' in Arabic, is an Islamic militant organisation in Somalia, comprised of radical young Somalians as well as foreign jihadists. It supports the Saudi-inspired Wahhabi version of Islam, and its aim is to establish an Islamic state (Most Somalis are Muslim). Al-Shabab may have links with other militant groups in Africa, such as al-Qaeda in the Islamic Mahgreb, based in the Sahara desert, and Boko Haram in Nigeria. The USA and the UK have banned it as a terrorist group, and the USA has issued a reward for the capture of its leader, Ahmad Umar.

While still lethally active today, al-Shabab was at the height of its power in Somalia between 2009 and 2010, having spread terror with jihadist violence, suicide bombings and kidnappings. In areas under its sway, it imposed strict Sharia law, stoning to death women accused of adultery and amputating the hands of thieves.

It controlled most major towns, including Mogadishu, earning millions of dollars in tax revenues [1]. However, it was forced out of Mogadishu in August 2011 following an offensive spearheaded by about 22,000 African Union troops. The US carried out targeted airstrikes, killing al-Shabab's then leaders. Moreover, al-Shabab lost support from the people when it rejected Western food aid to combat drought and famine in 2011.

Al-Shabab was forced to leave the vital port of Kismayo in September 2012. The loss of this port hit al-Shabab's finances, as it used to earn money by taking a cut of the city's lucrative charcoal trade [2].

Nevertheless, al-Shabab continued to carry out bombings in Somalia and surrounding states. In September 2013, it was in the world's spotlight with its bombing of Nairobi's Westgate shopping mall in neighbouring Kenya, leaving more than 70 dead.

In 2015 al-Shabab attacked a university in Kenya's Garissa University, near the border with Somalia. Its gunmen targeted Christian students in a dawn raid and left a total of 148 people killed. Further, the Somalian government blamed al-Shabab for the killing of at least 500 people in a truck bombing in Mogadishu in October 2017.

In March 2017, US President Donald Trump approved a Pentagon plan to escalate operations against al-Shabab. The US put more than 500 troops into Somalia and conducted 30 airstrikes in 2017. Troops of the African Union countries have also been fighting against al-Shabab, but in 2018, the EU cut the funds that support the AU force. Nevertheless, al-Shabab is much weaker than it was in 2010 at the height of its power.

The chaos that al-Shabab has caused has meant that it is still too dangerous for Somalia to hold democratic elections. The last one was in 1969. At present, the parliament and president are elected through a complex system involving the clan elders playing an influential role.

The government of Somalia and its people cannot be expected to act in a forgiving way to al-Shabab and to try to negotiate or be reconciled with it since it is determined to create an Islamic state, which most Somalis do not want, by carrying out the most heinous crimes such as massacres to achieve its goal. This organisation is not open to negotiation and compromise. The Somali people need protection from it, and the Somali government's military forces, together with those of the AU and of the USA, rightfully provided this and should continue to do so.

When Nelson Mandela decided, in 1961, that Gandhi's ideas were not effective when dealing with the Afrikaners, he persuaded the African National Congress that sabotage, such as the blowing up of railway lines should be used because this involved no loss of life (or so he argued) and would make reconciliation later easier.

Al-Shabab has not bothered with such concerns and is guilty of killing many innocent people. While their relatives may later forgive al-Shabab, forgiveness and reconciliation is not an appropriate response from the government.

It is true that the main support for al-Shabab has come from young people without any job prospects. Somalia is one of the poorest countries in sub-Saharan Africa due to decades of civil war and political fragmentation [3]. Clearly, besides a military response, an effort has to be made to help the poorer countries of Africa improve their economies and standard of living, including educational opportunities to avoid the development of extremism. However, because the Somalian government needs to protect its people from al-Shabab, the military response to its attacks is the most reasonable one.

20.2 Mozambique: Al-Shabab

Mozambique has long experienced instability, but the insurgency involving Islamist militants began in 2017. They call themselves 'al-Shabab' or 'the Youth', but are not affiliated with al-Shabab in Somalia. However, the USA has claimed it is linked to ISIS and has declared it a terrorist organisation [4]. Its members belong mainly to the Muslim minority in Mozambique where they believe they are discriminated against regarding jobs, although most Mozambican Christians are also are poor.

In 2021, in Cabo Delgado, the northern province of Mozambique, this Islamic militant group caused shock internationally for carrying out beheadings of children [5] as well as adults. Indeed, it once beheaded 50 people in a sports field. [6]. Besides mass murder, it has also caused the displacement of 670,000 people [7].

The key to these horrific actions in Cabo Delgado lies in the rich off-shore natural gas reserves that are being explored by the Mozambique government in collaboration with multinational energy companies, in particular, the French company Total. This has promised to use some of the profits from the local gas to improve the lives of the people in Mozambique. But al-Shabab wants all the profits from the gas exploitation to be used for the Mozambicans who, they say, should control it. In pursuit of this goal, al-Shabab wants to drive away all the foreign workers and executives in Cabo Delgado through terrorism.

Although al-Shabab is misdirected in its thinking, it is clear that Total should work at putting a large part of its profits back into Cabo Delgado so that the people can see the benefits which could be in health education and jobs. In Cabo Delgado, there is much poverty and disputes over access to land and jobs, which has contributed to local grievances. In addition, Mozambique has suffered greatly from natural disasters, such as hurricanes, probably caused by climate change which can encourage the development of extremism in third world countries by causing poverty. It is therefore important that richer countries tackle this problem urgently.

While one can have sympathy with the impoverished young people with few life chances, al-Shabab's horrific methods of beheading children and adults do not invite forgiveness but a military response to protect the rest of the population. To this end the Mozambican government has invited US military advisers who will train local forces fighting the militants [8]. Portugal, Mozambiques's former imperial master, has also sent a training mission, as will the EU [9]. Obviously, the development of the economy with the job and educational opportunities for young people, Muslim as well as Christian, is also important, but the protection of the Mozambican people demands a military response.

20.3 Boko Haram

Boko Haram is a terrorist organisation [10] founded in 2002 in northeastern Nigeria where it extended its power over vast swaths of territory. In 2015 it pledged allegiance to ISIS, which also operates in Chad, Niger, and Cameroon. Boko Haram is responsible for thousands of deaths and the displacement of millions of people. It aims to overthrow the government of Nigeria and establish an Islamic state under strict shariah law and then extend its power further afield. (In 2021, just under half the population was Christian, the same proportion was Muslim.) Boko Haram is responsible for Nigeria's coming third in the Global Terrorism Index for being most impacted by terrorism in 2020 [11].

The group's name, 'Boko Haram', means 'Western education is forbidden'. 'Boko' means 'fake' and is often used to refer to Western education by Islamic jihadists'. Haram' is Arabic for 'forbidden'.

Boko Haram is against Western education because this encourages critical, independent thought that challenges authorities. It is usually secular and fosters toleration of opposing views and holds that girls, as well as boys, should be educated.

The meaning of the name Boko Haram was dramatically illustrated in 2014 when the militant group kidnapped 276 girls, who were mainly Christians, from their school in Chibok, northern Nigeria. This hit the international headlines.

It seems the group not only wanted to deny the girls a secular education but also to use them as pawns to negotiate the release of some of their imprisoned commanders. Boko Haram threatened to sell them in the marketplace as slaves or force them to convert to Islam and marry. The USA, France and the UK helped locate and rescue them but, by 2019, over 100 of the girls were still missing [12].

20.3.1 Boko Haram and the Islamic State of West Africa Province

Boko Haram carried out many more abductions, often to gain ransom money but also as a campaign against Western education. As well as girls, it kidnapped young boys who became child soldiers. In 2016 the organisation split into two militant groups Boko Haram and the Islamic State of West Africa Province. The latter, in February 2018, kidnapped 110 girls from their boarding school in the village of Dapchi in northern Nigeria. They were released almost 5 weeks later, but five did not survive the ordeal [13].

The attitude of these Islamic jihadists to Western education can be contrasted with that of Nelson Mandela, who once said that ‘Education is the most powerful weapon which you can use to change the world’ [14]. He was so concerned at the high drop-out rate of girls from the school in South Africa that he asked the African American television host Oprah Winfrey to found an academy for girls from deprived backgrounds like herself. This has become very successful [15]. However, the Islamic jihadist does not regard Western education as a weapon for change. They want to use real weapons for death and destruction. As such, they deserve a military response from the Nigerian government. They believe their actions are right despite their obvious cruelty and therefore are not given remorse.

In May 2021, the Islamic State of West Africa Province captured the leader of Boko Haram, Abu-Bakr Shekau, who blew himself up with a suicide vest. It seems that the two organisations will become a single very powerful jihadist movement. It is clear that Nigeria will have to deal with Islamic jihadists for a long time in the future.

20.3.2 Military Response

Besides Western help to deal with the terrorists, the Nigerian government has been aided militarily by Benin, Chad, Cameroon, and Niger. Indeed, armed force is the appropriate response to protect the rest of the population from the extremist groups. They do not accept Western values of negotiation and compromise but want to force their beliefs on others through terror. Attempts at forgiveness and reconciliation would be inappropriate and encourage further terrorism.

Nevertheless in 2016, Nigeria did introduce a de-radicalising programme ‘Operation Safe Corridor’ for ex-combatants, but it is not clear whether it has helped them to reintegrate into society and probably lacked resources [16]. More international financial aid should surely be given to countries like Nigeria that have attempted to provide de-radicalisation programme. While deradicalisation is not, of course, the same as forgiveness, it is in the realm of mercy and hope of a change in the prisoner’s character.

20.4 The Spread of Jihadists in the Sahel

Islamic State-linked groups have spread over Africa as they did in the Middle East. Besides being in Somalia, Nigeria, Mozambique, they are already in the countries of the Sahel (the vast semi-arid region of Africa separating the Sahara Desert to the north and tropical savannas to the south). It is afflicted by drought and poverty. Mali, Chad, Niger, Burkina Faso and Mauretania comprise the Sahel countries and have all suffered from insurgents' attacks.

When the Western interventionist powers overthrew Gaddafi in 2011, they unwittingly destabilised the sub-Sahara region. For decades Gaddafi had been recruiting the Tuaregs (nomadic Berbers renowned for their desert-fighting prowess) into his military. When he was killed, they fled home to Mali, bringing with them their sophisticated weapons with which Libya was now awash. (Nearly half of Malians live in extreme poverty, and many are without access to education or employment [17].) Some of the Tuaregs joined forces with the local Islamists, many of whom had come from other Maghreb countries and belonged to Al-Qaeda in the Islamic Maghreb (the AQIM).

In northern Mali, the AQIM imposed Sharia law, including the veiling of women, hand amputations of thieves and the stoning of adulterers. There were also reports of vandalism in the World Heritage Site of Timbuctoo, an ancient centre of culture. In January, the AQIM 2013 moved southwards, seeming to threaten the capital Bamako and causing the alarmed Malian government to asked France for military help as Mali had ties with France as a former colony. The UN Security Council had authorised in December 2012 over 3000 troops from the Economic Community of West African States (ECOWAS), but they had still not arrived as AQIM moved towards Bamako. In early January 2013, France sent some 2000 troops to Mali to prevent it from falling into the hands of the Islamists. Britain sent two transport planes. Owing to France's bombing and the Malian soldiers' efforts, the Islamists and Tuaregs were driven back. However, they were not defeated.

At the time of writing (2021), for the last 8 years, France has been fighting the extremists in the Sahel. In 2020, the UK sent 300 troops to Mali to join Operation Newcombe, a 3-year mission using a force of around 15,000 UN multinational troops, spearheaded by the French, to help stabilise the Sahel region. The jihadists fight not only against the African governments but amongst each other for support. There is a rivalry between al-Qaeda and ISIS, which uses far more graphic, horrific atrocities than does al-Qaeda, attracting sociopaths but repelling many Muslims [18].

The Global Terrorism Index published on 25 November 2020, reported that the 'centre of gravity' for the Islamic State group IS has moved away from the Middle East to Africa and to some extent South Asia, with total deaths by IS in sub-Saharan Africa up by 67% over last year. "The expansion of ISIS affiliates into sub-Saharan Africa led to a surge in terrorism in many countries in the region," reports the Global Terrorism Index, 'Seven of the 10 countries with the largest increase in terrorism were in sub-Saharan Africa: Burkina Faso, Mozambique, DRC, Mali, Niger, Cameroon and Ethiopia' [19].

At the beginning of this chapter, I argue that forgiveness is not appropriate to dealing with the jihadists, yet it is clear that merely to kill them with military power is not a method that will completely eliminate them, nor is it humane. While there is a need to respond militarily to terrorists to protect the population and a need to try to deradicalize prisoners taken, the international community should, at the same time, consider the causes of jihadism and reflect on what can be done to remove them.

20.5 Causes of Unrest in Sub-Saharan Africa

The cause of some of the unrest in sub-Saharan Africa is obviously influenced by Islamic jihadism in the Middle East. However, poverty is another root cause. Drug trafficking, kidnapping and migrant smuggling are the important sources of the jihadists' income. This enables them to pay Africans to fight for them. These followers receive money and hope of a life better than poverty and inadequate governance, poor educational and health provisions, which have resulted in widespread discontent and ignorance. Weak, corrupt governance is another source of unrest in Africa.

To a large extent these problems can be laid at the door of the European imperialist countries which, fortified by racism, exploited the continent until forced to leave after the Second World War. There are five main reasons to blame them for Africa's present plight.

Firstly, the Europeans did not encourage their African colonies to manufacture goods and build up a strong economy based on manufactured exported goods. Instead, the Europeans exploited the continent by taking its raw materials, minerals, and agricultural produce. As a result, no enterprising manufacturing classes arose. An entrepreneurial middle class is important in a liberal democracy. (The relationship of former colonies with the EU has continued the trade pattern of their sending agricultural produce and minerals, not manufactured goods, with the 'Stabex and Sysmin' agreements.)

Secondly, the Europeans provided the African countries with no tutelage for democracy. They did not even give them the civil service that Britain created in India, for example.

Thirdly, during the Second World War, African soldiers fought for the Europeans. After it they used their military training against their imperial masters whenever they were denied independence. As a result, new African states emerged, often led by those who had fought militarily for independence and were usually one-party states that depended on the army's support. The leaders could not be removed without a military coup.

Fourthly, the imperialists put together, in one state, tribes which had no wish to be under the same government, such as Nigeria. This resulted in further wars as tribes tried to break free.

Fifthly, the Europeans did nothing to eradicate the massive corruption that pervades Africa and is one of the reasons why the governments cannot deliver effectively. Foreign aid goes into the wrong pockets.

Moreover, today the situation in Africa is made far worse by climate change and its extreme effects, which is partly the result of the West's excessive consumerism.

Given the legacy of the European imperialists it is not surprising that the African countries cannot govern themselves competently. The question is, therefore, can the people of Africa forgive the European imperialists for their greedy exploitation of the African continent which even now harms the indigenous peoples? It is not enough for European countries to apologise. They need to make amends.

20.6 Macron's New Deal

In April 2021, President Emmanuel Macron proposed a New Deal, financed by the richer countries, to help African countries develop their economies. He observed that without it, there would be more African migration to Europe and terrorism [20].

The international community should do more to develop African countries' economic and political well-being before it is too late and the continent becomes the breeding ground for the global spread of Islamic terrorism, which speaks the language of revenge, not of forgiveness.

References

1. Bryden, Matt 'The Reinvention of al-Shabab', Centre for Strategic and International Studies, February 2014, p. 1
2. 'Who are Somalia's al-Shabab?' www.bbc.co.uk/news/world-africa 22 Dec 2017
3. Pape, Utz and Karamba, Wendy 'From Data to Development: Poverty and Policy in Somalia' World Bank Blog Dec 9th 2019
4. 'Isis-linked militants beheading children in Mozambique, says aid group' The Guardian' 16 March 2021
5. Ibid
6. 'Mozambique conflict: What's behind the unrest? Giles, Christopher, and Mwai, Peter BBC Reality Check 29 March 2021
7. Ibid
8. 'Isis-linked militants beheading children in Mozambique, says aid group' The Guardian 16 March 2021
9. Rettman, Andrew 'EU preparing to send soldiers to Mozambique', EUObserver.com 7th May 2021
10. Global Terrorism Index 2020 www.visionofhumanity.org
11. Ibid
12. 'More Than 100 Chibok Girls still Missing Seven Later' www.voanews.com.africa April 14, 2019
13. 'Islamic State and the kidnap of Nigerian schoolgirls from Dapchi.' www.bbc.co.uk/news/world-africa43570488 29th March 2018

14. The Times May 22nd 2021
15. Ibid
16. Congressional Research Service In Focus March 2021
17. Felter, Claire, and Bussemaker, Nathalie 'What to Know About the Crisis in Mali', Council on Foreign Relations, August 12 2020 (www.cfr.org/in-brief/what-know-about-crisis-mali)
18. Gardner, Frank, 'Is Africa overtaking the Middle East as the new jihadist battleground?' BBC 3rd December 2020 https://www.bbc.co.uk › news › world-africa-55147863
19. Ibid
20. https//:northafrica post.com/category/international April 29th 2021, Africa: Emmanual Macron calls for a 'New Deal'

Chapter 21
The Limits of Forgiveness (2): Myanmar Under the Generals

Besides finding the right response to Islamic jihadism, the international community has today to face other situations where forgiveness seems irrelevant, as when a dictatorial power is killing unarmed protesting citizens. A dictatorship which has not improved the lives of most of its citizens, nor believes, however wrongly, that the use of force is necessary to preserve political stability, may warrant a different response from one which does. I have dealt with issue of the Tiananmen Square massacre in 1989 in chapter on China and in an earlier chapter considered the situation of Belarus. Each situation is different yet demands usually a response from the international community. Here I shall consider the case of Myanmar where, at the time of writing (May 2021), the military government is continuously shooting unarmed protesters. The junta's aim is simply to stay in power and has not improved the lives of its citizens.

21.1 The National League for Democracy

Myanmar gained independence from Britain in 1948. It was ruled by the armed forces from 1962 until 2011. In 1988, the National League for Democracy (the NLD) was founded when the ruling junta brutally oppressed a student pro-democracy uprising and displaced many Burmese ethnic groups who fled to neighbouring countries. In 2011, a new government began introducing a return to civilian rule. In 2015, the NLD became the country's ruling party after a landslide victory in the general election.

Throughout its struggles, the NLD has always had a policy of non-violence. Aung San Suu Kyi was influenced by Gandhi who forbade any violent harming of the enemy which hopefully would be persuaded of the rightness of the protestors cause by their moral example.

A. Wells, *The Importance of Forgiveness and the Futility of Revenge*, Contributions to International Relations, https://doi.org/10.1007/978-3-030-87552-7_21

21.2 The Coup 2021

In November 2020, Aung San Suu Kyi and her National League for Democracy (NLD) party won the general election in Myanmar. However pro-military protesters claimed there was wide spread fraud (although there was no evidence of that) and demanded a rerun of the vote.

On Feb 1st 2021, the military (or 'Tatmadaw') seized control of Myanmar in a coup. State Counsellor Aung San Suu Kyi, President Win Myint, and other NLD members were detained under house arrest.

The Burmese people took to the streets to protest but the military government opened fire, killing hundreds of people including children. At the time of writing (May 2021) it is still shooting the unarmed protesters. This action cannot be forgiven either by the protesters or the international community, as the aim of the junta in crushing protest with disproportionate force is simply to stay in power.

21.3 International Response

The argument advanced earlier in this book that the West should be less hostile to China is relevant here, as China is the one power that could probably persuade Myanmar's military government to stop the bloodshed. If the West were friendlier to China, the latter might be more cooperative with the former regarding intervention.

Also, the Association of South East Asian Nations (ASEAN) of which Myanmar is a member might use its influence. However, at their meeting in April with Myanmar's junta chief, General Min Aung Hlaing, South East Asian leaders said that the General had agreed on a plan to end the crisis that but he did not explicitly respond to demands to halt the killing of civilian protestors. Moreover, the ASEAN countries have rejected the idea of placing sanctions on Myanmar.

By contrast, the USA and UK have imposed sanctions on Myanmar's two military conglomerates, Myanmar Economic Corporation (MEC) and Myanmar Economic Holdings Ltd (MEHL), which control significant portions of Myanmar's economy and have interests across many major industries, while the EU, which already has an arms embargo on Myanmar, has imposed sanctions on several individuals linked to the military. However, as Myanmar's biggest trade partners in Asia have rejected that approach, the effect of the sanctions has been weakened [1].

There have been calls for the French oil company, Total, which supplies gas to Myanmar to stop its production. However, it has said that it would cut off essential electricity to the people of Myanmar and might result in its workers becoming forced labour [2].

21.4 The National Unity Government (NUG)

In the absence of international support, sadly the National League for Democracy is now turning away from its non-violent struggle and with it any sense of forgiveness and of avoiding killing its enemy.

The members of Myanmar's parliament who were deprived of their parliamentary seats on February 1st and other opponents of the coup who are in hiding or in exile, have formed the National Unity Government (NUG) and announced in May the creation of people's defence force.

The force seems to be formed by anti-junta activists who have gone to Myanmar's borders to undergo military training and will join with the armies of other ethnic groups persecuted by the military. The situation could develop into civil war in Myanmar [3]. If so, the United Nations could be actively involved. The UN has already condemned Myanmar for its appalling treatment of the Rohingya Muslims which shows the brutal nature of the regime.

21.5 The Rohingya Muslims

The Rohingyas are an ethnic Muslim group in Myanmar which is mainly Buddhist. The government regards them as migrants and denies them citizenship and excluded them from the 2014 census. The Rohingyas, however, claim they are of Arab descent and have been in Myanmar for generations. They have been subjected to much persecution. Indeed, the UN Secretary-General Antonio Guterres described them as 'one of, if not the, most discriminated people in the world' [4].

In 2017, the Myanmar government claimed 30 police posts had been attacked by the Rohingya militants in Rakhine where most of them live. Myanmar troops brutally cracked down on the Rohingyas, burning their villages, killing them, and raping the women. At least 6700 were killed including 730 children under the age of five [5]. Over 270,000 Rohingyas fled to Bangladesh [6].

'The situation seems a textbook example of ethnic cleansing', said Zeid Ra'ad Al Hussein, United Nations High Commissioner for Human Rights [7].

Appalled by the treatment of the Rohingyas, the tiny Muslim state of Gambia admirably took their case to the International Court of Justice in the Hague, alleging Myanmar was committing genocide against them. In January 2020, the International Court of Justice ordered Myanmar to take measures to protect the Rohingyas from genocide while it was hearing the case which is still continuing.

21.6 Responsibility to Protect

If the situation in Myanmar regarding the pro-democracy protesters deteriorates, one solution could be intervention by the United Nations in the form of Responsibility to Protect (or R2P). This has been endorsed by the UN General Assembly at the 2005 World Summit and can be traced back to 1999 when the British PM Tony Blair, in a speech at Chicago University, invoked such a principle to justify NATO's intervention in Kosovo where it was successful, as it was in Somalia in 2008. It was seen by many as a hope that massacres would in future been prevented by UN action. However, unfortunately the actions of NATO in Libya may have rendered this hope ill-founded. Russia and China felt betrayed over Libya as they did not realise that NATO forces would overthrow Gaddafi's regime. They would have vetoed the UN Resolution 1973 on the 'no-fly zone' if they had known that would happen rather than just abstaining from voting. Therefore, China and Russia refused to support Western countries over a similar Resolution on Syria. For an R2P intervention to be authorised by the UN the resolution for it must be passed by the UN Security Council and not vetoed by a permanent member of the Council.

This demonstrates the importance again of the West's maintaining friendlier, more forgiving relationships with Russia and China, instead of taking the moral high ground and being harshly judgemental, ignoring our mutual chequered histories. If the permanent UN Security Council members agree on joint action against Myanmar's military government, the mere threat could make it hand over power to the NLD or at least negotiate with it.

The UN is only as good as its members. There is a need to devise a way for UN to intervene when unarmed civilians are being killed by their governments.

An interesting idea suggested by Professor Kishore Mahbubani is that the West's harsh condemnation of Aung San Suu Kyi for not opposing the generals' brutal treatment of the Rohingya Muslims when she was State Counsellor, gave the generals the courage to act against her. This shows the enormous effect harsh condemnation without any attempt to understand forgivingly the difficult position of the accused can have [8].

The junta is clearly not composed of people who are given to compromise and negotiation, or compassion. Their lethal methods are simply to keep them in power and cannot be forgiven on any grounds.

References

1. McDonald, Tim 'Myanmar coup: Could sanctions on the military ever work?' BBC News 9 April 2021
2. Regan, James, 'Total's CEO cites humanitarian reasons for continuing Myanmar gas production' Bloomberg 4th May 2021
3. Parry, Richard Lloyd, 'Aung San Suu Kyi allies create armed force to combat Myanmar's junta' May 5 The Times 2021

4. https://www.bbc.co.uk/news/world-asia-41566561 Myanmar Rohingya: 'What you need to know about the crisis 23 January 2020'
5. Ibid
6. Human Rights Council 36th session Opening Statement by Zeid Ra'ad Al Hussein, United Nations High Commissioner for Human Rights https://www.ohchr.org/
7. Ibid
8. Mahbubani, Kishore, 'Myanmar coup could jump-start US-China co-operation' South China Morning Post 10th Feb 2021

Chapter 22
The Forgiveness of Debts

The word 'forgiveness' is often used to mean 'cancellation' in relating to debts. In the first chapter I referred to Hannah Arendt's opinion that Jesus of Nazareth was the 'discoverer' of the role of forgiveness in human affairs [1]. There has been much debate as to whether Jesus spoke in Aramaic or Hebrew. If, as seems likely, it was the former, then the words in the Lord's Prayer, 'Forgive us our trespasses (or sins) as we forgive those that trespass against us', can also be translated as 'Forgive us our debts' as the Aramaic word for trespass or sin had connotations of debt. This did not only have the meaning of financial obligation but also a wider sense of what is owed to us and what we owe to others. Indeed, Presbyterian churches do pray 'Forgive us our debts, as we forgive our debtors'. In this chapter, however, I shall be using the term 'debts' in the narrower financial sense and arguing that, particularly where irresponsible lending is involved, they should be forgiven.

22.1 The Third World Debt

In the late twentieth century developing countries were struggling to repay their debts to developed countries and lending institutions, resulting in the Third World's further immiseration. It seems that much of the Third World Debt arose through petrodollar recycling. OPEC countries, having raised the price of oil in 1974, lent their excess dollars to Western commercial banks which then lent the money to developing countries needing it to pay the increased price of oil. When later interest rates rose globally the developing countries were plunged further into debt. In August 1982, Mexico announced it could no longer meet the repayments of its external debts.

The problems of Mexico and other countries in similar straits were eventually temporarily ameliorated by the World Bank and the IMF launching the Heavily Indebted Poor Countries Initiative (HIPC) in 1996. However, this only meant loans were dependent on developing countries' cutting their expenditure on education and

A. Wells, *The Importance of Forgiveness and the Futility of Revenge*, Contributions to International Relations, https://doi.org/10.1007/978-3-030-87552-7_22

public welfare. Therefore, there developed a movement demanding that Western countries and banks forgive the debts owed to them by the poorer countries. Critics of this idea argued that such a policy encourages irresponsibility on behalf of the indebted countries, but supporters of the idea countered that the irresponsibility was on the part of the lenders in the first place.

Jubilee 2000 was an international coalition movement in over 40 countries which called for the abolition of the Third World Debt by the year 2000. The idea was based on the Biblical Jubilee Year or Fiftieth Year, referred to in the book of Leviticus, when those who have been enslaved or lost their lands because of debt have it forgiven or cancelled. In the Catholic Church the celebration of the year 2000 was to be the Great Jubilee.

The Jubilee 2000 campaign was founded in the 1990s by Martin Dent, a retired lecturer in politics at the University of Keele, and William Peters, a retired diplomat. Together with other churches the Church of England strongly supported the movement. In 1998, Archbishop Carey made the cancellation of the international debt a major topic for debate at the Lambeth Conference. A briefing paper for the conference stated:

'the poor nations of the world can make a fresh start. For those in debt, this would be an occasion to experience the redeeming love offered by Jesus on the Cross as he personally, spiritually and physically embodied the values of mercy, forgiveness and reconciliation, recognised in the Jubilee tradition. Creditors of the world would experience the offering of sacrificial love in the true unity of humanity, thereby being liberated from the weight of the burden of guilt from the oppression and poverty they help foster' [2].

Initially, the campaigning was through church channels but it spread to trade unions and charities. Then pop stars such as Bono and Bob Geldof took up the cause which soon became an international campaign with many countries participating. In Britain at a rally in St Paul's Cathedral in 1999, the UK's Chancellor of the Exchequer, Gordon Brown, gave debt cancellation his support and the USA did likewise at a meeting of the G7. Eventually a large part of the Third World's debts was cancelled. Archbishop Justin Welby described this as:

'perhaps the churches 'finest hour' in dethroning Mammon ...Sustained support from Christians and others across the world led to the cancellation of more than $100 billion of debt owed by 35 of the poorest countries' [3].

After 2001, Jubilee 2000 split into a number of organisations dealing with poverty and debt around the world.

Forgiveness of a poor countries' debts makes clearly sound political and economic sense. If there is extreme poverty, ill health, and illiteracy in a country which has to use its funds to pay the interest rates on debts, there is an increased likelihood of its people supporting extremist leaders or organisations which cause regional instability and might well invade other countries. Furthermore, its citizens will be unable to buy foreign goods to the detriment of those countries wanting to sell them.

22.2 Germany

My book opens by referencing the fact that after the First World War Germany was obliged to pay crippling reparations by the vengeful Versailles Treaty. This caused immense suffering to the German people but initially the USA helped them with repackaging and a loan. This unfortunately, after the collapse of Wall Street in 1929, was recalled. To repay the debt Germany had to impose further austerity on the German people as unemployment rose to 6 million. The resulting misery and social unrest helped pave the rise of the Nazis.

After the Second World War West Germany's treatment by the Allies was very different from that meted out to it after the First World War. This was partly because East Germany was already under Communist control and the West feared that West Germany, if in extreme economic distress, might also turn to Communism. In 1953, an agreement, the London Debt Accords, was signed between Germany and the USA, the UK, France, and other countries. It forgave Germany half its debts involving 16 billion marks of debt resulting from the Versailles Treaty and owed to government and private banks in the USA, UK, and France. Another 16 billion marks represented post-war loans by the USA.

The total amount owed was halved to 15 billion dollars and was to be paid over 30 years only while Germany ran a trade surplus. The forgiveness of Germany's debt together with generous terms Marshall Aid helped bring about Germany's strong economic recovery after the Second World War.

22.3 Greece

However, when, during the Greek Debt Crisis (which began in 2008 and lasted a decade) Greece asked the EU to forgive its debt, Germany, being the economically dominant member of that organisation, refused. Instead, it demanded an austerity programme that causes much hardship to the Greek people. Thousands left their country for good while pensioners died in poverty, some losing their homes, while the young saw their teachers sacked and their future as hopeless. The enraged Greeks took to rioting on the streets as their media likened German politicians to Nazis. Such treatment often results in hatred and a desire for revenge: Greece is now seeking reparations from Germany for the two World Wars [4].

An argument for forgiving the Third World its debt was that the lending of funds had been irresponsible. This argument could well be applied to Greece's borrowing from the EU. Indeed its budget deficit had been too high for the eurozone's Maastricht Criteria and it misrepresented its circumstances to enter the eurozone in 2001 [5]. A closer monitoring of the Greek economy should have been undertaken by the EU.

Today there are many Third World countries and even some in the West still struggling with debts. They cannot hope to spend as much as they would like on the public services in their countries and therefore their development is stalled.

For centuries Christian churches forbade usury, the taking of interest on loans. This resulted in Jews taking on the role of money lenders and eventually establishing some banks. The world today is more aware of Islamic thought and might well seriously reflect on the fact that Muslims are forbidden to profit from irresponsible lending. In Islamic banking great emphasis is made on the banks assessing the viability of a project for which a loan is asked. If the project fails, then the lender suffers along with the borrower.

This practice could well be adopted by Western banks and indeed until the whole system of capitalist banking is overhauled, it could help millions of people. Until that time the forgiveness of the debts of poorer states by richer creditor countries, particularly where irresponsible lending is involved, should be widely practised.

References

1. Arendt, Hannah, 'The Human Condition' (University of Chicago 1958) p.238
2. Thrall, James H., 'International Debt Emerging as Central Issue for Lambeth Conference' 7/1/1998. www.anglicannews.org
3. Welby, Justin, 'Dethroning Mammon, Making Money Serve Grace' (London 2016) p.154
4. Squires, Nick, 'Greeks repeat claim for war reparations from Germany', Daily Telegraph, 11 January, 2019
5. Little, Allen, 'How 'magic' made Greek debt disappear before it joined the euro', BBC News 3 February 2012. www.bbc.co.uk

Conclusion

I hope this book has demonstrated that the world is better served by forgiveness rather than revenge which can cause a colossal loss of life. Vengeance should therefore be speedily discerned in international relations, vigorously condemned and discouraged. Apart from politicians, the people who have a platform and a moral obligation to do just that are Christian leaders, since forgiveness is central to their faith. Indeed, Hannah Arendt, the distinguished political theorist quoted at the beginning of this book, called Jesus of Nazareth 'the discoverer' of the role of forgiveness in public affairs. Yet throughout the twentieth century and the beginning of the twenty-first, the voices of Christians have not thundered as loudly as they might have done in situations where forgiveness was the most noble and wise option, as was the case regarding the Treaty of Versailles in 1919.

1 The Christian Response to the Versailles Vengeance

As I explained in the first chapter, this vindictive treaty did not make the Second World War inevitable, but it was an important factor in the rise of Hitler, who vowed to repudiate it.

Had the Versailles Treaty, before it was signed, been roundly condemned by all Christian churches as vindictive, it might have been changed to be more forgiving and kinder towards Germany. Indeed, in 1928 the then Archbishop of Canterbury, Cosmo Lang, did condemn the treaty as 'vindictive and arbitrary' and saw Hitler's rise as a consequence of it [1]. However, this was too late. His predecessor in 1919, Randall Davidson, had not spoken out against it. The Anglican church could also, in 1919, have used its presence and influence in Parliament to lobby against the Treaty, but it did not. Furthermore, worldwide Christian leaders should have strongly criticised the Treaty for its vengeful nature. If they could have persuaded France to be more generous to Germany, millions of lives might have been saved.

A. Wells, *The Importance of Forgiveness and the Futility of Revenge*, Contributions to International Relations, https://doi.org/10.1007/978-3-030-87552-7

However, the Pope, Benedict XV, who had called the First World War 'the suicide of civilised Europe' did condemn the Versailles Treaty as 'vengeful' [2]. The Vatican objected to the 'War Guilt clause' and the size of the reparations as too harsh and said that they threatened the stability of Europe [3]. The Pope had in fact put forward proposals for a peace initiative in his Peace Note in 1917 when he had suggested that both sides should agree to a mutual renunciation of indemnities [4]. He had also proposed a general limitation of armaments and courts for international arbitration. Indeed, although he was given no credit for it, some of his ideas may well have influenced President Wilson's later Fourteen Points [5]. But the Pope was not invited to the Peace Conference in 1919 at Italy's insistence (because of the dispute over who governed the Papal states) [6]. He therefore sadly could not influence the conference.

Perhaps if Pope Benedict had written a letter to be read out in all Catholic churches asking his flock to urge their governments to treat Germany with forgiveness and generosity, he could have had an impact on the peace negotiations. But even here, he might not have had the support of the bishops. During the war, his peace initiatives were shamefully undermined by Catholic bishops in France and Britain (where the establishment was traditionally anti-Catholic). According to the Catholic scholar Fr Ashley Beck the Catholic bishops:

'like other Christian leaders, were determined to be seen as patriotic and completely behind the war effort: men like Cardinal Bourne (Westminster) and Bishops Amigo (Southwark), Casartelli (Salford), Keating (Northampton), and Burton (Clifton)were frankly embarrassed by the pope's actions, as was the Catholic press. They wanted all-out victory, not negotiations. In 1916 a group of Catholic lay people set up the Guild of the Pope's Peace, to disseminate the pope's teachings and prayers for peace. It was openly attacked by the bishops' [7].

In 1915, in his Exhortation to the belligerent powers to seek a negotiated peace, the Pope had warned of the cycle of vengeance '...Nations do not die; humiliated and oppressed, they bear the weight of the yoke imposed upon them, preparing themselves for their come-back and transmitting from one generation to the next a sad legacy of hatred and vendetta' [8].

2 Robert Schuman and Forgiveness

After the Second World War, it was a devout Christian politician, the French foreign minister, Robert Schuman, who, believing strongly in the importance of forgiveness, ended the age long vendetta between Germany and France. He knew that France must not act vindictively as it had in 1919 but instead forgive Germany. In this spirit, Schuman founded the European Coal and Steel Community (the ECSC) in 1951 so that France and Germany could produce coal and steel together with the Benelux countries. The ECSC eventually grew into the EU.

3 Western Revenge on Muslim Countries

At the beginning of the twenty-first century, however, no politician equivalent to Robert Schuman in stature, integrity, and motivation emerged. Vengeance was still the default response for a country attacked by another, not forgiveness with reflection on the cause of the hostility, as was shown in 2001 by the USA's response to the 9/11 attack. This last was itself a futile act of revenge (for the USA's support of Israel and its troops' presence in Saudi Arabia), but America's military response, which resulted nearly 20 years of war in Afghanistan, was also partly vengeful and largely futile. The USA finally made peace with the Taliban in 2020, having achieved little but destroyed much. When the 9/11 attack had occurred in 2001, church leaders in the USA did not publicly urge forgiveness of the terrorists. In the UK Archbishop George Carey actually supported the war in Afghanistan [9]. However, Dr. Rowan Williams, then Archbishop of Wales, raised a lone voice warning against mere revenge and later condemning the bombing of Afghanistan [10].

In 2003 President Bush' decision to attack Iraq, believing it was linked to 9/11, did provoke more protest from Christian leaders, but the protests did not stop the war. The British Prime Minister, Tony Blair, was one person who might have influenced President Bush to reconsider his decision, but he did not do so and instead committed Britain to the invasion. Thus, two avowed Christian leaders invaded Iraq, resulting in thousands of deaths, colossal destruction and the rise of ISIS. Had Blair urged Bush to clamp down on his desire to lash out, thousands of lives could have been saved.

Libya was also the victim of revenge cycles culminating in the overthrow of Gaddafi and resulting in a massive loss of life and destruction, while thousands of refugees and migrants flooded to Europe through Libya, many drowning in the Mediterranean.

In Iran too, a cycle of revenge has played an important part in its relations with the West. Unfortunately, it is a cycle that is not yet played out and may lead to further conflict.

In all the above-mentioned wars, Christians could have been instrumental in turning political leaders away from conflicts that were partly vengeful, urging forgiveness, which in this context means restraining a desire to immediately harm the assailant while reflecting on the reason for the attack and on non-military responses to it.

In the USA, unfortunately, churches are reluctant to speak out on political issues for fear of losing their tax concessions, although politics is about morality in the public sphere, which is precisely what Christians should be concerned about. Moreover, almost anything can become a political matter if it is the subject of political debate, government policy or proposed legislation.

The USA has been called a vengeful society by some scholars [11], not only because of its recent military history but because of its employment of the death penalty, which can also be regarded as a form of revenge and is a characteristic of many militarily aggressive states. This should also be of great concern to American Christians.

4 Syria

There have been many internal and external factors involved in the Syrian civil war, among them some leaders who are very vengeful and, on the other hand, some leaders who are forgiving. President Bashar Assad's younger brother, General Maher Assad, who has been responsible for atrocities in the conflict, belongs in the first category. In the second is Ali Haidar, Syria's Minister for Reconciliation, who has implemented a policy of forgiveness to the rebels against his government and to the killers of his own son. Unfortunately, it has been the actions of Maher Assad which have received the most publicity.

5 Russia

The age long hostility between the West and Russia might be relaxed by a more forgiving and empathising relationship on both sides. Instead of taking the moral high ground and retaliating with sanctions, the West could remember its own chequered history, attempt to see Russia's actions from Russia's own viewpoint and extend goodwill to that misunderstood country. Meanwhile, the Archbishop of Canterbury, Justin Welby, is doing a good job holding friendlier meetings with the Patriarch of the Russian Orthodox Church [12].

6 China

Similarly, with China, now rising to become the dominant world power, the West needs to give it credit for its colossal achievements and not be so harsh and unforgiving of its mistakes, remembering that China has only recently modernised. Former Western imperialist countries need to remember their own trespasses. More can be achieved in the spirit of friendly discourse and negotiation than lecturing a country without attempting to empathise with it. The West has been unforgiving towards some of China's policies without trying to excuse or understand the reasons behind them, or find alternative ways of viewing them, or reflecting on their own chequered histories. Indeed, such is the judgemental hostility of the West that some commentators speak of a new cold war with China [13]. This might turn into a hot war with all its catastrophic consequences if Sinophobia is not checked.

7 Revenge and Forgiveness in One Country

Between different conflicting peoples within one country, forgiveness means not retaliating harmfully to the enemy, but it does not mean accepting oppression and the abuse of power. Mahatma Gandhi, deeply influenced by Christ's teachings, showed how resistance without harming the enemy in return for its violence is possible. But Gandhi was protesting against the British who could be driven from India.

Nelson Mandela believed that Gandhi's methods would not be effective against the Afrikaners for whom South Africa was their home, so he introduced selective violence against them, yet it is probable that this method was not as effective as the economic boycott and withdrawal of international banking support from South Africa. After the collapse of apartheid, Mandela led his country by his example of forgiveness and reconciliation. The Truth and Reconciliation Tribunal helped alleviate the hatred and desire for revenge, but such tribunals in other countries where there had been ethnic conflict were not always so effective. Besides confessions and forgiveness, there needed to be a resolution of the issues that had given rise to the conflict in the first place.

The conflict between Israel and the Palestinians continues. The USA could help resolve it by encouraging talks between both sides that also involve Hamas (which is not a monolithic group), in a spirit of forgiveness while attempting to understand each others' viewpoint. This will be when both sides have reached a higher moral plane. The fact that some Palestinians on the West Bank are attempting to practice non-violent resistance is a sign that they are attempting to do this.

The peace in Northern Ireland is one that should give hope to all nations torn by ethnic strife. Forgiveness played an important part in it, as did skilful negotiators and geopolitical developments.

In former Yugoslavia, Rwanda, Sierra Leone, and Colombia, after ethnic conflict, there have been attempts to set up truth and reconciliation systems. However, they have not been as effective as the one in South Africa, partly because in those countries, there did not emerge leaders of the calibre of Nelson Mandela and Archbishop Desmond Tutu who could introduce a culture of forgiveness in their country, based on their Christian faith and example.

It is important to understand how such leaders emerge. I hope I have shown that how Mahatma Gandhi was greatly influenced by the teachings of Jesus Christ, Nelson Mandela was a deeply committed Christian as, of course, is Archbishop Desmond Tutu. Robert Schuman, who ended the revenge cycle between Germany and France, was also a devout Christian politician. Mikhail Gorbachev, who introduced a policy of openness, of forgiveness of mistakes in his country and who extended the hand of friendship to the West in ending the Cold War, was baptised a Christian. He probably learned about the faith from his parents despite the atheism of his communist country. One of the first things he did on coming to power was to allow the churches to be opened in Russia. In 2008 it was reported that when Gorbachev visited Italy, he went to Assisi and spent half an hour on his knees in silent prayer next to the tomb of St Francis [14].

8 Responsible Leadership

Political and religious leaders should understand their potential power to stop colossal bloodshed by querying the necessity and motivation of a military attack, unless of course, their country is clearly about to be invaded. It is surely time to put away the politics of the playground, of tit-for-tat, and show mature leadership as Mandela, Gandhi, Schuman, and Gorbachev have done.

Mutual empathy and forgiveness between previously hostile peoples cannot be beyond human achievement, nor can it be impossible for political leaders in any country to control their impulses of revenge, especially when encouraged to do so by others In such situations, besides fellow politicians and religious leaders, the mass media, instead of stirring up the mob to demand revenge as has often been the case, could play an important role by demanding that their government shows restraint in response to foreign hostile acts. It is pertinent here to remember how the influential Fox News host, Tucker Carlson, probably persuaded President Trump, in June 2019, to call off a proposed retaliatory attack on Iran at the 11th hour as there would be a disproportionate number of people killed [15]. This shows how prominent people in the media can save lives and prevent the escalation of conflict. Indeed, academics specialising in international affairs could also do this by lobbying governments effectively against military action that they see as gratuitous and vindictive. Unfortunately, such worthwhile actions do not help forward their careers which depend on writing books for other academics and students. It is to be hoped that, nevertheless, for those who do take such actions, that their fellow scholars will applaud their efforts to stop vengeful political responses and feel inspired to follow their example with a firm wrist. Those with a platform in society should surely use it to prevent vengeful policies that can result in unnecessary loss of life.

A country's defence is best served not by huge expenditure on weapons but by a constructive and creative foreign policy that seeks to understand putative enemies empathetically and makes every effort to cultivate their friendship, as well as showing concern for the political and socio-economic rights of their citizens. A country with such an enlightened foreign policy does not take the moral high ground when relating to others but remembers its own past critically, does not impose harsh punishments on other states and does not retaliate with military force unless there is no alternative. Countless lives may be saved in this way, and colossal sums of money released that can be used for the relief of poverty throughout the world.

References

1. Hill, Christopher Rt Rev., 'Faith and Patriotism: Some Snapshots and Reflections on 1914 and Beyond' published in Anvil, Vol 30 Issue 2, 11th Sep 2014 p.43
2. Philpot, Terry 'World War I's Pope Benedict XV and the Pursuit of Peace' *National Catholic Register* 19th July 2014
3. Pollard, John F., 'Benedict XV: The Unknown Pope and the Pursuit of Peace' (London 1999) p.144

4. Ibid p.126
5. Ibid p.128
6. Ibid p.101–102
7. Beck, Fr Ashley, 'A Peacemaker Betrayed', *The Catholic Herald*, 27th Feb 2014
8. Pollard op.cit. p.117
9. Megoran, Nick 'God On Our Side? The Church of England and the Geopolitics of Mourning 9/11' Geopolitics (Routledge 2006), 11: p.570
10. Williams, Rowan, Presidential Address to the Governing Body of the Church in Wales, University of Wales, Lampeter, 20th September 2001, https://www.churchinwales.org.uk
11. Stein, Rachel M, 'War and Revenge: Explaining Conflict Initiation by Democracies', American Political Science Review Vol 109, No 3, August 2015, p.558–559
12. Binyon, Michael, 'Archbishop Welby and Patriarch Kirill agree to focus on shared interests', *Church Times*, 24th November 2017
13. Rachman, Gideon, 'A new cold war, Trump, Xi and the escalating US-China confrontation'. *Financial Times*, 4th October 2020
14. *Daily Telegraph* 19 Mar 2008, 'Mikhail Gorbachev admits he is a Christian', Moore, Malcolm
15. Baker, Peter et al., 'Urged to launch an Attack, Trump listened to the Skeptics. . .' *The New York Times*, June 20th 2019

Selected Bibliography

Ajami, Fouad, 'The Syrian Rebellion' (Stanford 2012)
Alderdice, Lord John, 'Risks, Rights and Respect-Essential Elements of the Irish Peace Process', The 11th Dudley Senanayake Memorial Lecture, Colombo, Sri Lanka, 24th September 2008
Amstutz, M.R. 'The Healing of Nations; the Promise and Limits of Political Forgiveness' (Lanham, MD 2005)
Anand, Anita, 'The Patient Assassin A True Tale of Massacre, Revenge and the Raj' (London 2019)
Arendt, Hannah, 'The Human Condition' (University of Chicago 1958)
Azzam, Abdullah, 'Defence of the Muslim Lands', www.religioscope.com
Badi, Archbishop Justin, 'Peacebuilding in South Sudan: Linking Local and National Approaches', Panel Meeting at Chatham House, The Royal Institute of International Affairs, Chatham House, 7th September 2018
Barclay, William, 'Insights: Forgiveness' (Edinburgh 2012)
Bearman, Jonathan, 'Qadhafi's Libya', (London 1986)
Blair, Tony, 'A Journey', (London 2010)
Bloch-Schulman, Stephen and White, David, (eds), 'Forgiveness: Probing the Boundaries,' (Oxford 2009)
Bole, William et al., 'Forgiveness in International Politics' (Washington 2004)
Bregman, Ahron, 'A History of Israel', (Houndmills, Basingstoke, England, 2003)
Brittain, Vera, 'Testament of Youth,' (London 1933)
Cantacuzino, Marina, 'The Forgiveness Project', (London 2016)
Cobb, John B. 'Resistance: the new Role of Progressive Christians' (Louisville 2008)
Congressional Research Service, www.crs.gov
Coogan, Tim Pat, The IRA, (London 1980)
Dikotter, Frank, 'The Tragedy of Liberation', (London 2013)
Enright, R.D. et al., 'The Moral Development of Forgiveness' in Kurtines, William and Gerwitz, Jacob, 'Handbook of Moral Behaviour and Development' (New Jersey 1991)
Fountain, Jeff, 'A Christian Europe: the Forgotten Legacy of Robert Schuman,' (Amsterdam 2014)
Frayling, Nicholas, 'Pardon and Peace: A Reflection on the Making of the Peace in Northern Ireland' (London 1996)

Fromm, Erich, 'The Anatomy of Human Destructiveness' (Penguin Harmondsworth, Middx., England 1973)
Frost, Brian, 'Struggling to Forgive; Nelson Mandela and Reconciliation' (London 1998)
Gandhi, Arun, 'The Gift of Anger' (London 2017)
Gandhi, Mahatma, Collected Works (CWMG) www.mkgandhi.org
Gandhi, M. Harijan
Gandhi, M.K. 'Hind Swaraj'
Gandhi, M.K. Young India
Gandhi, M.K., 'An Autobiography', (London 2001)
Gleason J.H., 'The Genesis of Russophobia in Great Britain', (Cambridge, Mass 1950)
Glenny, Misha, 'The Balkans Nationalism, War and the Great Powers 1804-1999' (London 1990)
Glenny, Misha, 'The Fall of Yugoslavia' (London 1996)
Gourevitch, Philip, We Wish to Inform You That Tomorrow We Will Be Killed With Our Families (London 2015)
Halliday, Fred and Alavi, Hamza, 'State and Ideology in the Middle East' (London 1988)
Halliday, Fred, 'Two Hours that Shook the World' (London 2002)
Hilsum, Lindsey, 'Libya in a Time of Revolution' (London 2012)
Holloway, Richard, 'On Forgiveness' (Edinburgh 2015)
Horton, Richard, 'The Covid-19 Catastrophe' (Cambridge 2020)
House of Commons Hansard Debates www.publications.parliament.uk/
House of Lords Hansard Debates www.publications.parliament.uk/
Hunter, A. and Rigby, A. 'Gandhi and the virtue of forgiveness.' Gandhi Marg. Vol 30
Judah, Tim, 'The Serbs History, Myth and Destruction' (Yale 1999)
Kets de Vries, Manfred, 'The Art of Forgiveness: Differentiating Transformational Leaders' (April 18, 2013) INSEAD Working Paper No.2013/52/EFE
Kramarenko, Alexander, Minister Counsellor of the Embassy of Russia to Great Britain, Lecture to the Great Britain-Russia Society, 30th October 2013
Kurtines, William and Gerwitz, Jacob, 'Handbook of Moral Behaviour and Development' (New Jersey 1991)
Lister, Charles R., 'The Syrian Jihad', (Oxford 2015)
MacMillan, Margaret, 'Paris 1919', (New York 2003)
MacFarquhar, Roderick, 'The Origins of the Cultural Revolution', (New York 1997)
Macfarquhar, Roderick and Fairbank, John (eds), Cambridge History of China, (Cambridge 1995)
MacFarquhar, Roderick, and Schoenals, Michael, 'Mao's Last Revolution' (Cambridge, Mass USA 2006)
Magee, Bryan, 'Popper' (London 1973)
Mandela, Nelson, 'Long Walk to Freedom', (London 1995)
Mandela, Nelson, 'Conversations with Myself,' (London 2011)
Mandela, Winnie, 'Part of My Soul', (Harmondsworth 1985)
Manningham-Buller, Eliza, Reith Lectures September 2011 http://www.bbc.co.uk/reithlectures
Mathai, M.P, 'Meditations on Gandhi' (New Delhi 2002)
Mazrui, A.A. and Tidy, M. 'Nationalism and New States in Africa' (Heinemann 1989)
McLernon, F., Cairns, E., Hewstone, M. and Smith R., The Development of Intergroup Forgiveness in Northern Ireland (Journal of Social Issues, Vol 60 No 3, 2004)
McMauley, Martin, 'The Rise and Fall of the Soviet Union' (Harlow, England 2008)
Megoran, Nick 'God On Our Side? The Church of England and the Geopolitics of Mourning 9/11' Geopolitics (Routledge 2006)
Meghoran, Nick Solly, 'The War on Terror' (Nottingham 2007)
Meisner, Maurice, 'Mao's China and After', (New York 1999)
Melvern, Linda 'Conspiracy to Murder: the Rwandan Genocide', (London 2004)
Middle East Intelligence Bulletin
Moise, Edwin E., 'Modern China', (New York 1999)
Morris, Benny 'The Birth of the Palestinian Refugee Problem 1947-9' (Cambridge 1988)

Mowat, R. C. 'Creating the European Community', (London 1973)
Nanda, BR, 'Mahatma Gandhi: A Biography' (New Delhi 1981)
Nathan, Andrew, and Link, Perry, 'The Tiananmen Papers', (London 2001)
Northedge, F.S. and Wells, Audrey, 'Britain and Soviet Communism', (Macmillan 1982)
O'Leary, Brendan and McGarry, John, The Politics of Antagonism Understanding Northern Ireland, (London 1994)
Pew Research Centre
PLO Information Dept., London
Pollard, John F., 'Benedict XV: The Unknown Pope and the Pursuit of Peace' (London 1999)
Pope, Alexander, 'An Essay on Criticism', in *Selected Poetry* (Oxford 1998)
Revolutionary Democracy, Vol V, No 2, Spet (1999)
Roberts, Adam and Ash, Timothy Garton, 'Civil Resistance and Power Politics' (Oxford 2009)
Schram, Stuart R., 'Mao Tse-tung', (Harmondsworth, Middlesex 1970)
Schuman, Robert, 'Pour L'Europe' (Paris 1963)
Sharett, Yaakov (Ed) The Reparations Controversy: The Jewish State and German Money in the Shadow of the Holocaust 1951-1952, (Berlin 2011)
Shaw, Rosalind 'Rethinking Truth and Reconciliation Commissions, Lessons from Sierra Leone', The United States Institute of Peace Special Report, February 2005, www.usip.org
Shindler, Colin, 'A History of Modern Israel' (Cambridge 2013)
Shlaim, Avi, 'The Iron Wall' (London 2000)
Shlaim, Avi, 'Israel and Palestine' (London 2009)
Shriver, Donald W., 'An Ethic for Enemies', (Oxford 1995)
Spence, Jonathan, 'The Search for Modern China', (New York 1999)
Stein, Rachel M., 'War and Revenge: Explaining Conflict Initiation by Democracies', American Political Science Review Vol 109
Storey, Peter, 'A Different Kind of Justice: Truth and Reconciliation in South Africa', *The Christian Century* (http:gbgm-umc.org/nwo/99ja/different.html)
Strawser, Michael, '*Forgiving Derrida: From Terrorism to Self-Forgiveness*', in 'Forgiveness: Probing the Boundaries,' eds Bloch-Schulman, Stephen and White, David, (Oxford 2009)
Taliano, Mark and Bartlett, Eva, 'As Foreign Insurgents Continue to Terrorize Syria, the Reconciliation Trend Grows', https://dissidentvoice.org
Taliano, Mark 'Syria's Minister for National Reconciliation', www.globalresearch.ca/
The Holy Bible, ESV (London 2012)
The Koran with a Parallel Arabic Text, trans by N.J. Dawood (Penguin ed, Harmondsworth, Middx England 1994)
Tolstoy, Leo, 'Letter to a Hindoo', (Natal 1910) reprint
Tutu, Desmond, 'No Future Without Forgiveness,' (London 1999)
Welby, Justin, 'Dethroning Mammon, Making Money Serve Grace', (London 2016)
Wells, Audrey 'The Rule of Reverse Results', (London 2016)
Williams, Rowan, Presidential Address to the Governing Body of the Church in Wales, University of Wales, Lampeter, 20th September 2001, https://www.churchinwales.org.uk
Williams, Rowan, 'Writing in the Dust Reflections on 11th September and its aftermath' (London 2002)
www.catholicherald.co.uk
www.churchtimes.co.uk
www.ft.com
www.gallica.bnf.fr/Le Petit Journal
www.theguardian.com
www.independent.co.uk
www.irishtimes.com
UN Human Development Reports www./hdr.undp.org

Index

A. Wells, *The Importance of Forgiveness and the Futility of Revenge*, Contributions to International Relations, https://doi.org/10.1007/978-3-030-87552-7

The manufacturer's authorised representative in the EU is Springer Nature Customer Service Centre GmbH, Europaplatz 3, 69115 Heidelberg, Germany. If you have any concerns regarding our products, please contact ProductSafety@springernature.com

Printed and bound by CPI Group (UK) Ltd, Croydon, CR0 4YY
30/09/2026
02225661-0017